GEORGE H. W. BUSH

George H. W. Bush

Character at the Core

CURT SMITH

Potomac Books

An imprint of the University of Nebraska Press

Portions of chapter 1 originally appeared in *Windows
on the White House: The Story of Presidential Libraries*
by Curt Smith (South Bend IN: Diamond Communications, 1998).

Library of Congress Cataloging-in-Publication Data
Smith, Curt.
George H. W. Bush: character at the core / Curt Smith.
pages   cm
Includes bibliographical references and index.
ISBN 978-1-61234-685-4 (hardcover: alk. paper)
1. Bush, George, 1924– 2. Presidents—United
States—Biography. 3. United States—Politics and
government—1989–1993. I. Title.
E882.S63 2014
973.928092—dc23
[B]
2014019781

Set in Minion Pro by L. Auten.

To my family

CONTENTS

ILLUSTRATIONS

AUTHOR'S NOTE

Retrieve a time of puppies, picket fences, and Masonic lodges—frozen in amber but fixed and sure—of the bespectacled librarian, uptown soda fountain, and streets laced by unlocked homes. Did such an age exist? It did, especially in the America between two world wars. George Herbert Walker Bush loved "a nation," he said, referencing a medium that existed only later, "closer to [television's] *The Waltons* than *The Simpsons*."

Bush forged what Whittaker Chambers in another context styled "some quality, deep-going, difficult to identify in the world's glib way, but good, and meaningful." Its Agincourt: what writer Robert Healy called that "Yankee trait of competing hard, then picking your opponent up off the floor." Politics prizes ego, power, and a Harold Hill type of flimflam. Bush aired generosity—giving boyhood classmates half his lunch (his nickname, "Have Half")—modesty, and self-deprecation.

What a conundrum wrapped in hard-to-get-a-handle-on. The moderate northeastern Episcopalian liked country and western music. The patrician enjoyed hunting, fishing, and horseshoes. America's forty-first president (hereafter, Bush 41) could war on language: "Zippity doo-dah . . . Don't cry for me, Argentina!" Yet his charm—"I'm president," he said of broccoli, "and I don't have to eat it!"—eclipsed prep school and the Ivy League, forming a mountain twang.

Bush belonged to the "Old Boy Network" of perquisite, expectation, and old-shoe chivalry, yet he offset privilege by seeming a regular fellow. "And that's the wonder, the wonder of this country," said Willy Loman in *The Death of a Salesman*, "that a man can end [up] with diamonds here on the basis of being liked!" What did Bush *stand* for? critics carped, aside from grace, refusal to gloat, and reluctance to offend. As it turned out, more than the Brahmin peaks of courtesy and face.

At home Bush was said to lack a philosophy—"the vision thing," he coined and gently twitted. Abroad he helped reshape the post–Cold War world. The Greek Heraclitus said you cannot stand in the same river twice. He would have liked the man who, tongue in cheek, Bush called "Mr. Smooth"—himself. Writing a book is discovery, not preconception; the result, *George H. W. Bush: Character at the Core*. I wish to thank those who helped me explore the surface and complexity of America's 1989–93 president.

I was speechwriter to the president, writing largely about values, politics, and philosophy. When Bush 41 left the White House, I informally headed his speech staff for the next three years. I write here about the person and president I know, helped by the recollection of many journalists. I especially want to thank the late *Time* columnist, White House correspondent, and president watcher Hugh Sidey and Tom DeFrank, former *Newsweek* White House correspondent, now *National Journal* contributing editor, and student of Bush 41. DeFrank contributed to *Newsweek*'s book *The Quest for the Presidency*, which captured Bush's brilliant 1988 campaign. I am also grateful for Peggy Noonan's must-read *Wall Street Journal* column.

In Bush's White House study hung a painting. *The Peacemakers* showed Lincoln and his generals near the end of the Civil War. Outside, battle rages. A rainbow denotes the passing of the storm. Bush was a peacemaker: the Berlin Wall down; Eastern Europe freed; the Soviet Union spent; Communism dead. The storm was a reelection that unhorsed that record's author. History will ask how Operation Desert Storm's hero got 37.5 percent of the vote in 1992. The why is that Bush was a world statesman and prosaic politician. He loathed campaigning's faux intimacy—the baring of your soul. I am indebted to campaign accounts and detailed polling analysis that show politics' bloodletting. In 1988 Bush caused it. In 1992 he endured it.

By definition a speechwriter's book reflects the craft—anecdotal, episodic. Bush was endearingly unhip. To him, Pac-Man was a camper, not a video game. Asking Aretha Franklin's phonetic spelling, he called "R-E-S-P-E-C-T" "respect." Bush liked kids, comity—the Leader of the Free World rose at 5 a.m. to type thank-you notes—honest sentiment, and family. Barbara Bush spoke daily with their five children across the country. Millions would have cheered had they known.

For a time Bush brooded about his 1992 loss, blaming himself, not what he called "the team": "I couldn't get through. There'd be all these people saying, 'Bush is out of touch.' I couldn't jump over the hurdle." In time he cleared it to begin anew. "Just think," he said, shining cowboy boots, "I don't need new suits for the rest of my life." He and Mrs. Bush built a new house in Houston, their home since the 1950s, dividing time each year between Texas (October–April) and the family compound in Kennebunkport, Maine (May–September). Each evoked the most overwhelming sense of coming home to some place that *belonged*.

In the 1990s Bush 41 enforced a new rule: Nearing grandpa, his then twelve (now seventeen) grandchildren had to "deimperialize the presidential retirement" by giving him a hug. Bush also was made an Honorary Knight Grand Cross of the Order of the Bath by Her Majesty Queen Elizabeth.

"How does it feel to be married to a real knight?" he asked Barbara later.

"Sir George, make the coffee," she said.

Gratefully, America's vision of the vision thing's architect changed profoundly in the post-1990s twilight of his life. Polling and anecdotal data showed that the country's appreciation of Bush as a person and president had soared.

"He built a great alliance and won a great war, so people think of him as a great Commander-in-Chief," said pollster John Zogby, whose full analysis of Bush graces chapter 13. "He was a war hero as a young man, became a father, grandfather, a father figure, and our last President from The Greatest Generation. It all fits together."

Stylistically, it had fit together too. In 1991 Bush had helped open the Ronald Reagan Library. "I learned so much from him," the Gipper's two-term vice president told the crowd, "about leadership, how to treat people." Bush withheld one story that I had drafted for the speech for fear that he would break down telling it.

In 2004 I reinstated that story in his June 11 eulogy for Reagan at Washington's National Cathedral, Bush telling it fine. "It's something Reagan taught," 41 told me. "Every time you practice something really emotional, you lessen its effect on you so that finally you can say it." By now I knew Bush so well as a speaker that I predicted his voice would break in *another* sentence. It did.

Next morning Bush, kindly and typically, phoned to praise "your Gettysburg Address," then apologized for having to abort the call. The reason was that he had to mark his eightieth birthday—as he has every fifth year since, including ninety—by parachuting from an aircraft 12,500 feet above the ground to honor two World War II "buddies" killed in 1944, when the Japanese shot down the then-twenty-year-old pilot's Avenger plane.

You can see an Avenger replica at the Bush Presidential Library and Museum, which opened in 1997 at Texas A&M University in College Station, Texas. Leadership is said to bubble down from the top. It does in people around Bush 41. I have visited each of the thirteen presidential libraries from Franklin Roosevelt to George W. Bush. Among others, Director Warren Finch, Deputy Director Patricia Burchfield, audio-visual archivist Mary Finch, and archivist Debbie Wheeler help make College Station's among the best. Let me also thank Roman Popadiuk, former director of the Bush Presidential Library Foundation, and Angie Cooper and Nonie Fisher for speaking and scheduling help. Fred McClure, a White House colleague, is the foundation's fine chief executive officer. Jean Becker is President Bush's longtime chief of staff. Linda Casey Poepsel, director of correspondence at his Houston office, is a dear friend and, like the entire staff, exceedingly loyal and able. I am grateful to each.

I want to thank White House speech colleagues, later described herein, who tried to help listeners glimpse the Bush we saw each day. Speechwriting researchers were invaluable, including Stephanie Blessey, Carol Blymire, Jeannie Bunton, Carolyn Cawley, Peggy Dooley, Ted Garmey, Jennifer Grossman, Christina Martin, the late Robert Simon, and Rett Wallace. Let me especially thank William F. Gavin, speechwriter to President Nixon, longtime aide to Congressman Bob Michel, and author of such novels as *One Hell of a Candidate*. His superb book *Speechwright: An Insider's Take on Political Rhetoric* inspired this work. The University of Nebraska Press's Derek Krissoff, Martyn Beeny, Marguerite Boyles, Alicia Christensen, Sam Dorrance, Tish Fobben, Acacia Gentrup, Kyle Simonsen, and Rosemary Vestal helped facilitate this project. Kathryn Owens and Julie Kimmel artfully brought the manuscript to print. Also helpful were my wife, Sarah, who carefully read the text; our children, Olivia and Travis; counselor Phil Hochberg; Gene Brissie; and Ken Samelson.

I wrote where I am privileged to teach: the University of Rochester, in Upstate New York, site of the public papers and audio, video, and other correspondence of former three-term New York governor and two-time Republican presidential candidate Thomas E. Dewey. In 2013 the university staged a popular exhibit, The Presidential Voice: A History of Presidential Speechwriting. This history shows how language can reflect an age—and often change it too.

Bush's library contains what the former president calls "the record of the history of what we made in this administration." His life was the history of an *American*, transcending race, ideology, or geography—architect of Desert Storm; conqueror of Communism; nonpareil diplomat; model dad; grandpa extraordinaire; U.S. *grandmère*'s husband; parachutist, in his ninth decade, recalling a special time and place.

As president, Bush began a pioneering "Points of Light" program. Think of his life as hug a child, touch a heart, and tend a wound. You might not be prudent, to use a favorite Bushism, to call it his greatest Point of Light. But you might be right.

In the end, I want to thank George Bush most of all.

GEORGE H. W. BUSH

ONE

Beginnings

George Bush was born June 12, 1924, in Milton, Massachu-setts, into the cloistered network of Eastern commerce. The second of Prescott Sheldon and Dorothy (Walker) Bush's five children was shy and more complex than is commonly grasped, less Babe Ruth than Lou Gehrig. He was taught that wealth did not enrich your worth. "George, you forget any *La-Dee-Lahs*," his mother quaintly said of patrician pretense. Later, George would say, "I hope I care when someone else is hurt, and I suspect that comes from my mother."

Lean and trim like her future son and husband, Dorothy Bush was runner-up in the 1918 national girls' tennis tournament. You had to hear this from others. "Dorothy Bush was of another era," *Time*'s Hugh Sidey wrote, "and her sense of propriety and modesty and self-control was cast in iron." It forged her son's firm founda-tion, to reference another hymn George could sing by rote. Remem-bering mother, Bush later shrank in speeches from even using the word *I*. "[It] hindered him, too," mused Sidey, "in a fuzzy and form-less era of national debate." The effect was a giving and forgiving DNA, a term not present until 1953. To use an older term, George was taught to be a gentleman.

Bush's father was the son of an Ohio steel company president, six foot four, stern, stately, a tenacious competitor, an affluent invest-ment banker, and 1952–63 U.S. senator. "Big guy, tough," Bush *fils* told television host David Frost in a 1988 *U.S. News & World Report* book, *The Next President*, which included interviews with the dozen candidates seeking the presidency. Teddy Roosevelt immortalized "Speak softly and carry a big stick." Prescott, George mused, "spoke *loudly* and carried the same big stick. I hope I got some strength from my dad."

In 1921 Dorothy and Prescott married, one High Church Episcopalian joining a like side of the clan. In 1923 they left Columbus, Ohio, for Milton; in 1924 George was named for Dorothy's father, George Herbert Walker, but she couldn't choose between Herbert and Walker as a middle name, so she took both; in 1925 they moved to suburban Greenwich, Connecticut, where Dad commuted to New York City and George entered Greenwich Country Day School.

At twelve Bush enrolled at Phillips Academy in Andover, Massachusetts, giving 24/7 new connotation for making friends and leading groups, of which there seemed a limitless supply. The boy spent each summer at his family's home at Walker's Point, on the Atlantic Ocean, in Kennebunkport, in southern Maine. Emphatic and sensitive by nature, George was not a hater and endlessly sought to grasp other points of view.

George Herbert Walker's children called him Pop. In time, Bush became Poppy. At Phillips Academy he was president, senior class and community fund-raising group; secretary, student council; editorial board member, school newspaper; and captain, varsity baseball and soccer teams. Bush was expert at social intercourse, with his grace and boyish front, always ready with the hospitable word and beguiling gesture.

In 1989 he visited Andover in his first year as the nation's president to laud the two hundredth anniversary of President Washington visiting Andover Hill. A copious notetaker and editor, Bush wrote "self-typed notes," in his phrase, on small sheets of paper on a typewriter in his office, like this note to White House speech editor Chriss Winston (Bush's typographical and grammatical errors are preserved):

> We should have a statement on excellence in education . . . Also short comment on Andover's History . . . Research Washington

Visit . . . What did he talk about then? . . . Maybe there is a tie in . . . The whole point of the visit was to celebrate to the very day the visit of George Washington . . . Phillips Academy always had Chairty Drive and other "Points of light" groups . . . a sentence or two on this theme . . . give3 something back to Socxiety . . . etc. For me the friendships formed at Andover remain. The participation in sports was a key—helped me all my life. Excellence of faculty. I loved this school, this place.

In the 1973 film *The Way We Were*, the leading man is a novelist who loves sports and collects friends. "In a way," Robert Redford wrote as Hubbell Gardner, "he was like his country. Everything had always come too easy for him." In a way, everything came too easy for Bush until "the date which will live in infamy"—pivoting his life and World War II.

December 7, 1941, was a Sunday. "It was duty, honor, country," Bush later said. "It is *our* country that had been attacked." Next day George, seventeen, tried to enlist at the Navy draft office but was told to return at age eighteen. In June 1942 he graduated from Phillips. A half century later, Poppy could still recite how the commencement speaker, Secretary of War Henry Stimson, defined the U.S. soldier as "brave without being brutal, self-confident without boasting"—a mot that seemed to apply to Bush himself.

In his 1989 note to Winston, Bush observed that it might be

more appropriate [for him, revisiting Andover] to read brief remarks in Chapel. It was in this very place in June 1942 that . . . Stimson spoke. In those days Chapel was compulsory . . . and yes, there was [a] lot of restlessness, squirming, yawning at the boring sermons, listening when a good one came along . . . But somehow what I got out of it all here was a sharpening of my own faith—belief in God—and perhaps more subtly, the recognition of our Country being one Nation under God. As president I know for [a] fact already that one cannot be President without Faith in God.

In 1942 Stimson had also urged Andover's graduating class to get a college education before putting on a uniform.

"George, did the secretary say anything to change your mind?" his father said about enlisting.

"No, sir, I'm going in," said Bush. "I listened to what he had to say, but I'm not taking his advice."

Bush "went on into Boston" and enlisted in the Navy as a seaman second class. He was sworn in the day he turned eighteen.

In 1942 Bush trained with, among other aviators, baseball titan Ted Williams at the Chapel Hill Naval Air Station. On June 9, 1943, completing a ten-month course, he got wings and his commission as an ensign in the U.S. Naval Reserve at Corpus Christi, becoming the nation's then-youngest naval aviator. Bush was assigned to a torpedo squadron (VT-51), which in 1944 was placed on the destroyer USS *San Jacinto* as a member of Air Group 51. Mates looked at Bush's lanky skin and bones and coined a nickname: "Skin." Little came "easy" any more. In the Pacific theater, now-lieutenant Bush flew missions over Wake Island, Guam, and Saipan.

On September 2, 1944, he piloted a VT-51 Grumman Avenger aircraft to destroy the radio transmission center on Chichi Jima. The Avenger was struck by Japanese antiaircraft flak and its engine set on fire, yet Bush completed his run, emptied the tonnage, and scored dead-on hits. Each wing burning, Bush flew out to sea to give himself, RM2 John Delaney, and Lt. (j.g.) William White a better chance to parachute. One crew member—it is unknown which—was trapped on the plane; the other's chute didn't open; both died. Piloting a low-wing plane with a high tail, Bush hit his head against the elevator, pulled his rip cord early, jumped out, and braved more fire. "I had this huge gash on my head as I hit the water," he told David Frost. "It was about as close to death as you can get."

Bush landed near an island controlled, he feared, by the Japanese. He waited four hours in an inflated raft, had his opened parachute wash onto the beach, and "paddled like hell, I mean, set a world record trying to stay away from that island." Glad to be alive, blaming himself for the loss of his crew, he was courageous under tension, facing death with stark resistance. Finally, Bush was spotted by U.S. fighters, who circled above till the lifeguard submarine USS *Finback* arrived. A bearded ensign climbed up the conning tower. "A lot of other guys came around, pulled me out of the water, and down we went," he said to Frost. In 1960 John F. Kennedy's presidential campaign ballyhooed his wartime PT-109 boat heroism. In 1988 Bush barely mentioned his Avenger attack on the Japanese. Even that triggered Dorothy, still averse to self-importance.

"George, I understand you're bragging about your war record," she said in her son's telling.

"No, ma'am," he insisted. "I'm not bragging."

"Well, you be careful about that," Mother said. He was.

Bush stayed aboard the *Finback* for a month, helping rescue other pilots. "I went on deck at night, stood watch on the tower, and looked out at the dark. The sky was clear. The stars were brilliant." As a boy he had heard "Mother or Dad give a Bible lesson each day at breakfast." Now, alone, Bush felt "calm, inner peace—God's therapy." Dorothy and Prescott Bush's son grew up in a hurry. He soon returned to the *San Jacinto*, the Philippines, and then, his squadron replaced, America in late 1944. His scorecard listed fifty-eight combat missions, a Distinguished Flying Cross for completing his mission under fire, three Air Medals, his destroyer's Presidential Unit Citation, and a reverence for Lincoln's "last full measure of devotion."

Once Hugh Sidey asked John F. Kennedy, born in 1917, what he recalled of the Depression. "Really nothing," said JFK, his family worth north of $400 million, making the Bushes look like hired help. "It didn't have an effect. But ask me about the war—that's what I remember." Bush remembered too. Until then he had lived a sheltered life in Greenwich and Andover: tended grounds, catered personnel, a chauffeur to and from the Country Day School. Many friends and their families thought, in Mike Huckabee's hand grenade of a phrase, that "*summer* is a verb," placing portfolio stock above human stock.

"You'd see it at Newport, the Hudson Valley near Hyde Park, today the Hamptons and Nantucket," said a friend. "Their 'The Twelve Days of Christmas' goes 'seven yachts a swimming, six homes a owning, five golden rings.'" It would have been easy for Bush to graduate from poor little rich boy to upper-class swell—a hedge fund manager, stock overseer, less working stiff than aging golden boy—someone who never dirtied his hands, sweat a mortgage, or fret about a bill. That didn't happen. Why?

Later, in the White House, I asked Bush how politics had taught priorities. Did perks and prerequisites matter? Power's promise—potential or achieved? Instantly, he answered, "What matters? Faith, family, friends." Sidey, the journalist who with *Newsweek*'s Tom DeFrank perhaps knew him best, understood. "What is left [when power passes] is the infinite tenderness and love within a caring family. He had the best. So much of George Bush is family." Above all, Bush's parents bequeathed a fierce belief in equality, theirs the Puritan canon of inner-directedness. I did not grasp this for a long time, knowing Bush, like the vast majority of Americans, from afar.

Bush's postwar biography typified his generation's, and especially an adopted Texan's. It personalized his new state's beauty of bluebonnet fields and peach orchards and distant scrub brush and vastness to the landscape—a sense of impatience with limits of any kind. In December 1944 Bush was reassigned to Norfolk Navy Base, put in a training wing for new torpedo pilots, then assigned as a naval aviator in a new torpedo squadron, VT-153, at the naval air station in Grosse Ile, Michigan. On January 6, 1945, Bush, on leave, married Barbara Pierce, daughter of Pauline and Marvin Pierce, the latter ultimately president of McCall Corporation, publisher of the enormously popular women's magazines *Redbook* and *McCall's*. The wedding was at the First Presbyterian Church in Rye, New York.

Born June 8, 1925, Barbara attended Rye Country Day School (1931–37) and boarding school (1940–43) at Ashley Hall in Charleston, South Carolina. She first met Bush at a 1941 Christmas dance in Greenwich, then was invited to Andover's 1942 spring prom. "Dear Poppy, I think it was perfectly swell of you to invite me to the dance and I would love to come or go or whatever you say," she replied.

Beginnings

"I wrote Mother yesterday or the day before and rather logically, I haven't heard from her, but I'm sure she is going to let me come or go, etc. I'm really all excited but scared to death too. If you hear a big noise up there, don't worry, it's just my knees knocking." They were engaged less than two years later. He was the first boy she ever kissed.

George had named three wartime planes for her—*Barbara I, II,* and *III*. She dropped out of Smith College to marry. They then shared their first home in a tiny apartment in Trenton, Michigan, near Poppy's assignment in Grosse Ile. The Bushes' marriage outlasted the typewriter, long-playing record, carbon paper, mimeograph machine, vacuum tube, flashbulb, eleven American presidencies, four major U.S. wars, and half a century of losing for the Chicago Cubs. Their six children were George Walker Bush (born 1946), Pauline Robinson "Robin" Bush (1949), John Ellis "Jeb" Bush (1953), Neil Mallon Bush (1955), Marvin Pierce Bush (1956), and Dorothy Bush Koch (1959). In September 1945 the Japanese surrender ended the war, Bush honorably discharged.

Bush had been accepted by Yale University, Dad's alma mater, before he joined the Navy. As Timothy Naftali's book *George H. W. Bush* notes, the young man in a hurry now began the school's accelerated program to graduate in less in three years, not in four. Again his schedule rivaled Phillips Academy's: member, later president, Delta Kappa Epsilon fraternity; member, Phi Beta Kappa and, like Dad, the cheerleading squad and the secret society Skull and Bones; Yale's baseball captain, a good-field, no-hit left-handed first baseman. A famed photo shows Babe Ruth, dying of throat cancer, giving Bush the manuscript copy of *The Babe Ruth Story* for the Yale library before a 1948 game at Yale Field. The yearbook includes Bush, in uniform, with a description: "Captain of championship college baseball team [making the first two (1947 and 1948) College World Series finals], while completing college in 2 1/2 years after war service. Phi Beta Kappa—Economics."

In lore, Bush, graduating from Yale, closed his eyes, threw a mental dart at a 1948 map, and chose remote rural Texas to forge an oil wildcat niche. In fact, Poppy had already found his example—Dad's.

Business became a self-sufficient means to the end of entering politics. (Prescott was 1947–50 Connecticut Republican Party finance chairman, barely losing a 1950 U.S. Senate bid.) "Yes," George said, "it's what he taught me. Make some money so that you can serve." He spurned a possible 1948 Rhodes scholarship, "figuring I couldn't afford to bring Barbara and George [now two] to England." Instead, packing their red Studebaker, Bush accepted family friend Neil Mallon's offer to start in Texas oil as an equipment clerk with Dresser Industries, a subsidiary of Brown Brothers Harriman, where Prescott had been a board director for twenty-two years.

The oil-field supply company transferred Poppy to California as a salesman, then back to Midland, Texas. Bush's Navy squadron training also shipped him from one base to another, from Michigan to Maryland. The Bushes became happy wanderers; by 1989, on entering the White House, they estimated having lived in twenty-eight houses. "They were can-do, like the age. Anything was possible, because there weren't any limits," said J. Roy Goodearle, a postwar wildcatter and Bush's first campaign manager for 1962 Harris County (Houston) Republican chairman. (Goodearle, now deceased, was also my father-in-law.) "You had to be agile, a lot of rivalries"—think TV's *Dallas*. "Background meant a lot less than ability." To the natives', and perhaps Bush's own, surprise, the Yalie found that skill and gift for friendship could dwarf even lacking a Texas drawl.

"Lived the dream," Poppy said of the postwar boom. "People from other states as neighbors, barbecues, helping each other. My four boys playing baseball. I coached it. And Barbara—there were tens of thousands of kids in Little League. There were times I thought she car-pooled 'em all." In 1953 their first daughter, Robin, became ill of leukemia. The Bushes called doctors in Houston and New York, tried every medical treatment, held Robin, and wept with her, said Barbara Bush. Nothing worked. In 1988, sensing that David Frost felt he had made her cry by referencing the illness, Mrs. Bush said, "I'm not sad. I only cry when I am happy. I think of Robin as a happiness now, so please don't feel uncomfortable."

Barbara's husband reacted to, then later recalled, the almost unbearable differently—still Dorothy Bush's son. Barbara had always been independent—as a child, swimming, tennis, bike riding, a rabid reader. Strength now yielded to depression—and to brown hair that became the white color it remained. As his wife anguished in a way only death can cause, Bush, stoic and protective, held *her*, "wouldn't let me go, saved me from falling into a dark hole," she told Frost. "I think we grew closer because of Robin."

Unable to save their only daughter—Daddy's girl, as any papa knows—Bush buried grief deep inside, immersed in how "it was inexplicable to me—why an innocent child?" At the same time, he believed that "God works in wondrous, mysterious ways." Instantly, the tragedy could resurface. More than half a century after Robin's death, describing her, Bush's voice caught, choking, unable to proceed.

"We felt helpless," Bush said about Robin. When she was diagnosed with leukemia in early 1953, the Bushes had never heard of the word. Eight months later they donated her body to science and began giving time and millions of dollars to cancer research. Robin is buried at the Bush Library at Texas A&M University next to where her parents will one day lie.

At least business allowed a measure of control. In 1951 Poppy and a neighbor, John Overbey, founded the Bush-Overbey Oil Development Company, an independent firm into which Bush parlayed heart, work, curiosity, and Wall Street family capital. Uncle George Herbert Walker Jr. contributed nearly $500,000. Other investors included *Washington Post* publisher Eugene Meyer, a family friend. In 1953 the firm merged with another independent to form Zapata Petroleum, Bush choosing the name of Mexican revolutionary Emiliano Zapata, portrayed in the 1952 Oscar-winning film *Viva Zapata!* Poppy evidently liked the crew: Marlon Brando in the lead; Anthony Quinn, Oscar-winning supporting actor; Elia Kazan, director; and John Steinbeck, writer.

In 1959 the company divided operations between inland, drilling in Texas's Permian Basin, and offshore oil and gas. Bush headed

Zapata Offshore Co., moving his firm and family to Houston. He was white, like Texas's hierarchy; Protestant, like most of the populace; slim, with an athlete's gait; and had manners Miss Manners would envy, with a self-mocking way, not newly formed, that was neither bogus nor offensive. All this drew a stranger to him in oil and later politics, making you forget his less hardscrabble than privileged youth. It also explains—this is crucial—why except for Dwight Eisenhower and Ronald Reagan, the Orion of the Grand Old Party (GOP), Bush is the only Republican of our time to become beloved in the autumn of his life.

In 1940 presidential nominee Wendell Willkie—to Franklin Roosevelt aide Harold Ickes, "a simple barefoot Wall Street lawyer"—was a supernova, a preternatural creation of Republican newspapers and businessmen. He died in 1944, largely a non-person in his party.

Bush, Richard Nixon, and Gerald Ford each told me that Thomas Dewey, the 1944 and 1948 Republican nominee, was the one person of their lifetime who should have been but wasn't president. "Dewey would have been a fine president," Bush said. "A stiff and formal candidate, but his record as [1943–54 New York] Governor and as a prosecutor was superb." He died in 1971, still easier to admire than like.

Another New York governor, Nelson Rockefeller, essence of the Eastern establishment, welcomed conservatives' hatred, wrapping his portfolio in arrogance: "I've never found it a handicap to be a Rockefeller," Rocky barbed. Long before his death in 1979, many said Rockefeller's handicap was that he wasn't a Republican. Barry Goldwater spent the last third of his life a GOP pariah for losing the 1964 election so badly that it made the liberal Great Society possible. Unfairly, Bush 41 vice president Dan Quayle became a late-night TV punch line. Ironically, two-term President George W. Bush aided Dad's rehabilitation.

Republican 2008 nominee John McCain earned his fortune— estimated net worth, more than $100 million, surpassing either Bush— the old-fashioned way: marrying it. His daughter Meghan also made Madonna appear square. Mitt Romney and Joe Average were Venus and Mars. Only Bush 41 wore so durably that he survived his own annus horribilis—the 1992 campaign, which cast him as more dilettante than family and working man—to become revered by Americans "who give birth and grow and love and laugh and die, bonded and sustained by the land," wrote Hugh Sidey, "which is the oldest way of life Americans know."

In December 2012, brooking severe bronchitis, Bush was hospitalized in Houston at eighty-eight, Chief of Staff Jean Becker saying that "most of the civilized world" had contacted her after he had been placed in intensive care. "Someday President George H. W. Bush might realize how beloved he is, but of course one of the reasons why he is so beloved is because he has no idea." Bush's response was typical, advising Becker, "Tell people to put the harps back in the closet." He left Methodist Hospital in January 2013.

What explained what Bill Clinton, by then Bush's improbable charity tag-team *frère*, called 41's "capacity for giving and receiving love? I guess it's surprising because we opposed one another. But George Bush is a man I love." Some of Poppy's traits were deep down, thus initially hard to spot; others superficial, yet telling. The most obvious denoted an old upper-class family. Only later were his middle-class values grasped, building a bridge that Willkie through Rocky to Romney and McCain never crossed. To me—my youth forged by Middle America—Bush's background had at first seemed so different as to inhabit a separate globe.

TWO

Finding the Water Fine

I was born in 1951, the first of a thirteen-year storybook of unusual national harmony. Pulitzer Prize–winning historian Theodore H. White observed, "I cannot now deny my recognition that the Eisenhower [later, Kennedy] years in Washington were the most pleasant of our time." Among other things, they began with Joseph Stalin's death, Mount Everest's conquest, and the birth of *I Love Lucy*, starring Charlie Chaplin's lineal heir. They ended on a sunglint Texas afternoon in November 1963. "Just another era?" said a friend. "Maybe. But somehow I think those years meant more." Even now, something remains, if but a vague recollection, of the oneness that Ronald Reagan, among many from an earlier steppe land generation, felt with his childhood. "Everyone has to have a place to go back to," Reagan said of his heartland Pleasantville. "Dixon [Illinois] is that place for me."

It appeared less simple at the time. *Living*, as opposed to critiquing, the 1950s and early '60s, you focused on polarity, not uniformity, and how America changed: from a country of tradition to a culture crazed by youth; an administration of businessmen to a government spiced by academe; a Protestant-only presidency to an office others could attain; politicians equating success with legislation to leaders feeling that style wrote the prose of the legend that was Camelot.

In shorthand code those scoring the 1950s—1952 and 1956 Democratic nominee Adlai Stevenson, tarring the "green fairways of indifference," or John Kenneth Galbraith, torching "the bland leading the bland"—thought America before Kennedy had been puritanical, inhibited. As a young, Presbyterian, and in Murray Kempton's phrase, "shabby-genteel" male, I came from people who discerned in the Age of Ike a Fred MacMurray type of affability that, in retrospect, seems almost virginal. Demographically and attitudinally, they dominated the GOP.

Only later did we see a close working compact that bound both then-opposing camps. Our pillar was the keeper of the faith, defender of the peace, and scourge of "Godless Communism." Who doubted that John Winthrop's "Shining City upon a Hill" was the last best hope of freedom? To most of the republic, said 1963–69 Texas governor John Connally, the compact helped sustain a system that "fed better, fed more, clothed better, clothed more, housed better, housed more" than any system ever devised by man. In what TV's Archie Bunker later called the "good old U.S. of A.," it was a good time to be alive.

"The Forgotten Americans. The Silent Majority. Hard-working, church-going people. Farmers. Shopkeepers," a 1990 PBS documentary called the people among whom I grew up. "People with an inbred respect for authority and an unyielding belief in the American Dream." From a small town's closeness to the earth, you seldom wandered far away.

Caledonia, population 2,188, straddled a line between the lowlands of Lake Ontario and rolling greenery to the south in Western New York. It was a factory village, settled by Scotch-Irish immigrants like *McPherson, Hinsdale, McIntyre*, and *Denoon*—names vaulting back more than a century earlier, when travelers paused on their sojourn west. It had the country's first fish hatchery, porches whose swings spied neighbors' comings and goings, five grocery stores, two car dealerships, a Masonic Temple, a barber shop, and a town tramp dubbed the Big R, abbreviating her surname. Unlike the America of a later age—assassination, Vietnam, Watergate, then malaise—it was a community of piety and place.

Caledonia was also integrated, unlike many northern and almost all southern burgs, blacks buoying my school band, choir, and Little League team. Near the baseball field, which paralleled a creek, stood the vortex of my youth—the First Presbyterian Church, or White Kirk, where adults read scripture, sent their children to Vacation Bible School, and in general believed what Margaret Thatcher, whom I came to admire as much as any leader of our age, later called "the things I and millions like me were brought up with: an honest day's work for an honest day's pay; live within your means; put by a nest egg for a rainy day; pay your bills on time; support the police." Bush's mother could have said each word. The voters he one day sought could too.

Our church was at least as large, though not as lavish, as the town's Episcopal Church and smaller, though less mysterious, than St. Columba's Catholic Church, and the singing was more reserved than in next-door Mumford's black Baptist Church—and it could be almost as much a social organization as a vehicle for salvation, hosting November's annual turkey dinner of takeouts, handouts, and fewer Democrats than pies. The year's other pleasance—July's Strawberry Festival, with its homemade ice cream and berries shucked by hand—graced Caledonia's other Presbyterian meeting place: the Stone Church, across the street—Church Street, naturally—from a small two-story house where I was raised.

My father was an agriculture teacher, then high school counselor, taking outside jobs to support five children. One day, driving a backhoe, he raised an Indian skeleton that revealed a world not of bloodthirsty savages but of hunters and fishermen and New York counties that bore their name—Onondaga, Seneca, Oneida, Wyoming. My mother reminded me of no one as much as actress Eve Arden. Before becoming a high school librarian, she had taught Latin in the small Upstate town of Rushford. At five I accidentally told a teacher, "My mother taught in Russia." Recalling Alger Hiss, the Rosenbergs, and Joseph McCarthy's "list" of 205 State Department employees who "belong to the Communist Party," my parents expected J. Edgar Hoover to knock at our front door.

Behind our house the Lehigh Railroad's whistle voiced distant ven-

Finding the Water Fine

tures that spoke of impossible dreams. I walked its tracks to school, crossing hazy swampland ankle-deep in water—or rode a bicycle festooned with streamers and cards attached to spokes that scent of fingers on a mandolin. Returning home was equally self-dramatic. First, I passed aging Scotchy Tennent—a rumored veteran of the charge up San Juan Hill—sitting on the American Legion Building stoop. He dispensed candy to hangers-on, talking of combat and the flag and temptations assailing the small-town faith. (Ninety) proof lay a hundred feet away, slumped beneath a tree—our town drunk, Red Ned, half the size of Otis Campbell of TV's *The Andy Griffith Show*, set in mythical Mayberry, North Carolina, but just as gassed.

Law 'n' order crested up the hill in Bernard Hayward, Caledonia's chief of police, who resembled Mayberry policeman Bernard P. Fife in more than name. He packed but rarely used a gun, relying on sturdy citizens to, as TV's Barn' would say, "nip it [crime] in the bud." Complying, we frequented Moonwink's Restaurant, where after school-league Biddy Basketball victories the owner donated banana splits, and the village library, founded in 1826, with quotations on the wall urging a more moral and fruitful life.

One day my best friend and I, each ten, visited O'Brien's Drugstore, not far from the veterans statue in the middle of town. It was not long before I noticed the proprietor looking over our shoulders.

"What would your parents think?" asked Mr. O'Brien, a courtly, soft-spoken man, to my friend, holding *Playboy* magazine. Oblivious, I was reading *Mad*'s latest issue, no more knowing what *Playboy* was than how $E = MC2$.

I waited for my friend, then stepped outside and headed home, unaware how Dwight Eisenhower often hailed "the great and priceless privilege of growing up in an American small town."

All of the banal and towering, self-assured and un-self-confident, devious and trustworthy people who are the people of the United States have something central to their life. To Mario Cuomo, it is the immigrant experience; commentator Bill O'Reilly, his Catholicism; George Bush, noblesse oblige. The small town was Ike's central fact—and a large part of the America that made Bush president. Church Street and Wall Street, high school and prep school, blue-collar and Connecticut chic, believed in its chivalries and its codes.

Eisenhower was perhaps the most beloved man in American history. In late 1954, 84 percent of the American people in a Gallup poll couldn't name *one* thing Ike had done wrong in his first two years as president. A year later 60 percent of *Democrats* wanted the Republican as their 1956 nominee. "Everybody ought to be happy every day," he said. "Play hard, have fun doing it, and despise wickedness." Five years later I witnessed on TV my first act of political theater—Ike at the 1960 GOP Convention in Chicago, deplaning, speaking, waving; in writer Richard Cohen's words, "a buoyant and humane man, encircled by a captivating grin."

Eisenhower is remembered not only as a "great and good man," to quote biographer Stephen Ambrose, but as a great and good president. He knit eight years of peace and prosperity—1.5 percent inflation, the Interstate Highway System, St. Lawrence Seaway, the first civil rights bill in eighty-two years, domestic unity, and nonpareil prestige—a decade more Americans would choose to relive, I believe, than any of the century. Wrote Theodore White: "Never did the sun shine fairer across a great Nation and its prospects than it did in the age of Eisenhower."

On January 21, 1989, President Bush had his first White House meeting with the speech staff in the Roosevelt Room, a rich, mahogany chamber off the Oval Office, where he talked of policy, language, and the Ghosts of Presidents Past. To my left was a large fireplace; to its side, a patchwork of flags—one of the United States and another bearing the presidential seal. Across the room was Theodore Roosevelt's 1906 Nobel Peace Prize. Western art and a Remington bust enhanced the effect.

I asked Bush what predecessors he most admired. The president said Lincoln, because he abolished slavery and saved the Union. TR, because he was what Bush hoped to be—the conserver of lands and wildlife for unborn generations. Finally, he named the Sunflower son who graduated from West Point, becoming general of the Army, Columbia University president, first Supreme Commander of the North Atlantic Treaty Organization (NATO), and thirty-fourth president.

"I always liked Ike," Bush began. He revered him as a person, chief of World War II's Allied Expeditionary Force, and what Andrew Jackson became to Harry Truman, Truman to Gerald Ford, and FDR to Ronald Reagan—a presidential frame of reference.

"Why?" I asked.

"He was bipartisan. It was Congress and the president on the same side. We've lost so much of that since then," Bush said, unguardedly twirling glasses in his hands. "He got the country moving in one direction—representing our best values along the way."

Bush hoped to govern like Eisenhower—more as president than politician, his model a plaque that sat on Ike's desk: "Gently in manner, strong in deed." Soon speech references dubbed "Dwight Eisenhower—beloved Ike" sprouted like fireflies, aides joking that "beloved Ike" was Eisenhower's surname. Finally, the word came forth from staff secretary Jim Cicconi, Bush's fellow Texan: *No mas.* "If I see that phrase again," he said, partly tongue in cheek, "I'll go back and vote for Stevenson." Pity—our research file still bulged with beloved Ikeisms. I am sure Bush never knew of Cicconi's decree.

Eisenhower was not the kindly stick figure / father figure drawn by critics and admirers. Reserved, he was mercurial. His fuse was limited to intimates. Most people despair over big things—separation, death. Ike exploded over the little—a lousy seven iron, a balky jeep ignition. (Years later I used Ike as a scapegoat: "If temper was good enough for Eisenhower, it's good enough for me.")

Ike could be cold. Journalist Hedley Donovan shocked friends by saying that Eisenhower was smarter than Stevenson but not as nice. He used aides to deflect criticism. Nixon, his vice president, noted how Gen. Walter Bedell Smith, Ike's wartime chief of staff, tearfully recalled, "I was only Ike's prat boy. Ike always had to have a prat boy." Yet he was also adored by crowds in India and Italy, Budapest and Berlin. Many leaders are loved in their own countries or admired in others. Ike was loved *internationally* as America's sine qua non. Hearing Bush, I wondered, What *was* it that so set Eisenhower apart?

To begin, he was a man of inordinate goodwill. "In politics," Nixon observed, "the natural reaction is to have strong hatreds one way or the other. Ike didn't fit that pattern. He didn't think of people who disagreed with him as being the enemy. He thought, 'They don't agree with me.'" At home Eisenhower felt that "the road to success must be down the middle"; abroad, *knowing* war, he *hated* it—"I've had enough of war," Ike told the Soviets in 1955— thus began the age of summitry, the belief that "open skies" could open hearts. Three decades later what Bush called the Revolution of '89 flowed from the morality and humanity of a soldier, diplomat, and five-star general.

Ike encapsulated his age and land. He liked Zane Grey novels and TV Westerns, Bush's kind of escapist lilt. As the president told Eisenhower's Centenary Commission in a 1990 speech, Ike's favorite band was Fred Waring and the Pennsylvanians. (Sadly, Bush axed my line "Of course, his [Eisenhower's] fox trot was better than mine. As Barbara says, whose isn't?") Ike played baseball and football at West Point. Bush played baseball at Yale. As president, each attended the Army-Navy football game, culled from America's psychic attic. Eisenhower installed a putting green a few feet from the Oval Office, his love of golf a national belly laugh. (Out too went the Centenary line: "You'll know I've had a similar impact if the next few years bring creation of a seniors' fishing tour." The president could be wary about equating himself with Ike.)

It is true Eisenhower was not a linguist; to many, that affirmed his honest sense of identity. "He was one of us—we trusted him to act on *behalf* of us," Bush told the Eisenhower Commission. Next came a passage the president kept in: "In fact, fracturing syntax, Ike even *spoke* like us." Smile and self-effacement. "Come to think of it, now I know *why* he's among my favorite presidents."

Above all Ike was beloved because he acted—*decided*—as a president should. Bush had a splendid résumé when he ran for president— but it didn't include the words "preserved civilization." Eisenhower's

Finding the Water Fine

did. He provided what he prescribed for democracy: "faith, love of freedom, intelligence, and energy." Eclipsing biography's flesh and bones, Ike *was* as much a citizen of London as Abilene.

After one fit of Eisenhower temper, his mother told the then ten-year-old, "He that conquereth his own soul is greater than he who taketh a city." He did, and as Bush said, enriched the nation's. Beloved Ike, indeed.

After reading and writing millions of words about Eisenhower, Stephen Ambrose concluded that the secret to his success was trust: "I never found him in a personal lie." This account will show how Bush, in his starched white shirts trekking the oil fields, proving that Prescott Bush's son could make it on his own, and mentally readying to join Dad's craft of politics, was a man of honor too, speaking and listening with respect for people as *individuals*.

In 1990 Ann Landers wrote that "manners are" an inheritance to "children who are taught kindness, generosity, and respect at home." The downside was naiveté. My father tells how at eight, I beat up a bully, then ran after him, asking forgiveness. Two years later, visiting my mother's home city, Worcester, Massachusetts, I gave a stranger twenty-five cents to buy baseball cards for me, which he pledged to, but did not, return. Small towns can leave you more smart than street-smart, needing to learn how to treat life warily. Ike learned in the Army. Nixon learned in the Navy, playing poker. As we shall see, America's forty-first president could be excused for feeling cynical after Democrats reneged on their 1990 tax agreement to trim multiyear spending.

Republicans felt taken, as they had in the phantasmagoric election of 1960. "We were babes in the woods," said Nixon, running against Kennedy for president. Much of the theft occurred in Texas and Chicago: people registered in the graveyard; the same people voting in different districts; more backing Kennedy than resided in a district. "The stealing was outrageous," said Bush, whose Harris County voted solidly GOP. "If we'd had more people in Chicago that could count in those wards, Nixon probably would have been elected." The theft taught Bush a lesson *Nixon* would not forget.

Two years later Bush entered politics, running for GOP chairman of Harris County—for Republicans, historically more of a waif of the moon than bright noon sun. In 1952 Democrats had owned every southern U.S. House and Senate seat from Virginia to California. By 1956 Eisenhower peripherally cracked the solid South by taking four states, including his birthplace, Texas. In 1961 John Tower became the Lone Star State's first Republican U.S. senator since Reconstruction. At the same time, Texas was growing from without. Veterans from elsewhere came, enjoyed, and stayed. Many left the cities for Republican suburbia. Oil made Texas even more business friendly. Risk takers—entrepreneurs—felt at ease in the GOP.

As the state moved rightward, the ultraright John Birch Society also thrived, worrying some Republicans that it might seize the party apparatus. "Up to now, our primaries'd been small in-house affairs," said Bush's first campaign manager, J. Roy Goodearle. "The story is that one time the only folks showing up were two drunks and a Democrat at the meeting by mistake." Unless a strong candidate entered, "a Bircher might win a low-turnout county chairman race."

To Goodearle, "George's attraction was that he'd bring in enough voters to defeat the Birchers. Our folks thought he was conservative, but safe." Bush was also ready. "This was a challenge I'd been waiting for," Poppy said, "an opening into politics at the ground level where it all starts." He easily won the vote—his first election victory—then surprisingly tried to enlist the Birchers within the GOP base. Their toxicity eluded Bush, Goodearle said. "George didn't understand."

About this time Lewis Mumford termed Ike's successor, who never lost an election, "the first American President to give literature . . . a place of dignity and honor in our national life." If, quoting Kennedy, the presidency was "the vital center of action," language was its core. Only seven years older than Bush, JFK scored with his inaugural, Cuban Missile Crisis speech, and 1963 nuclear disarmament address, called by Soviet premier Nikita Khrushchev "the greatest speech by an American president since Roosevelt." Another speech confronted the Soviets' concrete and barbed wire wall, built in 1961, that divided Berlin, halted the refugee flow from the Communist East to democratic West, and separated families till its 1989 collapse.

On June 26, 1963, Kennedy addressed hundreds of thousands of people in the divided city, speaking briefly but unforgettably—"Ich bin ein Berliner"—I am a Berliner. Two and a half years into his presidency, JFK was still from, not of, politics' rock 'em–sock 'em maelstrom. In the 1960 Wisconsin primary, a drunk had tossed a glass in his face. Kennedy had picked it up and said, "Here's your drink." His style gripped reporters, even would-be pols—"JFK was understated," said Bush. "Never a false public step." He began the Peace Corps, formed the Alliance for Progress, braved the Bay of Pigs, and presented "a picture of total urbanity," one writer said, "the first true reflection in the Presidency of America at the turn of the mid-century, a country of city dwellers long gone from Main Street."

In 1990 President Bush introduced scholar David Donald before his White House Lincoln lecture. Aware of JFK's respect for Lincoln, I had called Kennedy Presidential Library director David Powers, who sent me an October 1960 campaign reference to Lincoln, writing, "Jack used this here [Illinois] and in other places [vs. Nixon]." Bush used it too, invoking how in 1861, leaving Springfield to assume the presidency, "Lincoln addressed his home people at the Great Western Railway Station." Listening, I drifted back to Middle America's 1960s split view. On one hand, it liked how JFK made of politics a sudden magic place—"Jack," said a Democrat, "is the first Irish Brahmin." On the other, it mistrusted his liberalism, beautiful people, and as Hubert Humphrey wrote, "win at all cost" code—thus, the 50-50 election tie.

In a fall 1961 Gallup poll meriting the phrase white lie or faulty memory, 62 percent of those surveyed said they had voted for Kennedy in 1960. (He actually got 49.7.) JFK might have won reelection in a breeze. Only the South resisted, civil rights' irresistible force facing the region's immovable object. Kennedy was in Dallas November 22, 1963, partly to slow the free fall; a Texas poll showed conservative senator Barry Goldwater—a libertarian, a true believer ("In your heart," said posters, "you know he's right")—narrowly leading him. A Goldwater tide might have helped Bush unseat liberal U.S. senator Ralph Yarborough in 1964. Poppy had planned to paint the incumbent as a zealot. Instead, Kennedy's death made Texan Lyndon Johnson president.

Suddenly, Goldwater's—thus, briefly Bush's—tide began running out. Attacked by Yarborough as "a right-wing extremist," Bush lost 56.2 to 43.6 percent but ran far ahead of Goldwater's 36.5 percent in Texas. In 1966 Yale '48 resigned at Zapata, selling his share for more than $1 million. Entering politics, Bush had found the water fine.

Franklin Roosevelt called himself a juggler, the left hand not knowing what the right was doing. Bush understood, trying to finesse the difference between his background and constituency. In 1966 he denounced the Birch Society but gave TV speeches scoring the United Nations. The perceived country club Republican opposed segregation, knocked busing, and hailed Ike's "sensible center." Bush had bought a home in Houston's Tanglewood area. As Harris County chairman, he used the Supreme Court one man–one vote ruling to file suit for congressional redistricting in Houston. Upheld, the suit preserved the new Seventh Congressional District as if it had been designed by Bush himself: affluent "Silk Stocking," overwhelmingly white, mostly Protestant, and three of every four voters from somewhere else. If Bush were a "carpetbagger," as Democrats huffed, so was his new district.

Bush beat Democrat Frank Briscoe, 57 to 43 percent, to become the first Republican to represent Houston. Upside: Bush was smart, attractive, and unlike Goldwater, not regarded as a nut. In 1964 Nixon and Reagan were the sole national Republicans to campaign for the Arizonan; years later he repaid each by trashing them. "I used to wonder whether Barry was evil or just dumb," Eisenhower would say. "No more. He's the dumbest person I've ever known." Helping Bush were Nixon and Ford, among other GOPers, each having known his dad. In particular, Nixon took a liking, Bush on his short list of possible 1968 vice presidential candidates. "Just one Congressional term, not a lot in his record to recommend him. It just shows how Nixon viewed his potential," said Goodearle. Downside: What *was* Bush, anyway, beyond a bright young man on the make?

Bush made the House Ways and Means Committee as a freshman—economics his leather. In 1968, reelected without opposition, he voted for the Civil Rights Act, which mandated open housing, reviled by many in his district. Bush backed gradual withdrawal from Vietnam, a litmus of Nixon's, narrowly elected president in 1968, but also birth control—the Right dubbed him "Rubbers." Some thought him pragmatic, a comer to get things done. Others deemed Bush's persona fuzzed, as Theodore White thought Nixon's was in 1960: "This is one of [his] characteristic and fatal flaws—that he presents too often a split image." The divide presaged Bush's presidency, when many in the media's peewee mind couldn't grasp how what they felt a Greenwich fop could like pork rinds, horseshoes, Johnny Cash, and Dolly Parton.

Bush entered politics at a time when the America for which he had nearly died seemed increasingly treated, to quote Ring Lardner, like a side dish the mid-1960s declined to order. Duty, honor, country yielded to EST, Zen, spiritualism, "Do your own thing," "If it feels good, do it," and other mindless mots. Looking back, the age was a bumper sticker, arrogance and a snarky meanness scaling a hidebound triumph undreamt of under Ike or JFK. "I think it would be difficult," sociologist Robert N. Nisbet wrote, "to find a single decade in the history of Western culture when as much calculated onslaught against culture and convention in any form, as much sheer degradation of both culture and the individual passed into print, into music, into art, and onto the American screen [and into its streets] as the decade of the sixties." More often we thought at cross-purpose, speaking *past*, not *to*.

A favorite college teacher said the '60s ended in 1973, "when Nixon began to drown [in Watergate] and Vietnam ended." Similarly, the 1950s ended November 22, 1963. Two days later Johnson told a diplomat, "I am not going to be the President who saw South Viet Nam go the way China went." LBJ rallied to Saigon's side. In August 1964, when two U.S. destroyers were said to be attacked in the Gulf of Tonkin, Johnson ordered a counterassault on North Vietnam. Next year he introduced American combat troops, initiated bombing raids up north sans retaliatory pretense, and dropped more U.S. bombs in Vietnam than hit *all* enemy targets in World War II. The stratagem, "gradual escalation," aimed to win the war while Johnson enacted his domestic "Great Society." Longtime friend John Connally told LBJ it wouldn't work: "The economy can't sustain guns *and* butter." Fatalities hit five hundred weekly.

To many, stalemate daubed the confusion of the president, not the courage of our troops. By 1967 Johnson was choosing bombing targets for his generals. Publicly, Bush backed his fellow Texan. (On January 20, 1969, he was the only GOP congressman at Andrews Air Force Base to bid the now ex-president adieu as Johnson flew home to Texas.) Privately, Bush thought LBJ should leave the military alone. Alabama governor George Wallace was less discreet: "What we've got to do is win. We've got to pour it on." By contrast, the Left termed the North-South conflict a civil war, the solution—get out *now!*—deserting the government the United States had helped install. Part of America dubbed Johnson's ministry of the war a revealing nihilism. The other saw the counterculture—that vacuous cliché—as unwilling to assume its responsibilities—even to know what they were. Bush, prizing civility, feared that America had become a dialogue of the deaf.

What part of the fracturing—right vs. left, hard hat vs. hippie, the rule of law vs. an activist who sniffed, "So we struggle, in our humble way, to destroy the United States"—stemmed from the war? Who knows, even now? Reaction against the pious '50s—a 1991 PBS documentary sniped, "Obey authority, control your emotions, fit in with the group, and don't even *think* about having sex"—might have been inevitable. Vietnam's magnifying glass showed a horror house at home. In 1967 Paris reported 20 armed robberies; London, 205; and Washington DC, 2,429. Riot ravaged Watts, Cleveland, Detroit (where forty-three died), Newark, and hundreds of other cities. Was the war an excuse or a cause?

Finding the Water Fine

University buildings were burned and scholarly works destroyed. Bombings, sit-ins, and vandalism maimed sites where panty raids once seemed bravura. Students tuned in, turned on, and dropped out. Trained antiwar protestors clashed with club-swinging police—crabbed radical Tom Hayden, "the shock troops of the Establishment"—at the 1968 Democratic Convention. Militant H. Rap Brown turned Phineas T. Bluster: "Violence is necessary. It's as American as cherry pie." Few Americans praised Cuban radical and pop culture sham Che Guevara. More merely rued their country, coming apart.

In August 1968 the Republican nominee for president gave an acceptance speech that MSNBC's Chris Matthews later called "a masterpiece" and George Gallup termed the most effective acceptance in polling history. "Millions of Americans cry out in anguish," the GOP speaker said. "Did we come all this way for this? Did American boys die in Normandy and Korea, and in Valley Forge for this?"

The question, you hoped, was rhetorical. The speaker was Richard Nixon, giving the address that made him president. Later, *Esquire* magazine said, "There was no player [of our age] in the national drama who came close to Nixon; the idea of Nixon was somehow central to the experience of being an American in the second half of this century." Next to Ronald Reagan, Nixon was also the person who most profoundly changed George Bush's life.

THREE

Perfectly Clear

T he Upstate New York town of my youth had one bar, six churches, and no traffic lights. Its people believed in work, God, family, a fondness for the familiar, and a reverence for everything American. Their hero was what journalist Tom Wicker called "one of us"—the quintessence of Middle America. Defending Richard Nixon, they defended their past and found what their parents and grandparents—bullied by a ruling class Congressman John Anderson dubbed the "Volvo and brie cheese crowd"—had rarely known. A voice.

Displaying pluralistic ignorance, where the members of a majority—here, the Silent—did not feel themselves a majority, they naturally admired Nixon's tenacity. "No matter what you say," jibed Jimmy Carter in 1976, "he was a leader." He regarded "trendies" and "beautiful people" and "academics who couldn't butter a piece of toast" as lepers at a bazaar. Meg Greenfield wrote of the "Nixon Generation. Half of America spent their adult lives hoping every day that Nixon would become President. The other half spent it passionately hoping he would not." After Watergate had forced RN to resign in 1974, aide Bryce Harlow compared him to a cork. Push Nixon down—always he resurfaced. Only FDR ran as many times for national office: five. Until 2012 more people had voted for Nixon for president than any man in history. In post–World War II America, his history was our history—Nixon 'R' Us.

Nixon began for me in the most theatric election of our time. I recall 1960 vividly, for even after the Great Debates—Mom saying of the first round, "He [Nixon] looks terrible"—and the turmoil of the final weeks—Kennedy stumping the Northeast, an election-eve Nixon telethon, two warriors spent by a hell-bent campaign—it was unthinkable that Kennedy would win. Election night went quickly, for I was in bed by eight: Nixon ahead, but Kennedy gaining; my father's pessimism auguring, for the first time, defeat. Next morning I raced to the front door and grabbed our daily newspaper, the Rochester, New York, *Democrat and Chronicle*. The headline screamed disaster: "Kennedy Wins." (The provincial subhead was cheerier: "Nixon Carries Monroe County.")

In 1962 Nixon lost to Pat Brown for governor of California. Mocked as a loser, derided for his squareness, incinerated, like Marley, *done*, Nixon proceeded to amaze by rising—*exhumed*—so that having served the GOP in good times and bad, he again became a leading candidate for the Republican nomination. Wrote Norman Mailer of Middle American delegates at the 1968 convention in Miami, which Bush attended as a Texas and Nixon delegate, "It was his comeback which had made him a hero in their eyes, for America is the land which worships the Great Comeback, and so he was Tricky Dick to them no more, but the finest gentleman in the land; they were proud to say hello."

There was nostalgia and love—akin to a gentle protectiveness—for wife Pat's cloth coats and the Nixon family, decent, much-wounded, and as straight and resolute as they came. In 1968 Mailer referenced Julie Nixon, then twenty. "No, she was saying, her father had never spanked them," he wrote of her and sister Tricia. "'But then,' the girl's voice went on, simple clarity, even honest devotion in the tone, 'we never wanted to displease him. We wanted to be good.'" Mailer said he had not heard a child make a remark like that about their father "since his own mother had spoken in such fashion thirty-odd years" before.

Upstate New York saw Nixon as brave and vulnerable and thoughtful and sentimental—a view so divorced from Washington's as to script another language. That may be why his stroke so stunned in 1994. There was no room in our view of Nixon for the finality of death.

In 1967 I mailed a handwritten letter to the senior partner at the Manhattan law firm of Nixon, Mitchell, Mudge, and Rose. I was president of my church's Ecumenical Fellowship, and our group would be in New York in August, and was there the chance we could meet, and if there was, it would be as fine as anything I had known.

In early April I received an answer from secretary Rose Woods. Nixon would be out of the country, writing for *Reader's Digest*. However, schedules change, and would I call on his return? I did and was invited to Nixon's office at 20 Broad Street, off Wall. For half an hour we talked of sports and college—Nixon suggested Cornell, my dad's alma mater ("Thank God," RN said, "the least Ivy of the Ivies")— and the need to work your way through school.

I still think fondly of how Nixon need not have met me but as a kindness did. Later I was to find this typical, not of the Old nor New, but of the Real Nixon—solicitous and shy. Two years later I entered college—1969–71, Allegheny College in Meadville, Pennsylvania; transferring because of tuition cost, 1971–73, State University of New York at Geneseo—as Nixon took the oath of office. It was then, as America cast herself in rancor, that he fused person and president like no chief executive since FDR.

It is hard today for post–baby boomers to grasp the early 1970s' fervor and division. Upheaval rent morality, civil rights, feminism, and drugs, and asked whether police were pigs, love should be free, grades abolished, and America—as 1972 Democrat nominee George McGovern said—"come home." The University of Pennsylvania avoided collision with student war protesters by putting its American flags in storage. Jane Fonda went to North Vietnam, railing against "those blue-eyed murderers—Nixon and the rest of those ethnocentric American white male chauvinists." Understatement went underground.

On April 30, 1970, vowing that we would not be "a pitiful helpless giant," Nixon announced the invasion of Cambodia. Campuses exploded when six students were killed at Kent State University and Jackson State College. Hundreds of schools closed or went on strike. Buses ringed the White House to ward off protestors. The heartland felt besieged, Nixon upholding it more by personality than policy:

welfare reform, revenue sharing, the all-volunteer Army, the Environmental Protection Agency. Despite Vietnam, Nixon's diplomatic summitry helped end the bipolar world. In February 1972 he ended decades of U.S. estrangement by visiting Beijing, Hangchow, and the Forbidden City. That May he became the first president to visit Moscow, joining Communist Party leader Leonid Brezhnev in the nuclear age's first agreement to limit strategic arms.

Like Bush, Nixon loved foreign policy—global, conceptual, moving chess pieces from a distance. He was more direct fighting America's cultural war. My generation loved the amplified beat of rock. Said Nixon at a White House event with the Ray Conniff Singers: "If the music's square, it's because I like it square." The liberal elite adored nothing if not fad. Nixon liked football and baseball; hated cocktail parties; despised "front-runners, the social climbers"; and thumbed his nose at the fashionable. "My family never had the wild, swinging times many trendies think of," he told me. "What we did have, of course, was a lot of fun. I, for example, and depending on the season, naturally, loved to sit down at the piano and belt out some Christmas carols."

Middle America could see Nixon as Father Christmas and not be deceived, accepting what writer Raymond Price called Nixon's "dark side"—the taped Milhous of "expletive deleted"—feeling that his good outweighed the bad. He began the habit of wearing the flag in his lapel pin; taunted draft dodgers as "idealistic? What they wanted was to protect their ass"; and grasped the Forgotten American's nobility and injury. Mocked by the maniacal 1960s, they felt not bigotry but injured pride. Sharing it, Nixon would "mobilize an immense, informal army of ordinary people," said biographer Conrad Black. "They identified with him in his lack of glamour, dedication to hard work, old virtues, and home truths, as well as his tactical political cunning, and above all his dogged indefatigability."

Nixon's public lay among the ordered and traditional—"good, law-abiding, tax-paying citizens"—not Eric Goldman's "MetroAmerican," privileged by lineage to rule. Duty mattered. To them, Vietnam was a test of character—whether as America conceded the limits of its power, its adversaries respected the power of its will. Religion counted too. Nixon, a Quaker, told aide Charles Colson, "You know, I could be a Catholic. I honestly could. It's beautiful to think about, that there is something you can really grab ahold of, something real and meaningful." Few politicians talk like that.

Even Nixon's awkwardness was endearing. At RN's July 19, 1990, library dedication, Bush told how one day at an airport Nixon heard a little girl shouting, "How is Smokey the Bear?"—then in the National Zoo. Nixon smiled as the girl kept repeating her question. Baffled, he turned to an aide for help. "Smokey the Bear, Mr. President," the aide whispered. "Washington National Zoo." Triumphant, Nixon walked over, took the girl's hand, and beamed, "How do you do, Miss Bear?"

Nixon's flaws some saw as virtues. His virtues others saw as sins. His solitude they termed isolation; reserve, arrogance; propriety, aloofness; sentimentality, corn. "This traumatic clash of cultures," Meg Greenfield wrote—Nixon as Grant Wood vs. the age's fashion cleaved families, legislators, and generations. As it lodged in the White House—in a man who detested, and was detested by, America's hip, camp, and pop-art intelligentsia—the split cemented his rapport with America's great middle before helping to bring about his fall.

Nixon prized nuance, respected the writing craft, and authored ten books—most best sellers. He told Ray Price, "I am an introvert in an extrovert's profession," yet he became the tribune of people who never read the *New York Times*. His goal was a new political, even cultural, majority. He almost made it. Instead, photos in his Manhattan office catapulted a visitor back in time—Nixon with Brezhnev or Golda Meir; Nixon with Chou En-Lai (now more often referred to as Zhou Enlai); Nixon speaking, waving, deplaning; Nixon in a motorcade, flinging high the V.

When I left college, the shadow on those walls was a president believing that "politics is poetry, not prose." When I saw him last, in 1991, he was frail and hunched, quizzing me about the Bush administration and suggesting that I run for Congress. He was wary of raising taxes, supportive of Bush in the then Persian Gulf War, and curious about the president in a way residual and personal. "I've known George since Prescott Bush was in the Senate," he told me, chuckling. "Both great competitors. Prescott'd play golf with President Eisenhower, who loved the game, and was famous—infamous—for never letting Ike win even once."

Nixon had lost Texas by 46,233 votes in 1960 and 138,960 in 1968. By late 1969 his popularity had bloomed in Bush's adopted state. He vowed peace with honor in Southeast Asia, nominated a southern justice for the Supreme Court, unleashed Vice President Spiro Agnew to bash "radiclibs" (radical liberals), and gave the unbeaten University of Texas his own national football title plaque when it edged Arkansas, 15–14, in December 1969. Nixon already regarded Bush almost as a protégé. Bush reciprocated the affection, worried only that RN resented his Ivy lineage—"this inferiority thing—such a waste."

About this time Nixon convinced Bush to vacate his House seat to again oppose Ralph Yarborough for the Senate. "This guy's a nut, really extreme," said Poppy, confidently, after swamping Robert Morris in the 1970 GOP primary, 87.6 to 12.4 percent. "We can knock his block off in the middle." He might have, except that Yarborough lost the Democratic primary to ex-congressman Lloyd Bentsen, who destroyed Bush's campaign strategy: keep the Dems on the liberal fringe. Bentsen appealed to each part of his party, ignored Nixon stumping for Bush, and belied Agnew's attempt to tar him with the Left: "Yippies, Hippies, Yahoos, Black Panthers, lions, and tigers alike," he said. "I'd swap the whole damn zoo for a single platoon of the kind of young Americans I saw in Viet Nam."

Bush had relished clubbing Yarborough from the right. Bentsen's upset threw Poppy off his game. It became an ugly race, old stereotypes again au courant: Daddy's little rich boy, Eastern dilettante, Ivy Leaguer. Years later Bentsen called Bush "the only Texan I know who eats lobster with his chili. . . . He and Barbara had a little down-home quiche cook off." (The 1988 election was Poppy's revenge eaten cold.) Bush lost to Bentsen, 53.4 to 46.6 percent—muddying and, some said, crippling his political future. "If not dead," said a friend, "he needed extreme CPR."

Bush had a dwindling base and growing reputation as a loser. He did, however, have two friends. One, inadvertently, was now-ex-governor Connally, a Democrat, whom Bush blamed for rallying Bentsen's base. A month after Poppy's loss, Nixon, wowed by Connally's command of a then-presidential task force, was set to name him treasury secretary. "You can't give me a job before you take care of him [Bush]," Connally warned. Bush's second friend agreed. Nixon had asked Bush to risk a safe House seat, vowing a high administration post—"a soft landing"—if he lost. Mr. Smooth, Bush's self-styled sobriquet, was also a Nixon loyalist. Each was a pragmatist: fiscally sane, hawkish on Vietnam, centrist on civil rights, tough on law and order. The difference was their background; among many things, Nixon had likely never eaten quiche.

"As a personal favorite of Nixon's," Theodore White wrote, Bush was considered for a White House post or Republican National Committee (RNC) chair. Instead, Bush pitched himself as U.S. ambassador to the United Nations to Chief of Staff H. R. "Bob" Haldeman, then Nixon. "He explained that the reason for his interest in the U.N. was . . . that for too long the President had not been represented there by anyone who was a strong [Nixon] advocate," Haldeman's notes recall. "There was a dearth of Nixon advocacy in New York City. . . . [Bush] could fill that need in New York social circles." Bush got the post, smiling when in 1972 RN became the first GOP nominee since Theodore Roosevelt to almost carry the city. By any reckoning, without Nixon's late 1970 help, Bush could not have leapt from Texas to DC—therefore, could not have erased his onus as a two-time loser—thus, almost surely would never have become president.

Bush's presidency, even vice presidency, accented foreign policy. It really began at the UN eighteen years before his presidential oath. On October 25, 1971, the People's Republic of China, the Communist government of 750 million people Nixon was to visit in February 1972, was admitted to the UN, and America's longtime ally, the Republic of China, Chiang Kai-shek's Nationalist government of 14 million

Perfectly Clear

people on the island of Taiwan, was ejected. Tanzanians danced in the aisles. "The problem is not Taiwan," Nixon told National Security Adviser Henry Kissinger. "The problem is the U.N." He never blamed Bush. That December NBC telecast *A Day in the Life of the President*. Nixon asked that a "show call" to Bush about Pakistan-Indian refugees be included. Next morning at the UN, Bush slashed $87 million of nonmilitary aid to India, calling it the "clear aggressor." Nixon was confident his new ambassador could finesse politics, not only policy.

Before the 1972 Watergate Office Building burglary and cover-up by the Nixon administration and campaign wrecked his grand design, the president had planned a government reorganization, telling Haldeman to "eliminate the politicians [from the cabinet], except George Bush. He'd do anything for the cause." To Nixon, government's cause should be the executive branch returning to the middle class constitutional power "that over the years elites have taken away," among them, the media, Congress, the judiciary, interest groups, bureaucracy, and think tanks. Each was arrogant, radical, and hostile to Mid-America.

Bush's new cause was to chair the RNC as the president's man, touting this New American Revolution. It began historically November 7, 1972. On NBC *Nightly News*, anchorman John Chancellor said, not liking it, "This is the most spectacular landslide election in the history of United States politics." Only 12 percent of blacks backed RN vs. McGovern—the only group in America to almost universally spurn him. By contrast, Nixon won more than one in three Democrats, nearly four in ten Jews, and a majority of the Catholic vote—the first Republican president to do so. He took half of the youth vote in the first election in which eighteen-year-olds could cast a ballot—and a vast majority of whites in every southern state. Nixon won 60.7 percent of the vote, 47,149,841 votes to 29,172,767—America's greatest-ever margin—and 49 of 50 states, losing only Massachusetts.

In a song of the season, Bush expected to hear Cat Stevens's "Morning Has Broken" in late 1972 and early 1973 at the RNC. Instead, Barry Maguire's "Eve of Destruction" soon seemed more applicable. "I knew people at the campaign were arrogant," said *Washington Post* publisher Ben Bradlee of Watergate. "It never occurred to me that they were stupid." As chairman, Bush, admiring Nixon's foreign policy, grateful for past help, and uncritical of his word, believed the president's profession of innocence. "I just never thought," he said, much later, "that the president would lie."

Officials were charged, plea-bargained, and pled innocent or guilty. Replaced by Gerald Ford, Agnew resigned as vice president, conceding graft as Maryland governor in 1967–68. Nixon's Gallup approval fell from 68 percent in February 1973 to 23 percent by fall. The Republicans lost a special congressional election in a bedrock Michigan district. Daily, Bush phoned, cajoling restless GOPers for time: *things will turn.* The president, he said, had been ill served by aides. Enemies, wanting a last pound of flesh, were all around. Ironically, given the 1980s, Ronald Reagan, completing a second term as governor of California in 1974, was perhaps the sole Republican to match Bush's public loyalty. "Someday," he said, "I think people will look back at Watergate and say, 'Now, what was that all about?'"

That Monday, August 5, the White House released a June 23, 1972, tape of Nixon's voice telling the Central Intelligence Agency (CIA) to halt a Federal Bureau of Investigation (FBI) probe of the break-in that would politically hurt reelection—an obstruction of justice. After being briefed, Bush attended a next-day cabinet meeting during which Nixon said he had committed no impeachable offense and would not resign, then proceeded to discuss every issue but the elephant in the room. "The atmosphere was entirely unreal," Bush recalled. After a time Nixon's new chief of staff, Gen. Alexander Haig, heard stirring from a person not sitting at the cabinet table.

"It was George Bush, who as a guest of the President occupied one of the two straight chairs along the wall," Haig wrote in his 1994 book, *Inner Circles: How America Changed the World: A Memoir.* "He seemed to be asking for the floor. When Nixon failed to recognize him, he spoke anyway. Watergate was the vital question, he said. It was sapping public confidence. Until it was settled, the economy and the country as a whole would suffer. Nixon should resign."

Perfectly Clear

Bush thought Nixon looked "beleaguered, worn down by stress, detached from reality." The cabinet looked shocked, Haig said, that an RNC chairman would ask a Republican president—his once mentor, having rescued Bush from 1970 eclipse—to resign. After Nixon had left, Bush approached Haig, asking, "What are we going to do?"

"We get him up to the mountaintop," Haig said of resigning. "Then he comes down again, then we get him up again."

That night Bush recalled his father, who had died two years earlier of lung cancer at Sloan-Kettering Memorial Hospital in New York. "I'm really glad he's not alive," Bush *fils* said. "It would have killed him to see this happen. He thought we were the party of virtue and all bosses were Democrats." Nixon alone, the party reeling, his loyalties irreconcilable, Bush penned a note. He delivered it Wednesday morn.

"Dear Mr. President," Bush's letter began.

> It is my considered judgment that you should now resign. I expect in your lonely embattled position this would seem to you as an act of disloyalty from one you have supported and helped in so many ways. My own view is that I would now ill serve a President, whose massive accomplishments I will always respect and whose family I love, if I did not now give you my judgment. Until this moment resignation has been no answer at all, but given the impact of the latest development, and it will be a lasting one, I now firmly feel resignation is best for this country, best for this President. I believe this view is held by most Republican leaders across the country. This letter is made much more difficult because of the gratitude I will always have for you. If you do leave office history will properly record your achievements with a lasting respect.

Bush was wrong, as Nixon might have told him. "History," he advised Henry Kissinger, "depends on who writes it." One survey after another shows historians leaning left. Loathing Nixon in life, they would hardly rehabilitate him in death. Thursday night the thirty-seventh president resigned his office in his thirty-seventh

Oval Office address. Next day Nixon bid his staff, including Bush, a tender, defiant, bitter, bittersweet, moving, haunting, and unforgettable farewell, his wife and family standing behind him in the East Room. He recalled his father; said, "My mother was a saint"; thought "the greatness comes . . . when you take some knocks, some disappointments, when sadness comes"; and sought lightness amid the dark—"only if you have been in the deepest valley can you ever know how magnificent it is to be on the highest mountain." It traumatized. It mesmerized. Tens of millions sobbed. The rest were glad to see him go.

To Bush, writing in his diary, entries he kept as president and before, "there was an aura of sadness, like somebody died. One couldn't help but look at the family and the whole thing and think of his accomplishments and then think of the shame." Bush felt betrayed. Nixon had put him at the point as RNC chair, then lied to his protégé, which meant that Bush inadvertently lied to the public— intolerable to the Bush code. Nixon's family was different: *almost* family to George and Barbara Bush.

The gulf between the Bushes on one hand and intellectuals, arts, and journalists on the other was especially wide toward the woman whose Gallup Poll approval-disapproval ratio hit a nonpareil 9 to 1 for American First Ladies in 1969 (54 percent approve, 6 disapprove, balance no opinion). Bush later said, "She became a mirror of America's heart, and love." Mrs. Bush recalled, "She was a sensational, gracious, and thoughtful First Lady." Asked what word would engrave his heart if it were opened after he died, Nixon said, simply, "Pat."

In March 1991, on the eve of Pat Nixon's seventy-ninth birthday, I took to the Nixons' New Jersey home a giant card arrayed with photos of her life and signatures of nearly two hundred Bush and White House career staffers who once had worked for her.

Unpacking it, I pled for patience: "I'm the most unmechanical person you'll ever meet." Playfully, she replied, "No, you're not. Dick is." I had never met Mrs. Nixon. For two hours we spoke of family, work, and travel. It was like talking to your mother.

The great CBS journalist Mike Wallace, who died in 2012 at ninety-three, interviewed hundreds of people in his life: Eleanor Roosevelt, JFK, Malcolm X, LBJ. In 2003 he named the one person he had hoped but failed to add. Pat Nixon "was a genuine, lovely, fine woman," the *60 Minutes* television host said. "Warm, smart as the dickens, a wonderful mother." In her case political correctness spurns self-evident evidence.

In an age of angst and change, Mrs. Nixon showed how a woman could fuse family and a career—her country. Too often feminism demands the freedom to choose a life—until it invokes motherhood and/or tradition. Sadly, such hypocrisy has found a home at the National Women's Hall of Fame in Seneca Falls, New York, the birthplace of women's rights. Like Nixon's presidency, its hall of fame opened in 1969, yearly inducting honorees—247 so far.

The hall hails Democrat Bella Abzug, but not Republican Jeane Kirkpatrick; Nancy Pelosi, not Condoleezza Rice; Eleanor Roosevelt, Hillary Clinton, Madeleine Albright, Shirley Chisholm, Geraldine Ferraro, Barbara Jordan, Barbara Mikulski, Janet Reno, Patricia Schroeder, and Donna Shalala vs. Betty Ford, Oveta Culp Hobby, Elizabeth Dole, and Margaret Chase Smith. Other GOPers need not apply, despite Mrs. Bush's enormous popularity shown herein and Mrs. Nixon making the Gallup Poll top-ten most admired women list an amazing sixteen times from 1959 to 1979.

At first the hall falsely said Mrs. Nixon had not been nominated—except that she and Mrs. Bush have. Its next excuse was that they hadn't passed a screening committee. How could they, given its uber-liberal tilt? Mrs. Clinton fancied a "vast right-wing conspiracy." In Pat Nixon, outcome-based bias snubs a woman who as a child nursed two dying parents, was orphaned, kept house for two brothers, then had five jobs in college. In 1968 journalist and future hall inductee Gloria Steinem asked what she had wanted to be growing up. Pat replied, "I never had time to think about things like that—who I wanted to be, or who I admired. I'm not like all you . . . all those people who had it easy. I had to work."

The cum laude Southern California graduate got her master's degree, earned an airplane pilot's license, and became a teacher, an economist, and 1953–61 U.S. Second Lady, ditching protocol to visit schools, orphans' homes, even a leper colony in Panama. In 1958 a communist mob in Caracas nearly killed the Nixons by attacking their car. Said a *Los Angeles Times* reporter: "Pat was stronger than any man." As 1969–74 First Lady, she became the first to visit the Soviet Union and China; travel alone to a foreign country, Peru, to bring earthquake relief; and receive its highest honor, Grand Cross of the Order of the Sun. At the same time, children mobbed her on four continents. "I have known the wives of six presidents," said Leonid Brezhnev's wife, "and Mrs. Nixon is the nicest."

Pat was the first First Lady to urge a woman Supreme Court justice, address a televised GOP Convention, attend a cabinet meeting, and back equal pay for equal work. In Yugoslavia Mrs. Nixon said its parliament and our Congress had too few women; in Liberia she became the first president's wife to officially represent America abroad; in Vietnam she rode an open helicopter into a combat zone to meet wounded servicemen in the line of fire. Snubbing her, how could any hall of fame be so out of touch, out to lunch? Mrs. Nixon began the "Right to Read" and "Parks to People" programs, lit the White House at night, and created tours for the blind and handicapped. "She did wonderful work in improving the White House history," said longtime curator Clement Conger of her restoring furniture, paintings, and other artifacts, leaving no time or wish for self-promotion. She answered by hand every letter addressed to her. Above all, as Bush observed, she raised two self-reliant, unspoiled daughters—difficult for a celebrity, especially in the mutually assured destruction culture of the early 1970s.

Amid Watergate, Pat's bravery stunned famed reporter Helen Thomas, who also should be in the hall. "God! Look at her!" she marveled at a White House reception. "What a woman! How does she do it?" Nixon thought he knew. "Incredible inner strength," he said. "My God, if she'd been the wife of a liberal, the press would have canonized her."

"I know the truth," Pat once said, almost biblically, "and the truth sustains me." In 1969 Duke Ellington marked his seventieth birthday by improvising a melody in the East Room. "I shall pick a name," he said, "gentle, graceful, something like Patricia." Pat Nixon was kept from the truth during Watergate. Today's truth is that a women's hall of fame without Pat Nixon—or Barbara Bush, as this work suggests—is unworthy of the name.

Most of the national media—if the reader doubts, simply Google—ignored all of the above, dubbing Mrs. Nixon pliant, Plastic Pat. America knew better, seeing a woman who thought of others, not herself. When she had a stroke in 1976, more than a quarter of a million letters flooded the Nixons' San Clemente, California, home. Her Secret Service code name was "Starlight." It is easy to see why.

FOUR

Looking for Mr. Right

George Bush attended Gerald Ford's swearing-in as president at noon on the day and in the room where Richard Nixon said, "Always remember, others may hate you, but they don't win unless you hate them, and then you destroy yourself." That night Bush wrote in his diary of "indeed a new spirit, a new lift." The sole U.S. chief executive not elected president or vice president would tie autobiography (Ford's *A Time to Heal*) and biography (Frank Capra's *It's a Wonderful Life*). Frank Merriwell or Chip Hilton? Both lived in the thirty-eighth president.

Ford is said to have calmed America. In truth, he taught it. He was impressed with policy, not himself, his hat size the same leaving as entering office. He was also comfortable with the presidency, treating pomp like Billy Graham did sin. James Fenimore Cooper wrote, "Truth was the Deerslayer's polar star." It lit Ford's first speech as president: "Truth is the glue that holds government together. . . . Honesty is always the best policy. . . . Our great Republic is a government of laws and not of men. Here the people rule." Who would not say he stilled our quiet desperation—right man, right time?

Born in 1913, Leslie Lynch King Jr. left Omaha for Grand Rapids when his parents divorced. Mom married Gerald Rudolph Ford; adopted, the boy took Ford's name. He worked odd jobs, was an Eagle Scout, and hoped to emulate legendary running back Red Grange. As president, the two-time All-American relived 1930s Michigan football by reading the sports section first. He liked its lesson: "the value of team play."

After Michigan, Ford spurned pro football's Lions and Packers to attend Yale, go to war, practice law in Grand Rapids, and begin a fifty-eight-year marriage whose longevity contended with the Bushes'. Another lesson is one that politicians who should know better violate at their peril: If a person is open and *reliable*, voters sense he is happy with their company. First elected in 1948, Ford began a twenty-five-year stint as Michigan's Fifth District's "Congressman for Life"—all he wanted till fate beckoned, garbed in the scandal of our time.

In 1965 Ford became House minority leader, "topping my all-time goal. I could have stayed there forever." Then, in 1973 Spiro Agnew resigned as vice president. Nixon wanted John Connally, by now a recently converted Republican, ex–treasury secretary, and as we shall see, Bush's bête noir. Instead, charred by Watergate, he tapped the tortoise, not the hare—loyal, familiar, and sure to be confirmed.

"They like you," Nixon stage-whispered after naming Ford Agnew's successor in October 1973. One reason is that few Democrats feared him. "I'm a Ford, not a Lincoln," he correctly told Congress. That month *Newsweek* assigned Tom DeFrank, twenty-nine, to cover the future accidental vice president. For nine months both crossed the country in tiny Air Force Two, fencing warily, then bonding, like two veins from a common mine.

DeFrank was younger, Ford more conservative. Jerry became president, Tom a superb president watcher—by turn *Newsweek* White House correspondent, *New York Daily News* Washington Bureau chief, and *National Journal* contributing editor. In 1991 he suggested recording Ford's views on policy, politics, and presidents—also, as it happened, life and love and faith and aging. Ford agreed, stipulating publication "only when I'm dead." He died December 26, 2006. The book, published in 2007, became *Write It When I'm Gone: Remarkable Off-the-Record Conversations with Gerald R. Ford.*

In April 1974 Ford prophesied Nixon's resignation four months before it happened, then, grabbing DeFrank's tie, swore him to secrecy. To Ford, the president had "not acted forthrightly" yet "had a terrific loyalty to people." He was a foreign policy savant yet "had a character where the bad part could take over." Upon Nixon's exit, his successor told the East Room audience, "Our long national nightmare is over." Ford then added, "May Richard Nixon, who brought peace to millions, find it for himself."

The new president found crisis. Unemployment hit 7.1 percent. Many wanted Nixon tried or hanged. Instead, Ford issued a "full, free, and absolute pardon" a month after taking office, creating a firestorm but freeing himself "to get on with the country's business." Improbably, the athlete took to falling down stairs. Two crazies tried to kill him. U.S. civilians left Saigon as Communists took South Vietnam. "To sit in the Oval Office and see Americans beaten," said Ford, "was not a happy experience for the President of the United States."

Unfazed, Ford forced Rhodesia to abandon white minority rule, met with Brezhnev in Vladivostok, and signed the Helsinki Pact, ensuring the sanctity of national boundaries. He ordered an attack on Khmer Rouge (Cambodian) forces that had seized a U.S. merchant ship, the *Mayaguez*, and refused to release it. Many Americans yawned. Increasingly, our ex-savior seemed Bill Mauldin's Sad-Sack Kid.

In January 1975 the incumbent said, "The State of the Union is not good." It was better by 1976: inflation down, America at peace. Still, not enough recalled 1974's breath of fresh air who rose at 5:15 a.m., worked eighteen hours daily, vowed "openness and candor," and seemed constitutionally unable to utter a nasty word. Ford trailed Democratic candidate Jimmy Carter by thirty-three points at August's GOP Convention. Then, like a timer clicking, America remembered Jerry College. He nearly won despite Watergate, the pardon, and claiming in the second presidential debate that Eastern Europe was not under Soviet domination. By election night Ford's voice was spent. Wife Betty read his concession.

Today many deem Ford just what the doctor ordered: substance over style. My first vote was for Nixon in 1972 over his opponent, George McGovern, whom in a spasm of arrogance I called Caligula's horse in a college newspaper column. Years later, at Washington's National Airport, I looked up to see McGovern sit next to me on a plane. To my surprise, I found him eminently decent, like Ford.

In 2012 Nancy Gibbs and Michael Duffy wrote a book, *The Presidents Club*, about the fraternity of former presidents, noting that Bush and Gerald Ford admired one another. I was not surprised. In 1999 Bush asked me to ghostwrite a remembrance for *American Enterprise* magazine of Ford's succession a quarter century earlier. Typically, Bush mentioned that I had helped, and Ford wrote a thoughtful note.

Politics, I would learn, need not differ from life. You could fault the other side and still allow for friendship. But I should have known this from 1974–77. Jerry Ford taught us that.

Unlike Nixon, Agnew, and later Ronald Reagan, Ford largely ignored targets of the counterculture. Their mid- to late 1970s voice was now inchoate—not for nothing were they still called the *Silent* Majority— robbed of the person who had demanded for them a decent measure of respect. Before Watergate burst in early 1973, *Newsweek* had termed Nixon "a stern, sure, and uncompromising man who disdained to conciliate his critics." To Ford, conciliation was means and end; he enjoyed advising a businessman, local banker, the Democratic whip on the Hill. With Nixon gone, the 1970s' frame of reference vanished. Liberals yearned for someone to attack. (They later found him in Reagan.) Others yearned for leadership, anywhere.

My time in college had split America into hawk vs. dove, religion vs. hedonism, Saukville vs. Woodstock, combatants trenched in belligerence—an age one might not want to relive but would not have missed living for the world. *Washington Star* reporter James Dickenson thought Ford unlikely to champion "traditional middle-class family values [like] busing, school prayer, abortion, and individual freedom," changing the last half of the 1970s landscape for almost everyone—including Bush. Poppy had been unable to advance electorally toward the presidency: witness 1964 and 1970. Building a curriculum vitae, he now tried appointively.

Since childhood I had read the Rochester, New York, *Democrat and Chronicle* (*D&C*). It was not a writer's paper like, say, the *Boston Globe*, but the then-money-in-the-bank flagship of America's largest chain, the Gannett Co. I wrote my first story for it the summer before my college freshman year. On a lark I called former Yankees manager Joe McCarthy. For two hours we spoke on his farm outside Buffalo of Babe Ruth and Connie Mack and Lou Gehrig—to McCarthy, a surrogate son. Next week I took the article to the *D&C*, dropped it on an editor's desk, and heard nothing till I woke one Sunday to see my byline and a headline, "Down on the Farm, Marse Joe Doesn't Seem So Bad." Nine days after college graduation, for $158 a week, Blue Cross coverage, and no expense account, I joined as a full-time reporter the newspaper of my youth.

By 1973 the *D&C* had waned, though memory of its 1930s through mid-'60s high meridian masked decline. The late publisher, Frank Gannett, considered people like Prescott Bush hopelessly left-wing. Al Neuharth, named chief executive officer (CEO) my first year there, was expected to restore balance (today's chain is as liberal as the late Gannett's was conservative) and profit (to get it, Gannett launched a new flagship, DC-based *USA Today*, in 1982). Working at night—the *D&C* was a morning paper—fused coffee and conjecture. Who was a better shortstop—Luis Aparicio or Maury Wills? (Little Looie.) Which was superior in its heyday, *Life* or the *Saturday Evening Post*? (Pick 'em.) Was "You're So Vain" about Carly Simon trashing Warren Beatty? (Only they knew.) Who would regret their choice in 1972—a Nixon or McGovern voter? (Depends on whom you asked.)

Sports intoxicated. They also were insufficient. A morning person, I disliked the bell curve of an a.m. paper. Moreover, politics gnawed, and I would not get there from here. In 1975 the *Chronicle of Higher Education* advertised for a communications official at Hamilton College, chartered in 1793 by a Presbyterian missionary, Samuel Kirkland, in Clinton, New York, overlooking the Oriskany and Mohawk Valley. In 1812 the school became known as Hamilton College, for Kirkland's friend Alexander Hamilton, whose Treasury Department statue stands next to the White House. What stunned—as anyone watching the 1969 film *The Sterile Cuckoo*, shot at and around Hamilton, can attest—was the area's cathedral of the outdoors.

After a year of campaigning across the country, John F. Kennedy was asked by Theodore White in 1960 what part he felt most scenic. "He thought for a moment, and then, like most Americans, chose home"—New England. Many might choose east-central Upstate New York, including Hamilton, with its changing seasons and wooded glens of oak and pine and maple and quadrangles, broad lawns, and redbrick buildings. Its 1827 chapel, designed by Philip Hooker, is America's last example of an early three-story church. Hamilton College extolled its faculty—most tying research and intellect—and students—many from private schools—and alumni—like diplomat Sol Linowitz, playwright Thomas Meehan, and psychologist B. F. Skinner. Bush knew a number of Hamilton men (till 1978 theirs was a single-sex college). Graduates anchored the wise men of the Boston–New York–Washington axis. Hamilton was "Little Ivy," tying privilege, discipline, courtesy, and expectation.

As profited Saul on the Damascus Road, scales fell from a newcomer's eyes on my arrival at Hamilton. I knew little of students' boarding school, a vacation in Belize, or alumni opening doors shut to state university graduates. Personally, many treated me with kindness—in particular, former *New York Times* book critic John Hutchens, then member of the Board of Trustees, became a friend. Meantime, I debated faculty over Ford vs. Reagan, the *Mayaguez*, and the fall of Southeast Asia. Some were thoughtful liberals. Some resided on what Reagan called the Loony Left. Others were content to live permanently in a state of compromise—what Margaret Thatcher termed the "wets," missing in action when the gloves came off.

Hamilton's student body was largely white, upper class, and Protestant—a bay window of Bush's 1940s education. A mile down the hill, the town of Clinton was middle-income WASP (white Anglo-Saxon Protestant) to the bone. The region's hub, Utica—working class, largely immigrant, and solidly Catholic—lay ten miles away. What a triangle! Like a candidate, I had to connect their points, somehow finding a denominator. "Easy," a friend proposed. "Just drink, swear, and talk sports." Truth was more complex. I could be myself and at home in Clinton—old style in a familiar style, polite and reticent, *Time* columnist Lance Morrow's "simple and virtuous small-town America." I could imbibe more, be more profane, and commune with Utica. As Bush found in 1988, to become president, a Republican, quoting Glendower, had to call *both* of their "spirits from the vasty deep."

In time Poppy found that Ivy and other academe had become prisoners of political correctness, changing mightily since he graduated Yale Class of '48. By contrast, Clinton's and Utica's differences were more superficial than substantive. Nixon, then Reagan, perceived, as the Gipper said, how "what unites us far outweighs what little divides us"—contempt for welfare, a need for work, and belief in faith, family, national security, and American exceptionalism. At heart, unlike Thatcher's "wets," each flaunted honest *emotion*.

Later, I often thought of this in a Washington of pretense and posturing vs. Upstate's love of home and people's feelings and how you grew up. If, as a newspaper wrote in 1991, I knew "as well as anyone at the White House the values of two groups central to a GOP majority—small-town Protestants and urban Catholics," the 1970s helped.

Asked about John F. Kennedy's view that "life is unfair," Bush said, "It's unfair to some people, yes. There are inequities, yes. Nobody is going to design a system that is totally, totally fair." His daughter's death of leukemia at three was unfair. Barbara Bush said simply, "We loved her more than life." Losing two crew members and almost Poppy's life at twenty was unfair. "These were," Bush said, "the molding events that most shaped my life." In 1974 his life was, above all, askew.

The last two years had made Bush a two-headed Janus—"serving without combat pay during Watergate." One head thought his benefactor "was entitled to a fair hearing. I thought he [Nixon] was entitled to it without a lot of fine-tuning out of the party apparatus." The second felt "the party was separate and apart from Watergate. The party was ongoing. The party had to be strong when all the Watergate mess was over." Two stacks of mail rose daily in his office. One attacked Bush for betraying Nixon: "The chairman of the party," he recalled, "he's head of the party. Why aren't you helping more?" The other stack ripped him for not attacking Nixon. "Hey, why are you keeping the party so close to the president?" Bush treasured fealty—but to whom?

After Ford's swearing-in, the president had to nominate a successor as vice president—the first simultaneous U.S. president and vice president not chosen by the people. Bush told Ford that if nominated, he would serve. In turn Ford cut the veep list to Bush and New York governor Nelson Rockefeller. Bush led a poll of GOP officeholders, but Chief of Staff Donald Rumsfeld reportedly wanted Rocky. Ford agreed. Rockefeller was thought to have more heft, *gravitas* not then stature's word of choice. He was also too liberal for party regulars, as the next year showed.

On August 24, 1974, Bush waited at Kennebunkport for Ford's call. "Mr. Bush, you don't seem to be too upset about this," a reporter said, moments later.

"Yes, but you can't see what's on the inside," said Bush, a profile in poise.

Rockefeller took his oath of office December 19. By then Bush had begun a campaign to gild his curriculum vitae in two places, eleven thousand miles apart. The first followed Ford's fall 1974 offer to become ambassador to France or the Court of St. James. Bush gently countered, asking to be sent to China. It was a shrewd, even career-making, move. Nixon's 1972 pilgrimage had given buzz to all things Oriental, Beijing née Peking now a dateline to rival London or Moscow. China would become a favorite congressional and executive travel destination. Bush's nonpolitical post could be a political boon. America then maintained official relations only with the Republic of China on Taiwan. Thus, the Beijing office lacked an embassy's official status and Bush the title of "ambassador," though he brought to the position everything but the name.

Ford made Bush chief of the U.S. liaison office in the People's

Republic of China, telling him to expect to stay there two years. Photos show Poppy and Mrs. Bush shopping with the natives, bicycling by the China World Trade Center, standing near a giant picture of Mao Tse-tung, and seeing the Great Wall, Ming Tombs, and Temple of the Sun Park—all the trappings of a pol. In October 1975 Bush's favorite baseball team, the Boston Red Sox, played Cincinnati in a World Series that next spring the *New Yorker* wrote "was replayed everywhere in memory and conversation through the ensuing winter, and even now its colors still light up the sky." Bush and the staff followed this keeper of an event. On October 22, at 12:34 a.m. eastern time, Carlton Fisk's twelfth-inning home run that hit the left-field foul pole won Game Six, 7–6, tying the Series, three all. It was noon at the office. Bush recalls "cheering almost as soon as Fisk's homer cleared the wall. Almost all of the people in our office were pulling for the Red Sox."

Missing America, the Bushes loved the Chinese, mannered and hardworking; Dorothy Bush could have mothered them all. "Mysterious, loving tradition, so much to discover in their people," said Bush. "China had been isolated by choice" until Nixon's trip—and inaccessible to the world. After a year in China, Bush wrote Ford that he wished to return to America, later saying, "I'd done all I could." Plus, he sensed opportunity. Republican politics rivaled a circular firing squad. On November 20, 1975, Ronald Reagan announced his candidacy for president, the Right already in revolt against Jerry B. Good: too dull, too inarticulate, too quick to capitulate. That month Rocky withdrew as Ford's 1976 vice president, a sacrifice to conservatives, saying, "I didn't come down [to DC] to get caught up in party squabbles which only make it more difficult for the president in a very difficult time."

Bush expected a cabinet position. To some, he seemed Rockefeller's ideal replacement: young, conservative, and Texan. Reading Bush's letter, Ford had another thought. For a year, revelations, including those based on queries by the Senate Church Committee about illegal and unauthorized activities, had rocked the CIA. The president and Kissinger sent Bush a "for eyes only" cable telegraph, asking him to come home and lead an agency charged, Poppy later said, "with everything from lawbreaking to simple incompetence."

Bush knew that this might make his tenure at the RNC look tame and that "some wanted me out of the way politically"—the CIA being theoretically nonpartisan. At the same time, he recalled what his parents had taught: you say yes when a president asks. Bush soon found that congressional Democrats were more obsessed by a question not yet posed. In retrospect, his confirmation hearing showed why the mid- and late 1970s were a Hades for conservatives in what polling called a right-of-center country. Not content with fairly judging his ability to head the CIA, majority Democrats on the Senate Armed Services Committee demanded that Bush not run for vice president in 1976.

"If I wanted to be vice president," Ford's nominee tartly stated the obvious, "I wouldn't be here asking you to confirm me for the CIA."

For several days dialogue rivaled pulp fiction. Democrats argued that the CIA might be a covert White House stepping-stone; Poppy countered that if anything, it would deter. The principle, he said, *was* principle. Bush would never desert "my political birthright" simply to be confirmed.

Finally, outflanked by Democrats ("They were perfectly willing not to *have* a director," Bush said later of liberal hardball; "it was all politics, nothing about the Nation"), he asked Ford to exclude him as a potential running mate. "I know it's unfair," Bush told him, "but you don't have much of a choice if we are to get on with the job of rebuilding and strengthening the agency."

In effect Ford told the committee that he would submit to Bush's mugging. On January 30, 1976, Poppy replaced William Colby as director. In *The Next President*, David Frost wrote, "A number of supporters [have] told me, 'If only George Bush could meet every member of the American public on a one-on-one basis, they would probably all vote for him.'" I have found that to be an understandable view. Bush's knowledge and personality helped rebuild the CIA's morale, so restoring the agency that its headquarters now bears his name.

Bush regularly briefed Ford on national security. In 1975 a former Democratic governor of Georgia became a nearly full-time resident of Iowa. Jimmy Carter made a heretofore asterisk of a caucus a springboard for his party's 1976 presidential nomination. He vowed never to lie to America, to be as "good and decent and fair as are the American people," and to be a great president—in his autobiography's priceless title, *Why Not the Best?* As CIA director, Bush briefed Carter as a candidate, then voyaged to Plains, Georgia, to regularly update the president-elect. The DC grapevine surmised that Bush might stay, but Carter wanted his own man and got him in Stansfield Turner.

Things are said to occur in threes. Ford dug that many potholes in Bush's White House road: picking Rockefeller as No. 2 in 1974; overlooking Bush when Rocky announced his withdrawal; and finally, not bucking Congress on Bush's possible status as veep. Instead, the president made Bob Dole his running mate, then heard the Kansas senator say in his October 1976 TV debate with Walter Mondale that "Democrats have started every war in this century"—ignoring, among other things, how fascism began World War II. Ford narrowly lost the general election to Carter, 297 to 240 electoral votes. Choosing Bush as vice president would have avoided Dole's visit to Mrs. Malaprop, won Texas, and helped elsewhere in the South, Carter barely taking many states.

At sea Bush returned to Texas. He became chairman of the executive committee of its First International Bank. He taught in 1978–79 as part-time professor of administrative science at Rice University's Jones School of Business. "I loved my brief time in the world of academia," Bush smiled, twenty years before he taught at the newly opened Bush Presidential Library, saying, "I plan to do some teaching, because when you teach, you learn."

In 1977–79 Bush was also appointed a director of the Council on Foreign Relations, burnishing his résumé for 1980. He would campaign not on ideology, rhetoric, or fanfare of the common man—rather, on his background, experience, and knowledge of government. In short, he would run as all that Carter was not.

As his presidency evolved, Carter diminished the office as few have or pray God will again. *Time*'s Roger Rosenblatt later wrote that the Georgian "oversaw a Presidency characterized by small people, small talk, and small matters. He made Americans feel two things they are not used to feeling, and will not abide. He made them feel puny, and he made them feel insecure." Carter pardoned most Vietnam draft evaders, handed the canal to Panama, proclaimed day number __ of the Iranian hostage crisis, and at one point fired thirty-four cabinet and staff officials. America seemed a nation *McGuffey's Readers* would scarcely recognize—of leaders who spoke of impotence; voters, crossing party, who expected things to get worse; and fear, greased by Washington, that problems were too intractable to solve.

In 2012 Mitt Romney campaigned solely on the economy, as if the average voter were a Texas Instruments calculator. In 1980 Bush campaigned on knowing more policy than any other Republican, as if the voter were taking a multi-choice exam. Later, as president, the Gipper taught Bush how politics, like life, was more intuitive than intellectual. If people liked you, they would forgive almost anything: you were *one* of them, trusted to do *for*, not *to*. I often marveled at (a) the public's curious definition of importance, and (b) how affinity could spur support. Reagan's fondness for TV's *Little House on the Prairie* may have meant as much as Bush's vow to lower the tax on capital gains.

If elected, Reagan, crowding seventy, would be America's oldest president. Was he up to the job? No one knew. Bush, fifty-four, announced for the office May 1, 1979. Adept at tennis, golf, fishing, hunting, and horseshoes, he soon campaigned as though possessed. In one year Mr. Smooth attended 850 political events and flew 250,000 miles. What counted, of course, was "Main Street," said a writer, "and specifically, the people reviled in *Main Street*." In 1991 Reagan described them at his presidential library dedication: "Our neighbors were never ashamed to kneel in prayer to their Maker. Nor were they ever embarrassed to feel a lump in their throat when Old Glory passed by. No one in Dixon [Illinois] ever burned a flag. And no one in Dixon would have tolerated it."

One question germane to 1980 was, which would-be president grasped Dixon's view? Another was, which could win? A decade earlier Nixon had watched Guy Lombardo's orchestra ring in 1971 on CBS Television, then called several friends, including evangelist Billy Graham, comedians Bob Hope and Jackie Gleason, and actor John Wayne. A better parade of Main Street household names did not exist. Nixon didn't merely know his constituency. Nixon *was* that constituency. Whoever earned—no one could inherit—it would be the likely Republican nominee.

Long before GOPers vied to unseat Carter, Graham had personally been beheld by more people than any human being in the history of the world. In 1949 publisher William Randolph Hearst used Billy's Los Angeles crusade—"Puff Graham," an in-house memo said—to help the Tar Heel tyro, thirty-one, lure a following he "never dreamt of, never expected." A year later *Time, Newsweek, Life*, and the *Saturday Evening Post* put him on their cover. By the late 1950s, Graham was a global institution, eclipsing Norman Vincent Peale and Bishop Fulton Sheen—a champion of frontier evangelism, a Calvinist's answer to the pope.

To Graham, Nixon's victory in 1968 seemed to verify America as civic Zion: "I guess," Billy said, "Dick is one of my ten closest friends." He was the nation's parish chaplain—said Gallup, America's most admired man. His umbrella Billy Graham Evangelistic Association achieved a scope distinctive of fundamentalism: "Go," Jesus told disciples, "and spread the word." Graham's *Hour of Decision* tied almost nine hundred radio stations; crusades aired in two hundred television markets; his monthly magazine and movie facilities grew like mushrooms in the shade. At a White House–sanctioned July 4, 1970, "Honor America Day," he was almost a cabinet official sans portfolio—said radical Angela Davis, "the Lord's American Son."

Graham scored the news media for "imposing a leadership on the American public which they do not want and for making heroes of radicals," criticized the United Presbyterian Church for giving $10,000 to Davis's defense fund, and was an electric speaker, neither con man nor intellectual, using religion to deliver America from the

1960s' dark and massy pull. One biographer deemed Graham "the indestructible American innocent." He helped save lives and souls, feeling that "governments," quoting Emerson, "have their origin in the moral identity of men." A service ended by inviting sinners to stride forward, the organ playing "Just as I Am," and rededicate themselves to Christ. It is fair to say that Graham buoyed Middle America's identity as no other clergy has.

The Reverend Billy was in apposition to another institution of the age: Bert Parks, his Atlantic City no Mount of Olives. It is true Bert could not sing, act, or dance superbly. It is also true that his ordinariness drew you toward him, his slickness a defense. If broadcaster Curt Gowdy meant the era's World Series, Rose Bowl, and All-Star Game, Parks sold more viewers than anyone on the Miss America Pageant. There he was, each September—girls parading down the aisle, smiles frozen on every face—joining the pageant in 1954 as master of ceremonies. It meant little but was deliciously square— millions could not go to bed until Bert crooned, "There she is, Miss America. There she is, your ideal." In Caledonia one would no sooner miss the evening than burn the American flag.

In December 1979, Parks, sixty-five, was fired. *People* magazine, gawking at the "hoopla," demanded his return. A decade passed before he revisited the event that involuntarily retired him. In 1990 Parks butchered lines, mis-lip-synched "There She Is," and forgot to introduce fifteen of the twenty-six former Miss Americas gathered at the pageant's seventieth anniversary. No matter. It was a trip back, as ratings showed, to a warmer, kinder time. Bert endeared like another middle-class totem. For half a century, a son of London, Ontario, Guy Lombardo and the Royal Canadians greeted each new year over CBS from New York's Roosevelt, then Waldorf-Astoria, Hotel. An early '70s comedian said, "I hear Guy Lombardo says that when he goes he's taking New Year's Eve with him." He did for many when he died in late 1977.

Looking back, it was not only "The Sweetest Music This Side of Heaven," to quote the publicists, that made Guy the nation's neighbor; or soloists like Kenny Gardner, crooning "The Band Played On";

or the Lombardo Trio, singing standards like "Give Me the Moon over Brooklyn"; or even the showman Guy, who made New Year's so remarkable. Though their feats were—ouch—instrumental, it was the evening's *whole*—the horns and party hats and magic—that let Lombardo join that closet of imagery in which, critic William Henry said, "purple mountain majesties, amber waves of grain, small-town school marms, the cavalry riding to the rescue, Norman Rockwell Thanksgivings, the flag-raising at Iwo Jima, the World Series, and astronauts landing on the moon somehow seem interlocked because they each in turn have evoked a swelling sense of personal participation in national pride and purpose."

Lombardo became America's umbilical cord for the rite of New Year's passage, corkscrewing into high society's apotheosis. Eyeing what the announcer called "Park Avenue's finest" in their gowns and tuxedos, all loaded, financially and boozily, and oblivious to the camera, and the lordly Guy, playing to the camera, made me wonder what it must be like to meet such a different clientele that it *had* to come from a different planet altogether. When my brothers and sisters were young, our parents invited friends to salute the turning of the calendar. Perched on the upstairs steps, we heard the bandmaster, a floor and generation away, count down the seconds to a new and unknown year.

I think of that January 1 and how Lombardo's memory has razed each solstice since 1978. In my heart, Guy *did* take New Year's Eve with him. On the cusp of the 1980 presidential election, which candidate could inspire the GOP in the new year still to come?

The late 1970s RNC slogan was—I kid you not—"Republicans Are People, Too," a communiqué guaranteed to make Democrats jeer, not fear. A joke of the time went, Why do Republicans oppose abortion? Answer: They are most comfortable in the fetal position. Depending on your view, potential presidential candidates were felt marginally or considerably better than the party's moribund elite.

Tennessee's Howard Baker was thought bright, moderate, and

squishy soft to some. Ronald Reagan was deemed too old—counsel that was widespread but not wise. Illinois boasted both conservative Phil Crane, sans name recognition and cash, and John Anderson, a Republican in Name Only (RINO) before the term was born.

At another time Bush might have run as liberty's Horatio at the Bridge from the UN and CIA. In the 1950s UN ambassador Henry Cabot Lodge used television to regularly bash Communism. Once Lodge called the Soviet delegate "a gentleman." The Communist chafed, "I'm not a gentleman. I am a delegate." Lodge replied, icily, "I had hoped the two were not mutually exclusive."

In 1962 U.S. ambassador Adlai Stevenson demanded that his counterpart, Valerian Zorin, answer whether the Soviet government had placed offensive missiles on the island of Cuba, ninety miles from Florida. "Yes or no—don't wait for the translation—yes or no?"

"I am not in an American courtroom, sir, and therefore I do not wish to answer," Zorin answered. "In due course, sir, you will have your reply."

"You are in the courtroom of world opinion right now, and you can answer yes or no," said Stevenson.

"You will have your answer in due course," Zorin said.

"I am prepared to wait for my answer until hell freezes over," Stevenson said, taking the stage to show reconnaissance photos of the missiles in Cuba to Zorin—and the world.

As we shall see, Bush's diplomatic work was effective, even brilliant one-on-one. Unlike Lodge's and Stevenson's, though, it was almost always private—by instinct, at the UN; by job description, at the CIA.

Many knew little of Bush, other than pedigree, Ivy education, and experience; polling showed little emotional link. I knew almost nothing then of his staff, background, and fidelity to Middle America, most of all.

That was not true of another Texan and 1980 Republican candidate: Navy secretary (1961), governor of Texas (1963–69), treasury secretary (1970–72), nearly killed in the front seat of President Kennedy's car in Dallas, tall, bold, and buccaneering, with his eagle profile and shock of silver hair—Big Jawn.

FIVE

Big Jawn

On August 15, 1971, President Nixon froze wages and prices. Defending him, Treasury Secretary John Connally held a regional press conference that week in my hometown of Rochester, brandishing what Nixon heretofore lacked—as Henry Kissinger said, "a second order of advocacy." Readying to return to college, I watched on television as Connally gave what columnists Rowland Evans and Robert Novak called "an incendiary performance." By 1978, with Main Street demoralized by Watergate, Jimmy Carter, and "Republicans Are People, Too," it was not altogether impossible that Connally might one day be president.

That December I called Raymond Price, former Nixon speechwriter turned columnist, out of the blue at his office in New York and asked, was there a chance that he and I could meet? We did, downing Bloody Marys in Manhattan as I explained my quandary: I could not penetrate Connally's palace guard. A man of kindness and humanity, Price knew that to leap from Hamilton College to big-league politics scent like something out of *Peter Pan*. He also knew that if doors could not be opened, they might at least be nudged.

Since Nixon's 1974 resignation, Price had moved to San Clemente; helped draft *RN: The Memoirs of Richard Nixon*; written a lyric memoir, *With Nixon*; and taught at the Kennedy Institute of Politics at Harvard. His humility and clarity clashed with DC's charlatans and shills. Perhaps Price liked my admiration of *With Nixon*—perhaps, as a politician, what he later described to Connally campaign manager

Eddie Mahe as my "combination of enthusiasm and level-headedness. Considering the knocking about that people in the Connally organization are going to have to put up with"—he got that right—"this could be a considerable asset."

In January 1979 Connally officially announced for president. After Mahe got a letter from Price, I flew to Washington to meet him. That June I put my dog in a car, loaded boxes in a van, and headed south. I arrived in Washington to find a psychotic patient: government. Gas lines, unemployment, inflation, and interest rates had flown the cage. The president's approval rating would soon plunge to 17 percent.

Carter retreated to the presidential getaway at Camp David; consulted aides, experts, and solons; and wrote a speech decrying "a crisis of the spirit." He returned to Washington to give the address— Senator Edward Kennedy used the word *malaise* to engrave it—that put the public in the dock. Most Americans disagreed, thinking Carter the problem—leadership, the solution. But from which party and which candidate—and how?

John Bowdoin Connally thought he knew. He had announced for president, four months before George H. W. Bush, starting his marathon with a sprint, almost as if he could swallow the nomination in a single gulp. In a day he flew from Indianapolis via Milwaukee to Concord, New Hampshire, wowing the party faithful and outspending the field. JBC saw himself as a younger, brighter, tougher Gipper, sure the race would become an old B-grade actor vs. a born-to-be president. It is hard to capture how awesome Connally then seemed. The *Washington Post* conceded "rave reviews." George Will, who detested him, fretted about his appeal. "Among Republicans, only Connally seems to [understand] Teddy Roosevelt's legacy that the Presidency is the only engine the central government has."

At Connally's zenith, it seemed a question only when, not if, he would return Reagan to Hollywood. The Fortune 500 adored him, helping raise a then-record $12 million. His experience—businessman, lawyer, farmer, governor, cabinet official, and global traveler—made him, said CBS Television, "perhaps the most qualified man to be president in this century"—unless that was Bush: businessman, congressman, UN ambassador, RNC chairman, chief liaison officer in China, and CIA director. Poppy was an outlier, slighted by the media, trying to replicate Carter's 1976 Iowa upset, parlaying delegates one by one.

Connally was above—in truth, bored by—such petty politics. What counted was to rivet an audience, his deep, rich voice addressing issues from nuclear power to international trade. He was more urbane than Huey Long, Theodore Bilbo, and George Wallace but heir to the same southern tradition of stem winding and storytelling. Not reticent—unlike Clement Atlee, of whom Winston Churchill said, "He is a modest man. But then, he has much to be modest about"—nor bland, polls said, like rivals Bush and Howard Baker—nor vapid like, presumably, the Gipper, dispensing simple truths—nor daunted by detail like Carter, missing the forest for the trees—Connally seemed molded for Mount Rushmore. How could he miss?

As it turned out, noted Bushies, in the shorthand of the day, historically.

Across the Potomac River from Washington, Connally headquarters moored the polyglot suburb of Arlington, Virginia. (Reagan inherited the office space next spring when Connally withdrew.) When Democrat JBC became a Republican in May 1973, he profited from Mahe's GOP Rolodex. He also benefited from a round and jovial press secretary, Jim Brady—to Connally, "The Bear." On March 31, 1981, Brady, now Reagan's press secretary, was severely wounded in an assassination attempt on the new president's life. By then the Connally campaign had long ago gone belly up, costing aides like Brady countless unpaid bills. In 1987, spotting an ex-Connally aide, Brady passed a note: "Would you ask the Silver Thatch [his name for Connally] if my check is in the mail?"

From the start, opinion split on how to conduct the campaign. Mahe wanted to divide time and cash across the country—the "fifty-state strategy"—accenting Connally's strengths: donors, speaking style, and energy to leapfrog Reagan's activist network in early primaries. Having helped JBC win three landslides as governor, his old Texas Democrats wanted him to blanket a state, becoming instant front-runner in Iowa and/or New Hampshire. For the moment Connally sided with his campaign manager—mostly, I believe, because he trusted Mahe's grasp of the GOP.

On July 16, 1979, I left DC for San Antonio. Connally's boyhood home, Floresville, was thirty miles southeast. Another seven miles brought you to his Xanadu, the Picosa Ranch, in the peanut country of Wilson County, where I met what the *New York Times* called "the most captivating performer on the American political stage."

Floresville's population was circa four thousand. Connally's father—"a big man," the son said, "over six-foot-six, about 250 pounds; he never finished the eighth grade"—drove a Greyhound bus from San Antonio to the Rio Grande Valley, the rich citrus and vegetable region near the Mexican border. Connally *fils* ran two blocks from their home to a street where he could wave to John Sr. as the bus left town. At night, like Nixon and Connally's mentor, Lyndon Johnson, he heard train whistles that spoke of "child's dreams," Connally said in a 1973 eulogy to Johnson, "[that] could be as wide as the sky and his future as green as winter oats because this, after all, was America."

The fourth of seven children helped butcher hogs, make lye soap, render lye, and haul corn into town on a wagon. Connally studied by kerosene light; his mother cooked on a wood stove; their home, on a dirt road, lacked electricity and indoor plumbing. Floresville was unforgiving even for the 1930s. Connally was glad to leave, at sixteen, for the University of Texas. It still intrigues how such poverty—JBC walked barefoot behind a plow—produced his persona as centurion of the rich. "You know the difference between LBJ and Connally?" said ex-Johnson aide Bill Moyers, who hated Connally and was hated in return. "LBJ wants to be the best president in United States history. Connally wants to be lionized in the best country clubs of Houston." The charge stung—and stuck.

Picosa tied a Lone Star State of Bermuda grass and Santa Gertrudis cattle and streams, falling away in endless sequence, and an airstrip for corporate jets. At the door Connally appeared in jeans and cowboy boots, showing me the home's two-story beamed den and living room. He vaunted gemstones and antiques, discussed a recent speech, then veered to Western art and back to politics. Next day the ministers would come to call. They did not include Billy Graham, a longtime friend whose crusades Connally had spoken at and who, scarred by Watergate, had vowed to boycott politics. Instead, Jerry Falwell, Pat Robertson, and Bob Jones were among those there, most tilting to Reagan. I sent a memorandum: "The GOP's conservative base must see that only you have the courage to talk about what most Americans think, but no one else has the guts to say." Connally hoped to convert the choir, and I saw him at his best.

He began as what *Time* called "an old-fashioned man in many ways." Unlike Ted Kennedy, about to oppose Carter for the Democrat nomination, Connally understood the clergy. Unlike Carter, he would be the middle class's spokesman, not pseudo friend. He spoke of his childhood, stern and disciplined, and of a Silent Majority wanting social justice, not social engineering. For two hours Connally seemed the leader those ministers had been praying for—also the mechanic wracked by inflation, textile worker hurt by unfair trade, and mother to whom pop culture seemed a sewer. He closed by vowing to restore "prayer to our schools and order to our streets."

An hour later, clergy gone, I approached Connally near his backyard pool. "You were terrific," I told him. "What I especially liked is that you didn't swear."

Connally, a gentleman around ladies, relaxed his guard among men. "Yeah," he fairly whistled, "I was pretty Goddamn good, wasn't I?"

Straightaway Big Jawn resumed his pursuit of Reagan, not announced but the clear front-runner. In Dallas, before the International Association of Police, Connally opposed a federal suit against alleged Philadelphia police brutality. The suit by "muddled do-gooders" insulted "Philadelphians perfectly able to look after themselves," he said. "Police departments should be respected, not hostage to ideological inquisitions and political kangaroo courts." Columnist Pat Buchanan loved it: "Connally's assault upon the Department of Justice, and the 'untouchables' within, signals an intention not to evade the social issues." Another columnist, Ernest Ferguson, hated how it "showed Connally . . . eager to renew the emotional rhetoric so familiar a decade ago. Few have remarked on its absence . . . but that rhetoric has been heard very little since the departure of the Nixon Administration, of which Connally was a part." To me, it was as natural as a smile.

In one speech after another, Connally attacked: "If weakness is an art form, Carter is the Rembrandt of our age." (He didn't speak, as he told the staff, of his disdain for "everything about that little man in his sweater," Carter having given a White House TV speech in a cardigan.) In Detroit Big Jawn backed a $50–100 billion tax cut over four years. In San Francisco he hailed "developing the ninety-two nuclear reactors now under construction in one-half the time presently required." In Pittsburgh Connally's brief season of triumph led to the City of Hope Medical Center, where he lashed Carter's caress of reverse discrimination. "We need equal rights for all Americans— not preferential treatment for some." The innocent were paying "a debt owed by society as a whole."

At this point, Connally was scoring even with those who detested him. *Newsweek* hailed his "breakaway positions on the issues"; James Reston termed him "the figure of real Presidential substance, the politician unafraid to take bold and tough positions." Each ignored how you have to be nominated to get elected.

By fall 1979, under media radar, George Bush was shaking hands, breaking bread at Rotary, and talking wherever an Iowan paused to listen. "George didn't just know each county's area code," said an aide, "but the GOP leader, the town banker, who got drunk, who went to church." By contrast, Connally "had grown up with a heroic concept of the Presidency," said Eddie Mahe. "This fit perfectly with his vision of himself" spurning the intellectual fashion of the time—"a man of ideas, fearless, Churchillian, longing to give his nation resolve."

On October 11, 1979, Big Jawn brought that longing to the National

Press Club in Washington, where he gave a talk drafted by ex–National Security Council (NSC) staffer Sam Hoskinson, former LBJ press secretary George Christian, and himself. The speech addressed diplomacy's Bermuda Triangle, the Middle East, unveiling a "new approach" that treated Israel as a colleague, not a client. Connally called on it to withdraw from all civilian settlements in territories gained in the 1967 war and argued for some kind of Palestinian state—autonomous or, preferably, a region with self-determination. In return, Arab nations would ensure America's flow of oil at a relatively stable price.

To guarantee Israel's security, Connally proposed a new U.S. military presence in the region—an air force base in the Sinai and a "Fifth Fleet" in the Indian Ocean—and the demand that the Arabs endorse UN Resolution 242, recognizing Israel. At the same time, he predated by a decade Bush's view that "a clear distinction must be drawn by the United States," Connally said, "between support for Israel's security, which is a moral imperative, and support for Israel's broader territorial acquisitions. We must act in America's interest—not Israel's or the Arabs'."

The address was visionary—a blueprint in part for Presidents Bush 41 and Clinton. Yet Connally was not president. October 11 ensured he never would be. His speech enraged the media, the Israeli lobby, and most fatally in the GOP, the evangelical Right that interpreted the Bible literally—Christ would return when Jews ruled the Holy Land. The *New Republic* braided "his naked trade of Israel's security for oil." Wrote the *New York Times*'s William Safire: "After John Connally's speech last week, supporters of Israel . . . made a reassessment of Ronald Reagan and decided he looked ten years younger."

Much later Mahe talked of the Press Club debacle. "It's just something he felt he had to talk about. Connally said, 'Goddamn it, I believe it—I'm going to say it.'"

"And you told him not to," I said.

Mahe smiled sadly. "If anything, I didn't alert him strongly enough to the political risks, especially among evangelicals. And even if I had, the rest of our problems might have sunk us."

Those "problems" loomed "like a ball and chain," said Jim Brady. The heaviest was Connally's image as a "wheeler-dealer," consisting, in no special order, of JBC's 1974 indictment in a milk fund scandal, symbiosis with Nixon and Watergate, and longtime union with LBJ. (Connally's campaign postmortem was "I reminded everyone of Lyndon.") He was called a turncoat by Democrats but not accepted by Republicans. The criticism was unfair—Reagan too had been a Democrat—becoming, to quote Shakespeare, whose work Connally playacted in college, the stain that would not out.

A second stain also concerned image. Connally "seemed to be the fulfillment of the mythology of Texas," ex–LBJ writer Horace Busby said. In 1979, as oil prices and gas lines spiraled, Texas became the incarnation of Big Oil. The public, in turn, blamed domestic oil—not the Organization of the Petroleum Exporting Countries (OPEC) or a presidency adrift—for the crisis. Connally and Bush were experts on energy. Feared more by Democrats, only Connally drowned in the *hysteria* over energy.

A campaign misjudgment was another stain. "Republicans would never nominate Reagan if Kennedy seemed the nominee," Mahe was certain. "Given the difference in energy and age, Republicans thought Teddy'd eat the Gipper alive." Connally yearned to oppose him, despising the Kennedys' liberalism, their nouveau wealth, and how the media and academe forgave their sins, from college cheating by way of adultery to Kennedy's letting Mary Jo Kopechne die in a 1969 car incident he caused at Chappaquiddick, Massachusetts.

"Teddy Kennedy!" Connally told a reporter. "Now that would be a classic confrontation. There are so many things—personal lives, lifestyles, family, philosophy."

Big Jawn would become, as his first network TV ad in 1979 said, "the candidate of the Forgotten American," which is the America that I knew. Only, paraphrasing the musical *Oklahoma*'s "Poor Jud Is Dead," it didn't turn out that way, "so nobody ever knowed it."

That November 4 Kennedy appeared on CBS *Reports* and, like Connally a month earlier, committed political suicide. Roger Mudd asked the simple question of why Kennedy wanted to be president.

His response was almost incoherent; millions of TV sets turned off. In spring 1940 the Nazi rape of Western Europe made foreign policy dominant, harming then–GOP favorite Tom Dewey, only thirty-nine, dubbed "the first American victim" of Hitler's aggression. After Mudd, Kennedy's erosion of support inverted the Democratic field— Connally its first victim. Republicans would not need him now to prevent Camelot II.

Finally, Connally suffered from Iran's November 1979 seizing of fifty-two Americans. "What a case of Murphy's Law," said Mahe a decade later. "We were trying to redress October 11's damage and the way to do it was in foreign policy—Connally's forte. Now [Ayatollah] Khomeini takes the hostages. Suddenly, that dominates foreign policy, and we can't even discuss it." Big Jawn had declared a post-hostage-taking moratorium of Carter's foreign policy.

Longtime Connally aide George Christian grew easy at the memory. "That was Connally at his purest," he said. "I was worried he'd incinerate Carter—way too partisan. Instead, he told me, 'The poor bastard's doing the best he can.'"

"What explains it?" I said.

"Connally had no respect for Carter—but total respect for the Presidency," Christian said. "It's just too bad the crisis came when it did."

Comparing generals, Napoleon once said, "Ability is fine, but give me commanders who have luck." Luck was the avenging angel of Connally's 1980 campaign.

In October I flew to San Clemente to spend three days at Ray Price's condominium. Like Nixon, about to move back east, Price wrote speech drafts, suggested policy themes, and helped edit his still-boss's books. The final day Ray took me to the villa and nearby stucco building once called the "western White House," to meet with the man the *Washington Post* had recently called "the one true superstar of the 1970s." Entering, we passed the Situation Room, where Nixon, Kissinger, and the Joint Chiefs of Staff once plotted war and peace. Nixon's office was adjacent. The former president was alone, removed from the pinnacle, standing, slightly hunched, in a dark blue suit, beside an illuminated globe.

"How's Ray been treating you?" he asked, tanned, sixty-six, and younger than I expected, settling in his chair.

"Fine, Mr. President—he's showing me California," I said.

"Let's talk some politics," he replied. For two hours Nixon etched Carter, whom he pitied ("too small for the world's biggest office"); Kennedy, whose candidacy he said would fail ("Democratic bosses don't want a divided party"); and Republican candidates whom he knew and found wanting.

"Howard Baker," I said.

He stiffened, leaning forward in his chair. "Nice smile, not enough steel."

"George Bush."

"Good background, fine mind, especially on foreign policy. The questions are his strength and if he can connect." Behind him, through the window, the lawn of *La Casa Pacifica*—"the Peaceful House"— sloped sharply to the sea. A railroad track split its grounds. Surfers littered the beach where once Nixon walked in wing tips.

Next came the Gipper, a hybrid of Dixon and Eureka College and WHO Radio Des Moines. "A good man, a loyalist, man of principle. But can you imagine him going up against Brezhnev?" he asked. "That's quite a stretch." Pause. "But who knows? He's been under-estimated before."

That left Connally. Nixon was worried about his friend. In 1971 the treasury secretary had scolded White House staffers. "If you gave the average person the choice," he asked, "what do you think they would like to hear—about revenue sharing, taxation, government reorganization, or what Tricia's boyfriend is like?" Correctly, JBC chose the latter. Yet what he urged as Nixon's counselor, he ignored as Nixon's candidate.

A job of mine was to monitor Reagan's 1979 speeches—opposition research. Listening, I found them more anecdotal than factual. By contrast, even ad-lib Connally remarks were structured; he was a lawyer making a case to the jury—the electorate. Yet "politics," Price once wrote Nixon, "is only minimally a rational science, and no matter how persuasive our convictions, they will be effective only if we can first get people to make the *emotional* leap."

Many had or would with Reagan—despite or because of what Norman Mailer called his "tripped on my shoelaces, aw-shucks variety of confusion." In Tennessee, Idaho, or rural Ohio, his vision was their vision—as actor David Ogden Stiers later narrated in the PBS documentary *Reagan*, "inheriting the values of the American heartland—a clear sense of right and wrong, and self-reliance."

Nixon agreed: "The American voter doesn't vote as an adult—on fact. He votes on images and impressions and how they relate to him," he said.

"But the public's instincts can be right," I said, "especially if it knows what's at stake."

"Sure," he replied, "and that's what you appeal to. But the average guy with a beer watching TV doesn't spend his time reading *The Nation* or *National Review* or what have you. It's values, not detail, to which a voter responds."

Connally, who said he agreed, persisted in treating Americans as adults—less, I think, out of ignorance than pride. Refusing to talk down, he dealt in policy, not emotion. The upshot was that he won GOP minds, not hearts. "Listening to Connally is like eating a Chinese dinner," Reagan aide Lee Atwater barbed. "Ten minutes later, you've forgotten you ate."

Connally's résumé, which he thought superior to Reagan's, didn't stop his stalling in the polls. In November Reagan won a key Florida straw poll, 36–26 percent, over Big Jawn; out of nowhere, giving a fine extempore speech, Bush corralled 22. Early 1980 Connally losses in Iowa and New Hampshire followed. Big Jawn axed Mahe, turned more to old Texas Democrats, named future securities fixer Charles Keating his campaign chair, and increasingly scalded aides about being overbooked—scheduler David Parker began holding the phone a foot from his ear. Thinking he could outraise everyone, Connally had spurned federal spending limits—thus, was ineligible for matching funds. In January the $12 million candidate ran out of cash.

His last stand was the March 8, 1980, South Carolina primary. Atwater leaked a story to Lee Bandy, a writer for the state's largest newspaper, *The State*, that "Connally was trying to buy the black vote," said Bandy. "That story got out, thanks to me, and it probably killed him. Lee [Atwater] saved Ronald Reagan's candidacy." Atwater died in 1991. Other Reagan aides deny the story. At any rate Reagan won decisively, whereupon Connally withdrew three days later. He won one delegate: Ada Mills of Clarksville, Arkansas.

I remember a meeting with advisers as the walls began closing in. Connally got out a pen and piece of paper and began drawing a brochure.

"Here's what I want it to say," he began. "On one side, 'Connally,' the other side, 'Reagan.' On my side it'll read, 'Governor, Texas,' on his, 'Governor, California.'"

I watched in fascination.

"Next comes cabinet experience," he said. "'Connally—Secretary of Navy and Treasury. Reagan—Nothing. Business experience—Connally, rancher, lawyer, businessman. Reagan—actor.'" For a long pause I eyed George Christian.

"'Foreign policy—Connally,' find out the number of trips I've taken. 'Reagan'—if any, there'll be far fewer." Connally stopped, theatrically. "Now we come to the personal side. 'Connally—married, thirty-nine years. Reagan—divorced.'"

An aide said quickly, "Governor, you can't *say* these things. The media will slaughter you."

Connally looked past him. "Why not?" he demanded, planting his jaw. "It's not an exaggeration—it's the *truth*."

Connally hoped that speeches like Dallas's and Pittsburgh's might right his ship. So he spoke of capital punishment, permissiveness, and social leeches to lure independents and conservative Democrats—but his heart wasn't in it. Touting America's civil religion, Reagan said, "[My favorite] historical character was the man whose simple teachings in a three-year span between the ages of thirty and thirty-three set down rules which, if we had the courage to follow them, would solve all the problems of the world today, the Prince of Peace, the Man of Galilee." Connally couldn't talk that way. He liked to speak about productivity, regulation, and tax relief—unlike Reagan, never grasping the kind of coalition that could help conservatives usurp power.

Bush did, belatedly, in 1988, as we shall see, addressing nonpolitical concerns of character, faith, and spirit—what a *Time* columnist called a blend of "nostalgia; religious simplicity; stoic heroism; reverence for family as the mainspring of society; a belief that truth dwells in inner conviction rather than facts"—issues like the Pledge of Allegiance and voluntary prayer. To use Connally's favorite phrase, such an agenda would have "personally offended" him as not the province of a president. On one hand, Big Jawn was a most impolitic pol, scrapping lines that told "groups what they *want* to hear, not what they *need* to," said Christian. On the other, I will admit, part of me loved his going for the jugular.

When a voter doubted nuclear power plant safety, Connally snapped, "Your problem is, you're afraid of the future." He whipsawed his favorite Kennedy: "The milk fund—what about it? I never was thrown out of college for cheating. I never killed anybody." At a Denver business breakfast, I gave him a last-minute note about Jane Fonda, "who said that if America left Southeast Asia, there would be no bloodbath—only peace and harmony. They were wrong—dead wrong—and millions are dead *because* they were wrong." Connally used it because Connally believed it. Because he did, it brought down the house.

In 1991 Nixon likened George Bush, to whom we are about to return, to quarterback Joe Montana. "Nothing flashy—no long bombs— but he'll short-pass you to death. Dependable—and he makes few mistakes." Going for the bomb, Big Jawn was too often intercepted. Later, writing for a very different Texan in the Bush White House, I recalled Connally's instinct for ad hominem combat. "I've been rich and I've been poor, and rich is better," he said, quoting Sophie Tucker. In his world, "Second is fine and third is worse, but neither of them are acceptable. You don't win at any price. You just win."

Risking all, Connally lost all. Spurned politically, he plunged into real estate, made a fortune, then went bankrupt in 1988 from the collapse of his state's economy—to the last, as Horace Busby said, "the fulfillment of the mythology of Texas."

One night in November 1979, on a flight from Houston to the nation's capital, Connally suddenly recited lines from Byron's "The Prisoner of Chillon":

> My hair is grey, but not with years,
> Nor grew it white
> In a single night,
> As men's have grown from sudden fears.

In college, Connally's favorite poets were the romantics. His romantic notion of leadership was not a wet finger in the wind.

SIX

A Phone Call from the Gipper

For Bush, John Connally's humiliation was almost as delicious as had he won the GOP nomination itself. He felt that Connally's machine had resuscitated Lloyd Bentsen's comeback in the 1970 U.S. Senate race. Moreover, Bush knew that the native Texan thought him somehow effete, despite Poppy's remarkable record of heroism and success. He would have recoiled at Connally's Weltanschauung: "You are judged in Washington," snarled JBC, "by the enemies you destroy." I had not known of the bile—"dislike" hardly describes it—between the candidates when I began to write for Connally. Gradually, I became aware as the two staffs drank each Friday night at the Alexandria, Virginia, bar Chadwicks. Each partied in a separate corner of the second floor, my few meetings with the Bush staff pleasant. It seemed mostly Texan and northeastern, heavily Ivy League, largely upper class and prep school. Connally's staff was overwhelmingly Lone Star, also upper class, largely University of Texas, and more conservative than Bush's. I was one of few New Yorkers—and likely the only person ever to have written for Connally and Bush.

Michael Kramer of *New York* magazine was with Bush in his hotel the night of the January 21, 1980, Iowa caucus, when Connally, conceding, came on the screen. Bush reached out as though to shake his hand through the screen. "Thank you, sir, for all the kind things you and your friends have been saying about me," Poppy said, then raised his hand, slammed it on top of the set, and said, "That prick!" Dorothy Bush must have forgiven her son's lapse, this once.

Announcing in November 1979, Reagan intended to spend most of his time in New Hampshire before its February 26 primary. Like Carter in 1976, Bush applied retail politics to virtually every Iowa cattle call and caucus, aware that the Gipper was the default GOP incumbent, having almost upset a sitting president four years earlier. Bush sent a million pieces of mail to party members across Iowa a week before its caucuses. The outcome stunned his principal rival, almost a native son since his 1930s suzerainty as WHO play-by-play man Dutch Reagan: Bush, 31.25 percent; the Gipper, 29.4 percent; balance, other candidates. Later Reagan thanked Iowans for a needed "kick in the pants," the caucuses briefly crowning a new front-runner.

Certainly the victor thought so, claiming momentum—"The Big Mo," he exulted, joining "deep doo-doo" in classic Bushspeak—preppyisms likely to limit the GOP's working-class appeal. Reagan, who would swell it, began for the first time to engage his future running mate. Still, many doubted if Dutch, at sixty-nine, was still Tom Mix by way of Jimmy Stewart. The answer came in Nashua, New Hampshire, at a February 23 debate the *Nashua Telegraph* had offered to sponsor between Bush and Reagan. Accepting, "we [then] worried that it might violate electoral relations," said a Reagan aide, "so we offered to fund the event with our money" and invited the other four candidates to participate.

When Bush arrived at the debate, he learned for the first time of the new six-man format. Feeling sandbagged, he understandably refused to compete, causing an impasse on the stage. "He'd been given the shortest of notice," said then–*Newsweek* White House correspondent Tom DeFrank. "It's also true that Reagan had a firm percent of the vote. With two guys debating, Bush would inherit the anti-Reagan vote, probably winning. With six, it would split." Reagan tried to explain the decision, prompting *Telegraph* editor Jon Breen to tell the sound man to mute his microphone, at which point Reagan steamed, "I am *paying* for this microphone, Mr. Green [*sic*]!"— perhaps subconsciously, one actor aiding another, Reagan borrowing the line from Spencer Tracy's film *The State of the Union*.

What a sight! Reagan, visibly furious, his phrase the most quotable quote in GOP primary history. The other candidates, offstage, having reluctantly agreed to the original two-man debate. The event continuing, uneventful and unnecessary. Leaving, Bush aides saw the parking lot littered with "Bush for President" badges. Trailing in the polls before Mr. Breen cut the Gipper's mike, Dutch romped next week, 50–23 percent. A quarter century later, his future close friend laughed at the memory. "Reagan had left Iowa before election night and paid big-time for it," Bush said. "He always learned from his mistakes. In New Hampshire he kept stumping there until the polls were closed."

We also recall the about to be ex-front-runner sitting, awkwardly, as Reagan took over: Bush did not know how to seize the moment (the actor did, brimming with self-confidence), having been taught as a child to defer, not dominate (usually a good thing, not here). Bush soldiered on without "the Big Mo," winning primaries in Puerto Rico, Massachusetts, Connecticut, Pennsylvania, Washington DC, and Michigan, his vote affluent and moderate-liberal, where Reagan, heading the ticket, would arguably be weak. "Why doesn't he get out of the race?" Nancy Reagan objected that spring as Bush lost one race after another. He did, May 26.

Reagan used a standard line when asked if he was nervous about an event: "I was on the screen with Errol Flynn" in 1940's *Sante Fe Trail*. The message was that he'd already been in the big leagues; one in two Americans at that time saw at least one film a week. The famed actor impressed the Gipper. At first Bush did not. Franklin Roosevelt said that wishful thinking could not rewrite history. To Reagan, Poppy's first role had been the Nashua fiasco. "Just melted under pressure," said the soon-to-be GOP presidential nominee. In May 1980 Bush called Reagan's supply-side stratagem "voo-doo economics." Neither increased the possibility that Reagan would make Bush veep. Aware of his largely self-made fix, Bush sold his house in Houston and bought his grandfather's estate at Walker's Point. To many, it seemed that the Connecticut Yankee was giving up on politics.

Every politician needs a base—his home. Which was Poppy's? In 1988 he told David Frost, "Texas is our home, and this [Walker's Point] is idyllic for a family to come home to. I lived there [Texas] since 1948, voted in every major election since '48 down there, and it's where I made my living. It's where most of our kids were born." Still, his mother, "the spiritual leader of our family," lived in a bungalow on Walker's Point. Their Maine home was "our anchor to windward in the summertime. Our kids live in five different states . . . and they come home here. We had twenty-two people in this house a few weeks ago. It was wonderful." The estate and home had been bought and built, respectively, in the early twentieth century by George Herbert Walker. Later the future "Summer White House" passed to Poppy's parents. What was home? There was no simple answer: no Lincoln bidding farewell at the Great Western Railway Station; no Johnson on a horse at the LBJ Ranch; no JFK as Hyannis Port's Young Man and the Sea.

Lance Morrow wrote the same of Bush, politically. "He sometimes seems to have misplaced America, and to be intently seeking it," Morrow observed in the 1980s. "Or perhaps fleeing it. Bush used to be a moderate Republican. Now, inheriting the Reagan legacy, he is constrained to run as a right-winger. Bush went from patrician Connecticut to the Texas oil fields as a young man . . . from one identity to another, from one appointive office to another, and these transitions seem at least to add up to a sense of permanent motion and quest, or search for something that is finally his own." The self-styled Mr. Smooth wanted consensus. Growing conservatism wanted its way. Connecticut Yankees were dying—literally. If Poppy was to reemerge to lead the GOP, he would have to turn right.

Before withdrawing as a candidate, Bush was in permanent motion, perhaps seeking his "identity." After Connally's losing campaign, so were survivors, his withdrawal robbing them of joy and definition. Casting about, I focused on a periodical that, in memory's rear-view mirror, embodied what Upton Sinclair once called "standardized as soda crackers." He meant the *Saturday Evening Post*—the first magazine that I recall reading and that, having backed Connally, offered me in spring 1980 the post of senior editor and national affairs editor. What I was about to help run now had offices, not in Philadelphia, as I remembered as a boy, but in Indianapolis, Indiana. (In 2013 the *Post* decided it would rather relocate to Philadelphia and did.)

There was no weekly with a more glorious name than the old *Saturday Evening Post*, characterized by imagination, great narrative, and a kinship with Middle America. "Through world wars and the Depression," it said, "the *Post* informed its readers of global events, entertained them with cliff-hanging stories that ran in serial form, and moved or amused them with evocative, sometimes sentimental, covers." It began in 1821, evolving from Benjamin Franklin's *Pennsylvania Gazette*. In 1897 Cyrus H. K. Curtis bought the magazine for $1,000. He hired a new editor, George Horace Lorimer, a minister's son from Boston, and founded the Curtis Publishing Company. For more than half a century, the *Post* was a weekly grandstand and mirror of a middle-class mentality; it lasted until 1969, when one of its best writers penned a eulogy.

By his count Stewart Alsop had done 126 articles and 147 columns for the periodical—about 750,000 words. Now twenty-five years after his first article—"a look at Harold Stassen's chances of being President, which I concluded were excellent"—he wrote of the magazine's love of words and editors "[who] considered a writer's style and political views his business, as long as he was accurate and readable." Generations of Americans displayed the *Post* in their waiting rooms or bought it at the corner drugstore or trekked each Thursday to their mailbox—as esteemed as *Life*, less dull than *Reader's Digest*, and more small-town than *Look*. The bylines of Paul Gallico and Ellery Queen; diaries of Alexander Botts and Scattergood Baines; Pete Martin's gossip profiles, breathlessly intoning Hollywood; and an artist whose work became the *Post* reflected the America of their time.

At seven I traced the covers of the illustrator Norman Rockwell, who painted, among a swarm of other things, the politicians of each season—in mine, JFK, Stevenson, Nelson Rockefeller, Ike with his pitching iron. His *Post* seemed impervious. What killed it—also, the magazine's treatment of politics, humor, and fiction—was an aging readership, slack advertising and circulation, and cultural disarray. *Newsweek* wrote, "More and more, Rockwell's America wasn't there anymore"—bound inextricably with the Great God Television. By its last weekly writhing, the *Post* had lost $62 million since a 1962 move from Philadelphia to New York—apparent proof of the general interest magazine's demise. Next year, 1970, Indiana businessman Beurt SerVaas bought the Curtis empire and became president. The *Post* relocated to Indianapolis, reemerged as a one-dollar-a-copy newsstand quarterly, and recycled golden oldies from Tugboat Annie to Ted Key cartoons, the old "gray narrative illustrations," custom headline type once used by the magazine, and Rockwell, puffing his pipe and preparing to paint a *Post* delivery boy on its initial cover.

The *Post*'s first two issues sold out their 500,000-copy press run. It became quarterly in 1971, turned to ten and now six issues a year, and temporarily revived the general-interest genre—a triumph for SerVaas and wife Cory, *Post* editor and publisher. Both hired me to succeed—no one could, or has, replaced—the glorious Ben Hibbs, *Post* editor from 1942 to 1961; later, William Emerson and Otto Friedrich; and 1970s former *Esquire* managing editor Fred Birmingham. A typical issue tied fiction, "Post People," medicine, entertainment, a tale about John Wayne sculpture, and right-center politics. Any GOP nominee would find a friend.

I enjoyed the creative cycle of building a magazine, each issue bred from scratch: story, photo, caption, theme. In two years we wrote cover stories about "Ronald Reagan's Greatest Role," the 1981 presidential inaugural, Robert Redford, and the Muppets; penned fiction and nonfiction book reviews; won a national cover award by putting the film star dog Benji in a barber chair, wrapping him in a towel, and simulating a haircut; and grasped why Wright Morris wrote of Rockwell, "His special triumph is in the conviction his countrymen share that the mythical world he evokes exists."

Dutch Reagan could evoke it too, especially after being sworn in as president on January 20, 1981. As our narrative will show, Bush, having almost left politics, took the oath that day as vice president. Looking back, the office's criteria seemed so tailored to Poppy—

discretion, hard work, intelligence, loyalty—that he wore it like a Savile Row suit.

As president, Reagan would quote the Founding Fathers, especially Thomas Jefferson, often using them to twit his age, sixty-nine when inaugurated—"I know that's true because Jefferson told me." Bush's frame of reference differed. "I'd rather quote Yogi Berra than Thomas Jefferson," he said in our first meeting. His favorite Berraisms included "It's always dangerous to make predictions, especially about the future." At July 1980's GOP Convention in Detroit, Bush apparently had little chance of being Reagan's vice presidential nominee. Nashua stung. Bush had shown finite appeal beyond the eighteenth hole. Nancy Reagan was still miffed that he hadn't dropped out earlier.

After the 1980 primaries, Jimmy Carter led Reagan and independent candidate John Anderson in the Gallup Poll, 39, 32, and 21 percent, respectively. Tellingly, though, six in ten were upset by the incumbent's "handling of the Presidency." Before the Republican Convention, the Georgian launched a TV attack blitz, dubbing the Gipper a lightweight right-wing warmonger. Henry Kissinger, hoping to (a) unify the GOP and (b) become secretary of state to a record third U.S. president, urged that (c) Ford become Reagan's vice president, at which time the thirty-eighth president warmed to the idea if (d) he could play "a meaningful role." Word of a "dream ticket" made the quadrennial event, held in Ford's home state, go bonkers.

On the convention's opening night, Ford traveled to the CBS TV booth, where the august Walter Cronkite held forth. America's "most trusted man" got the Accidental President to describe the parameters of his possible vice presidency, including the term "co-presidency." Watching, Bush reasonably assumed that Ford would not talk so brazenly unless Reagan had approved a pact, not knowing that the Gipper too was shocked. Reagan pollster Richard Wirthlin said the candidate literally jumped off the couch. "Did you hear what he said about his role?" Reagan said. "Sounds like he wants to be a co-president."

After the Cronkite telecast, Reagan summoned Ford to his hotel suite, where they met alone. Ten minutes later each emerged to say that the "dream ticket" had been scrubbed. Berra once said, "When you come to a fork in the road, take it." Reagan was about to take a road he perhaps had not intended. "The answer is no," the Gipper told his staff. "He [Ford] didn't think it was right for him or me. And now I am inclined to agree."

Reagan had been an eight-term president of Hollywood's Screen Actors Guild. He was intuitive, incisive, with a gamesman's gift for timing. With Ford now out, delay about who was in might help Carter paint him as naive. "Reagan picked up the phone," aide Michael Deaver wrote in his book, *Behind the Scenes*, "and to the amazement of everyone in the room, said, 'I'm calling George Bush. I want to get this settled. Anyone have any objections?'"

Reagan grasped the need for the ticket to lure non–true believers. It says much about Bush's ability to foster trust that Reagan instantly turned to him. No one, including Deaver, objected. The Gipper called Bush, saying that he would like to promptly announce his choice. Bush was delighted—and incredulous. Unintentionally, the Accidental President had made him the Accidental Vice President.

Only Reagan knew for sure if he would have chosen Bush had Ford not guest starred with Uncle Walter. For more than a decade, Bush had eyed the presidency—from before opposing Lloyd Bentsen via the UN to thrice being spurned by Ford to China and the CIA to campaigning more exhaustively in 1979–80 than anyone else in either party—all in vain.

Now, in one moment, Ford had inadvertently propelled Bush to the possibility, as John Nance Garner said, of being "one heartbeat" from the presidency. It all felt unreal—a miracle, looking back. For one who believed in God, as Bush did, immersed since youth, it was hard not to see the work of Providence.

Bush's new work now began.

In his acceptance speech, the new GOP vice president said, "If anyone wants to know why Ronald Reagan is a winner, you can refer him to me. I am an expert on the subject." Next day he met a news media that, if not as wholly an appendage of the Democratic Party as today's, still tried to split the Republican ticket. "I won't permit myself to get bogged down in trying to find or accentuate—or permit you to make me accentuate—differences that I had with the Governor because they had been minimal," Bush told reporters.

In the primaries he had clashed with Reagan on foreign policy, abortion, the Equal Rights Amendment, and taxes. En route from Los Angeles to the convention, aide Stuart Spencer heard the Gipper trash Bush's months-long rebuke of him for ten minutes, then say calmly, suddenly, again the pragmatist, "What'd you think?"—about Bush as vice president. He hadn't closed the door. Hearing Bush tell the media to forget six degrees of separation between number one and number two, many Reaganauts looked at him anew. By contrast, many pressies would have attributed to Bush T. S. Eliot's "We are the hollow men. We are the stuffed men," had they known who the poet was. "If I'd been a liberal," Bush later laughed, "they've have praised my fidelity to principle. It's just the way it is. The media has a double standard."

Going forward, Reagan-Bush could count on solid GOP support, though the liberal Republican congressman Anderson had become a third-party candidate. Would he hurt Reagan, luring the GOP leftist fringe, or the incumbent, giving the ABC (Anyone But Carter) voters a choice? No one knew. In cold text it was hard on the stump to separate the Republican ticket. Reagan urged a pronounced cut in "big government programs." Bush vowed a balanced budget within three years, the first time since Nixon's first year as president. Bush, like Kennedy in the early 1960s, said lower tax rates would mean higher tax revenues—supply side's core. Reagan said famously that "recession is when your neighbor loses his job. Depression is when you lose yours. And recovery is when Jimmy Carter loses his."

In August Reagan, touting states' rights to "help people do . . . as much as they can at the community . . . and the private level," spoke at the annual Neshoba County Fair in Philadelphia, Mississippi, where three civil rights workers had been murdered in 1964. Bush defended his own longtime National Association for the Advancement of Colored People (NAACP) record—and the Gipper's decency. Carter mocked Reagan for saying that trees caused pollution. He also had a Gallup Convention "bounce": from sixteen points behind, he leapt to one ahead. Bush, counterpunching, said that Carter's self-created misery index—the unemployment plus inflation rate, nearing 20 percent—polluted something worse: the economy. The lead bobbed back and forth, like a crew race on Long Island Sound. The debates seemed crucial—the League of Women Voters scheduled three presidential and one vice presidential—except that Anderson's presence skewered the cards.

Carter would not debate with Anderson. Reagan would not debate without the independent candidate. "He [Carter] couldn't win a debate," said the Gipper of himself and Anderson, "if it were held in the Rose Garden before an audience of Administration officials with the questions being asked by [Press Secretary] Jody Powell." On September 20 Anderson and Reagan met to little polling movement. Carter opposed a three-man duel, fearing that Anderson would take independents unable to back Reagan but unforgiving of Carter's record. Clock ticking, the first two presidential debates and Bush's duel with Vice President Walter Mondale were canceled. Finally, conceding Carter's criteria—"We led him by a point or two," said pollster Wirthlin, "but were concerned voters scared of Reagan would go back to Carter. We had to show he didn't have horns"—Reagan okayed an October 28 debate in Cleveland.

Too often debate rewards what doesn't count—appearance, glibness—and minimizes what does—character, maturity. The presidency and vice presidency need people as deep as a river. Today's culture spurs many candidates as shallow as a spoon. Carter attacked— "war hawk" and "dangerous right-wing radical"—and revealed how daughter Amy told him the election's greatest issue—"the control of nuclear arms." Reagan was devastating in a poised and wistful way. After Carter demagogued Medicaid and Social Security, the Gipper sighed and said, "There you go again." Closing, Reagan faced the TV screen that had been his home since the 1950s. "Are you better off than you were four years ago? Is it easier for you to go buy things in the stores than it was four years ago? . . . Is America as respected as it was four years ago?" To ask was to answer.

Reagan won forty-four states to Carter's six and the District of Columbia, 489 electoral votes to the incumbent's 49, and 51 percent of the vote to his 41; Anderson's 6 percent cost Carter as much as Reagan. Reagan won most key Gallup groups: independents, 54–30 percent; whites, 55–36; males, 54–37; females, 46–45; white Protestants, 62–31; Catholics, 51–40; households with incomes of $15,000–24,999, 53–38; $25,000–50,000, 58–32; over $50,000, 66–26; high school graduates, 51–43; college graduates, 51–35; people thirty to forty-four years of age, 54–37; forty-five to fifty-nine, 55–39; sixty or over, 54–40; the South, 51–44; white South, 60–35; Midwest, 51–40; Far West, 53–35; suburban/small cities, 53–37; and rural/small towns, 54–39. Carter won among Democrats, liberals, blacks, Hispanics, people eighteen to twenty-one years of age and in cities with populations greater than 250,000. He and Reagan tied among people twenty-two to twenty-nine years of age. Barack Obama used the same base in a different America to become a majority president a quarter century later.

To the degree that a vice president can matter, Bush did in 1980. He reassured moderates and independents, many in the East, where Reagan led only 47–42 percent, and cemented the Gipper's huge margin among Bush's natural clientele—whites, Protestants, households with incomes over $50,000, suburbia, professionals, college graduates, and people thirty to fifty-nine years old. Still, Bush knew Reagan only faintly and his inner circle less. He knew also that the Reagan campaign thought he had "folded at Nashua. No spunk," according to one. Heraclitus said, "A man's character is his fate." Slowly, Bush's character became *his*.

He had seen others showboat: Theodore Roszak, hailing irrationality; Margaret Mead, wallowing in Future Speak; Kenneth Keninston, terming baby boomers the best and brightest. They violated Bush's deepest sense of self. He would earn Reagan's respect his way, which was his parents' way—by his conduct, how he acted, treated others. A song, ironically, of that younger generation put it well: "Little things mean a lot."

Reagan chose—it is assumed, with Nancy Reagan's *selah*—James A. Baker III, Bush's campaign manager and longtime friend, as his White House chief of staff. For Poppy, it was like striking a vein of silver ore. Through January 1985, when he became treasury secretary, Baker ministered to Reagan's economic, political, and international agenda. He also fueled the Reagan-Bush friendship, kept his old friend abreast of decisions large and small, and helped facilitate what Bush would have been in any event—the ultimate team player, even at age ten at Greenwich Country Day School. His hero was Lou Gehrig, the Iron Horse, pride of the New York Yankees, a good and quiet man of whom Captain Bill Dickey said, "Every day, any day, he just goes out and does his job."

From 1926 to 1938, Gehrig drove in a hundred or more runs, including an American League record 184, another record thirteen-straight years. Bush and his father heard network radio convey seven Yankees World Series titles. "I remember Graham McNamee doing most of the play by play," Bush said, "and Lou's continuity"—ten Series home runs, thirty-four runs batted in, and a .316 average. "Gehrig was steadier, less flamboyant, and more dependable than the Babe . . . steadily achieving excellence"—a telling self-portrait.

In 1939, after a Major League record 2,130 straight games, Gehrig was felled by an enemy within: amyotrophic lateral sclerosis, a hardening and collapsing of the spinal cord—now called Lou Gehrig's disease. That July 4 the Yankees retired his number 4 at Yankee Stadium. Between games of a doubleheader, he delivered baseball's Gettysburg Address. "Some may think I've been given a bad break," said Gehrig, "but I've got an awful lot to live for." The peroration wed sweetest song and saddest thought: "I consider myself the luckiest man on the face of the earth."

Gehrig died in 1941. Half a century later, Bush called him "my hero not just as a child—still is"—one first baseman to another. "Lou Gehrig was a great example in his personal life, and showed courage as he faced death"—dutiful son, faithful husband. Bush talked baseball—also Washington Redskins football, politics, foreign and domestic policy, guests' families, and the day's odds and ends—at the many social events he and Mrs. Bush hosted at the vice president's residence at One Observatory Circle, two miles from the White House. Mrs. Bush had called him "the Pearle Mesta of the United Nations," the American socialite known as the "hostess with the mostest"; the name and instinct stuck.

Bush knew most members of Congress, had worked with some still serving, liked to kibitz, and was a quick study of the Hill's leaders and legislation. As president of the Senate, he briefed Reagan regularly—and well. Nixon once said, "If it weren't for people, this [the presidency] would be an easy job." To Bush, people were the job. As vice president he traveled 1.3 million miles, visited all fifty states and sixty-five countries, and attended so many funerals that Baker coined his fictional motto: "You Die. I Fly." Barbara Bush quietly bristled at the fuss, saying, "George met with many current or future heads of state at the funerals he attended, enabling him to forge personal relationships that were important to President Reagan—and later, President Bush." The 1991 Gulf War became exhibit A.

In 1988, looking back, Bush said, "If you're a supportive vice president, you sublimate your own priorities and your own passion for a team." He had, adding, "Ultimately, I'm not going into this game [of criticizing President Reagan]—and it is a game. I'm not going into that. It's talking about character, about fundamental honor. These are things that matter with me. Decency. Talk about what I learned from my dad. Let somebody else play that game. Not me." There are far worse ways to be recalled.

On March 30, 1981, Bush unveiled—ironically, events proved—an historical marker at the Fort Worth hotel where John F. Kennedy had spent his last night in 1963 before being assassinated next day in Dallas. In early afternoon Bush learned that Reagan had been shot

A Phone Call from the Gipper

and seriously wounded after giving a speech in Washington. A bullet by would-be assassin John Hinckley lodged an inch from the president's heart. Reagan was rushed to George Washington Hospital, was operated on, and came close to dying, America learned much later. "I didn't know I'd been shot when I heard that noise. I thought it was firecrackers," Dutch said. In Texas, Reagan's would-be successor immediately ordered that his plane return to the nation's capital.

Landing at Andrews Air Force Base, Bush was urged by many aides to helicopter to the White House. It would be dramatic, pitch-perfect for the kinetic tube, showing the government intact and functioning, freeze-framing Bush as a leader in absentia. Instinctively, he refused. "Only the president lands on the South Lawn," Bush said, doing what was proper—a little thing. When Reagan heard of the story, he was impressed—better, touched. The helicopter flew to the vice presidential home. Bush drove to the White House, went to the Situation Room, and joined the cabinet meeting already under way. Among issues discussed was the nuclear football—the button that, once pushed, would start a nuclear war.

In Bush's absence some officials had acted rashly. "As of now, I am in charge here," Secretary of State Alexander Haig, sweating, told the nation, harming his own credibility and rearranging the line of succession. By contrast, Bush's calm and Reagan's grace soothed many. "I hope you're all Republicans," the Gipper told doctors in the operating room. Weak and underweight, he returned to work April 11, ultimately using TV—"If Congress won't see the light, I ask you to make it feel the heat," he said in one address—and Bush on the Hill to help pass the Economic Recovery Act of 1981. The law lowered the marginal and lowest tax bracket from 70 to 50 and 14 to 11 percent, respectively. Another work of Providence: explaining the act to pols, the Yale economics major was able to make the dismal science clear.

In his 1993 book, *President Kennedy: Profile of Power*, Richard Reeves wrote, "There was an astonishing density of event during the Kennedy years": the Bay of Pigs, Berlin, the space race, civil rights, the Cuban Missile Crisis. Reagan's first years as president had a similar density. On Inauguration Day the American hostages seized in

1979 by the Ayatollah Khomeini were released. On January 29, 1981, Reagan held his first press conference as president. Asked about the Soviet Union, he said, "As long as . . . they reserve unto themselves the right to commit any crime, to lie, to cheat, in order to attain . . . a one-world Socialist or Communist state, I think when you do business with them . . . you keep that in mind." Said an adviser, incredulous, "Well, that takes care of that [détente]."

In early February Reagan addressed the nation for the first time on the economy. On April 28 the Gipper, still recovering from the bullet wound, spoke to Congress on behalf of his economic program like Caesar taking Gaul. In August he signed the act in California—"the most important economic law," he said, since his hero, Franklin Roosevelt, forged the New Deal half a century earlier. The economy tumbled into 1983, then rose for the rest of his presidency. On August 5, 1981, Reagan fired 11,345 air traffic controllers, the largest union to back him in 1980, for violating a federal law prohibiting a government union from striking. The Kremlin was stunned, U.S. intelligence later learned, to find a different kind of president.

In Britain Reagan told Parliament that "the forward march of freedom and democracy will leave Marxism-Leninism on the ash-heap of history." Boldly, he proposed a zero option: if the Soviets removed their ss-20 missile deployment, America would not install Pershing 2 and ground-launch missiles in West Germany. The Reds said no. Reagan went ahead. He proclaimed the "Reagan Doctrine," seeking to "roll back" Communism in, among other places, Latin America, Pakistan, and Afghanistan—and foresaw a strategic defense initiative to protect America from attack by a strategic nuclear ballistic system, making nuclear war improbable. When Soviet fighters downed Korean Air Lines flight 007, carrying 269 passengers, near Moneron Island, Reagan said the Soviets had turned "against the world and the moral precepts which guide human relations among people everywhere." To many, the United States was again standing tall.

On October 23, 1983, American peacekeeping forces in Beirut, sent by Reagan during the Lebanese civil war, were attacked by a suicide truck bomber—241 U.S. Marines died; more than 60 were wounded.

Bush led a White House team four days later to investigate. That week Reagan ordered U.S. forces to invade Grenada, where a 1979 coup d'etat had formed a nonaligned Marxist-Leninist government. The force helped protect several hundred American medical students at St. George's University and stem an alleged Soviet Cuban military buildup in the Caribbean. Symbolically, on a trip abroad Reagan might sing "Amazing Grace" with troops, eat in their mess, and beam when a soldier said he was from California. More tangibly, he rebuilt the armed forces hollowed out under Carter.

The different kind of president was helped by a different kind of vice president. For one thing, Bush knew the world—U.S. friends and enemies—better than any vice president since Nixon. "Here's where the United Nations and CIA really helped," said John Sununu, Bush's future presidential chief of staff. "He just wasn't socializing with countries' leaders at personal events and meetings. He'd been getting to know them—their families, how they worked." For another, the human element applied irrespective of rank. In the mid-1980s Bush's mother chided him for reading while Reagan gave a State of the Union address. Bush explained that he was just following the text. No matter, she said; it still showed bad manners. Reagan, whose mother had grounded him in fundamentalist religion, had been taught how to treat other people too.

The near assassination affirmed the Gipper's faith. "God must have been sitting on my shoulder. Whatever time I've got left, it now belongs to someone else," said Reagan, citing the phrase "I look to the hills, from whence cometh my strength." After March 30 he and Bush met every Thursday for lunch and conversation—"wide-ranging, from affairs of state to small talk," said Poppy, who, knowing Reagan's humor, began each session with a joke or story, often at official Washington's expense. The veep was judicious, increasingly synergistic with his boss, never divulging in eight years one syllable that he and Reagan said to one another. Incrementally, perhaps inevitably, Bush became a trusted member of the inner circle.

"You don't become president," Reagan said, in prose that Bush would echo. "The presidency is an institution, and you have temporary custody of it." Like every vice president, Bush was given special projects. Reagan asked him to chair a special task force on federal regulations—red tape as heinous to the GOP as a red cape to a bull. Bush studied hundreds of rules and admonitions, deciding specifically which to change and end. Reagan called "a Federal program the nearest thing on earth to eternal life." The more Bush could discard, the more he helped the country—and himself, with conservatives if he chose someday to run for president. That was also true of coordinating a federal war on international drug smuggling into America. The Right, often suspicious of foreigners, had reason to be here.

By early 1984 Bush seemed, if not someone who caused voter orgasm, at least a politician who seldom evoked a wrinkling of the nose. He was acceptable—to many, by fit and start much more. In particular, he was wooing the staff of the late William Loeb, publisher of the hard-right Manchester *Union-Leader*, and Jerry Falwell, founder of the conservative Moral Majority. Loeb's paper bestrode New Hampshire, site of the nation's first primary. Falwell's movement could affect a dozen state caucuses and primaries—and the general election after that.

Inexplicably, conservative columnist George F. Will recoiled: "The unpleasant sound Bush is emitting as he traipses from one conservative gathering to another is a thin, tinny arf—the sound of a lap dog." Perhaps he found them—huff—middle class. Most Republicans were reassured, thinking Bush a hunter who went where the ducks were. The sound they heard him emitting resembled a cash register—people giving to the presumptive next prez.

In 1988 *Time*'s David Beckwith wrote, "As the public became better acquainted with his [Bush's] personality and his sense of humor, they grew to like it, even viewing fondly his tendency toward malapropisms and scrambled syntax. In the end, despite talk of scripted events and control by handlers, the public got to know Bush and liked what it saw." That had been true even by 1984, which, Bush would tell you, was not his favorite year.

A Phone Call from the Gipper

In 1981 James Baker had listed Reagan's trifecta: "Economic recovery. Economic recovery. Economic recovery." By 1984 the recovery was, if not complete, irrefutable to even Democrats. Like a fever, Reaganomics broke before reviving. "It's funny how they [critics] don't call it that anymore," said the Gipper in 1987, "now that it's working." Unemployment peaked in December 1982, a highest-since-the-Depression 10.8 percent jobless rate. It dropped to 5.4 percent by the time Reagan left office. At the same time, inflation flew back inside the cage: 12.5 percent at the end of 1980 vs. 1988's 4.4. "Look back at 1981 and '82," said 1984 campaign manager Ed Rollins. "We had to cut government back, and give private enterprise some help. The economy was sick because we'd lacked leaders with spine." The correct prescription was liberty.

"When people are free to choose, they choose freedom," was a sure Gipper applause line. Under Reagan federal receipts grew at an annual 8.2 percent average. Even with 1981–82's recession, gross domestic growth increased yearly at 3.85 percent, including 1984's election year 8, a fortuitous patch of timing. Reagan's TV campaign that year remains a classic. "It's Morning in America," the voice-over began. Film shows hard hats building homes, ships trolling, weddings underway, people working farms, the flag being raised, towheads respecting it. "Today more men and women will go to work than at any time in our nation's history. With interest rates and inflation down, more people are buying new homes. And our families can take confidence in the new future. America today is prouder and stronger and better. Why would we want to return to where we were less than four short years ago?" America had come home.

More than sixteen million new jobs festooned 1983–89. The recovery lasted, with only a minor downturn or two, for almost a quarter century—the longest peacetime boom in U.S. history. The Tax Reform Act of 1986 dropped the top marginal tax rate to 28 percent, raised the bottom bracket to 15 percent, and cut the number of brackets to four. The prime interest rate fell by 60 percent, and the mortgage rate 6.4 percent from its peak. Meanwhile, the federal debt rose from $987 billion to $3.85 trillion under Reagan. "The president always told me that if it came down to a choice of somehow balancing our budget, or rebuilding our military which Carter had so decimated, he'd choose the latter," said Secretary of Defense Caspar Weinberger. It is true that a budget deficit was necessary to rebuild our defense. It also became the madam at the church cotillion.

By mid-spring 1984 Reagan-Bush was walking in tall cotton. "Here Comes the Recovery!" bannered *Time*. Then, on July 12, about-to-be Democratic presidential nominee Walter Mondale made history and momentarily rattled the GOP, picking America's first major-party woman vice president: Geraldine Ferraro, three-term U.S. representative, bright, liberal, and depending on your politics, barbed or snarky before the latter word was born. On one hand, she was smart and telegenic; would likely swell the gender gap, where Democrats led the GOP among women; and represented New York's multiethnic Queens district of TV's *All in Family*, its symbol malapropping Archie Bunker, who idolized "Richard E. Nixon." On the other, she was married to ethically checkered realtor John Zaccaro and had yet to hit big-league pitching.

In 2008, critiquing Barack Obama's candidacy, Ferraro panned affirmative action's double standard—which, ironically, she said, had profited her. "If you go back to 1984 and look at my historic candidacy, if my name was Gerald Ferraro instead of Geraldine Ferraro, I would have never been chosen as a vice president," said the Fox News contributor. "It had nothing to do with my qualifications." America agreed. In a summer 1984 poll of all voters, 60 percent thought "pressure from women's groups" caused her nomination, whereas 22 percent thought her "the best candidate" available. Mondale ignored the New Yorker's thin résumé, low name recognition, and lack of foreign policy experience. Needing to act boldly, he did.

Before Ferraro's pick, Mondale trailed Reagan by sixteen points in the Gallup poll. A week later the same firm showed them tied. At the convention in San Francisco, Mondale vowed to raise taxes—"an act of courage," he said—to cut the debt and that year's $185 billion deficit. It "wasn't courage," Bush retorted. "It was just a [Democratic] habit." As vice president, Poppy would visit most of the thirteen

A Phone Call from the Gipper

Latin American nations that, leaving Communism, held democratic elections in the 1980s. At August's GOP Convention in Dallas, Bush acted not as Reagan's attack dog—a veep's historic niche—but as a would-be president, quoting Dwight Eisenhower: "May the light of freedom . . . flame brightly, until at last the darkness is no more."

Aware of the Gipper's popularity—liberal congresswoman Pat Schroeder called him the "Teflon President," as in no criticism stuck—Ferraro assaulted his number two, becoming Bush's most elusive foe since Bentsen. Barbara Bush said, "Her name rhymes with rich"—a middle-class poseur. Liberal, Ferraro called herself a small *c* conservative. Catholic, she opposed the Church on abortion. Protecting her, the press ignored the dissonance. Virtually every survey shows most national journalists leaning left. What startles is the media's recent brazenness, unafraid to bare prejudice.

On October 7 the press fairly reported GOP self-inflicted injury. In the first presidential debate in Louisville, Reagan referred to going to church "here in Washington," called military uniforms "costumes," and confused military salaries and pensions, among other things. "Where was the Gipper?" Nancy Reagan, Rollins, and tens of millions must have asked. The likely answer: Reagan, seventy-three, America's oldest president, was showing age. His debate staff had showered him with facts and statistics—broadcaster Dizzy Dean termed them "statics." Reagan hated them, knew how they numbed. The next debate, he vowed, would be different. As conservatives said about policy, Let Reagan be Reagan.

In the interim Bush had to stop Mondale's momentum—1980's Big Mo now hung ironically—in the October 11 vice presidential debate. He was—choose your analogy—at High Noon, in the OK Corral, the Dutch Boy at the Dike. Surely Poppy would know more about foreign and domestic policy than Ferraro. So, however, had Nixon vs. Kennedy, or Ford vs. Carter. Substance—sheer knowledge—would matter less than style, and style less than wearability—the viewer saying over time, "Yes, that's my kind of guy. I trust him/her to act for me."

Retrieving the debate, Bush island-hopped in a quicksand sea. Many reporters in the press room, hoping that he would stumble, could be heard cheering loudly for Ferraro. Bush must be aggressive, but not menacing; courtly, not condescending; conservative, not chauvinistic; kind, not "Have Half" of Greenwich Country Day School. One mistake could, if not lose the election, fuel Mondale's Mo.

In 1945 Chicago writer Warren Brown had been asked about the wartime Tigers-Cubs World Series. "Frankly," he said, "I don't think either team can win." Ironically, both candidates won the vice presidential debate. Thrice panelists asked how Ferraro's experience equaled Bush's. She changed the subject, then used a preplanned zinger: "Let me just say, first of all, that I almost resent, Vice President Bush, your patronizing attitude that you have to teach me about foreign policy." Bush's mastery of the subject was so plain he didn't need—couldn't afford—to zing her. Instead, he mixed detail and praise of Reagan. A poll soon showed that men and women felt that Bush and Ferraro, respectively, had won.

Next day Poppy suggested he had "tried to kick a little ass last night"—for him, harsh profanity out of character, reflecting frustration in his attack-dog role. Bush did it loyally but joylessly, knowing that extreme makeovers rarely work. As we have seen, what did was Reagan campaign TV. In 1984 the United States and Soviet Union still grappled in the post–World War II Cold War. Reagan's policy toward Communism—the Bear—was Peace through Strength: rebuild, then negotiate. Liberalism refused to concede Communism was a threat. "The Bear" ad artfully split the difference. "There's a bear in the woods," the voice-over begins, the animal on the screen. "For some people, the bear is easy to see. Others don't see it at all. Some people say the bear is tame. Others say it is vicious, and dangerous. Since no one can really be sure who is right, isn't it smart to be as strong as the bear, if there is a bear?"

On October 21 Reagan and Mondale again met in Kansas City. The president's age had owned the past two weeks, policy advisers, speechwriters, and humor writers deluging Reagan with one-liners and memoranda, how-tos to defuse fear that he had gone around the bend. Reagan gently reassured them that he would neutralize the issue—not to worry. Most of the White House did.

Panelist Hank Trewhitt of the *Wall Street Journal* gave Reagan his opening. First, he noted that President Kennedy had "very little sleep" during the Cuban Missile Crisis in 1962. He then asked if Reagan, given his poor first debate, had any doubt that he could endure the demands of the presidency, especially in a crisis.

"Not at all, Mr. Trewhitt," the Gipper said, "and I want you to know also that I will not make age an issue of this campaign. I am not going to exploit for political purposes, my opponent's youth and inexperience."

The crowd erupted. Even Mondale couldn't help himself. "If TV can tell the truth, you'll see that I was smiling," he told PBS in 2012. "But I think if you come in close, you'll see some tears coming down because I knew he had gotten me there. That was really the end of my campaign that night, I think." Reagan's reaction shot is even more telling, like the eighth take on the back lot at Warner Brothers. He is smiling, not boastfully, but contentedly, tongue faintly in cheek, the canary in fatal trouble.

The rest was for history: Reagan, on the train from one small town through another, reliving his childhood with an itinerant father; Bush, touting "my friend and America's greatest president" and calling Mondale "the all-time tax raiser"; Mondale, knowing that defeat lay ahead, yet refusing to abandon the flag of liberalism; Ferraro, saying Reagan would outlaw abortion, ignore the poor, and raise taxes too—losing, yet proud of making history.

At every campaign stop, Reagan used Al Jolson's line "You ain't seen nothin' yet!" On election night he told the crowd, "You'll forgive me. I'm going to say it one more time!"—and did. Except for Nixon's in 1972, Reagan's statistics were nonpareil: 525 electoral votes to Mondale's 13 and 49 states to the Democrat's one (Minnesota, Mondale's home state, plus Washington DC). Reagan got 58.8 percent of the vote, 60 percent in 30 states, and 70 percent in Wyoming, Utah, Nebraska, and Idaho. He lost Minnesota by 3,761 votes.

Ferraro hurt, or at least didn't help. Reagan won 55 percent of the

Catholic and women's vote, first and second to Nixon in 1972, respectively, among GOP presidential candidates. "She was supposed to be a boon with each group," said Ed Rollins, "and wasn't." Bush likely helped, and clearly didn't hurt, especially in the moderate to liberal Northeast. Including 2012, 1984 is the last presidential election the GOP has won any of these states: Hawaii, Massachusetts, New York, Oregon, Rhode Island, Washington, and Wisconsin. Bush campaigned in each.

In December 1984 President Reagan was asked what he wanted for Christmas. He reportedly joked, "Well, Minnesota would have been nice."

SEVEN

To the Brink—and Back

Abattering ram for Reagan in 1984, Bush himself emerged battered, asking if he could run for president from the vice presidency in 1988. No veep since Martin Van Buren in 1836 had won election on his own immediately after the term of the president with whom he had served—then, Andrew Jackson. Fellow Ivies Nicholas Brady and Jim Baker, future and about-to-be secretary of the treasury, respectively, told Bush that if Van Buren could transition, so could a war hero, business whiz, statesman, and as we shall see, husband of a wife becoming as popular as her spouse. Van Buren became a frame of reference, someone to poke fun at. "Ask me who I'm going to put pictures of . . . on the walls of the White House," Poppy told a journalist. "Martin Van Buren." When it comes to role models, some would-be presidents get all the luck.

Baker's and Brady's case for running, Bush said in his twinkly, self-conscious way, was "unassailable." By Christmas 1984 they were charting strategy: Craig Fuller as vice presidential chief of staff; Baker and Brady, counselors; above all, Lee Atwater, as populist base-in-his-bones campaign strategist. A year later Atwater's political action committee, the Fund for America, had raised more than $2 million— far more than any other Democrat or Republican candidate. In their thinking, Bush would mind the jibs as Reagan's second term steered the ship toward 1988.

For one thing, Bush inflated the sails by swelling his already huge speech schedule. For another he made history July 13, 1985, becoming the first vice president to serve as acting president, Reagan having surgery to remove polyps from his colon. "I think the president was coming to trust George on about everything," said Barbara Bush. "They had that relationship." For her part, Mrs. Bush found the vice presidency a perfect place to divulge her opinions, of which she had many.

Even as a newlywed, she had found it hard not to express herself, once sitting in her in-laws' living room in Connecticut, smoking a cigarette.

Prescott Bush, most often described as intimidating, loudly asked the new Mrs. Bush, "Did I ever tell you that you could smoke?"

Instantly, she said, "Well, did I marry *you*?"

Reportedly, the elder Bush broke out laughing.

Since then Barbara had zealously helped Prescott's son as a wife, mother, and host. She had cautioned him to spurn the RNC position. She enjoyed China, bicycling with Bush to remote cities and regions unavailable to most Americans. The CIA was harder: Much of Bush's data were classified—thus, closed. At fifty, Barbara had many friends who had reached career goals—thus, increasingly, she felt isolated. Rejecting analysis—the Protestant canon of self-reliance—Mrs. Bush began lecturing about the China of the Ming Dynasty and Mao Tse-tung and 1972's Trip That Changed the World. It hadn't changed hers.

"For Bar, 1980 was a pivot," said her husband. "She'd done charitable work, been with party women's groups, met diplomatic wives, but this stage was bigger." She was his Boswell but not his party's, opposing, as it did, abortion and the Equal Rights Amendment. When Bush was nominated, his opinions became Reagan's. That, in turn, made Barbara's attitudes less germane as the vice president began a second term. As a child, she had gathered with her family at night to read together—not surprising, since Dad was a publisher. Now adult and childhood literacy became her issue. Son Neil had dyslexia. Mrs. Bush began working with firms to find what caused illiteracy, learning that 35 million adults and 23 million Americans could not read beyond an eighth-grade or fourth-grade level, respectively.

Here and around the world, Barbara found that homelessness was a curse. Everywhere she was careful to be correct, never uttering a

To the Brink—and Back

word remotely critical of Nancy Reagan. Like the Gipper, Mrs. Bush made fun of herself: the white hair, how she was more mature than hip, more L.L. Bean than designer clothes. Middle America looked in the mirror and saw itself—a person of substance, not style. Historian Henry Steele Commager said, "Ours is very much a presidential country." Mrs. Bush knew that it is also a canine country. In 1944 Republicans spread the tale that a destroyer had been sent to Alaska, at great taxpayer cost, to rescue President Roosevelt's dog Fala. At a labor dinner, FDR had taunted the GOP. "These Republican leaders have not been content with attacks on me, or my wife, or on my sons," he said. "No, not content with that, they now include my little dog, Fala."

In 1952, under assault for an alleged "secret fund," Republican vice presidential nominee Richard Nixon gave a network radio/TV speech known for the dog that gave the address its name. A man in Texas, hearing Pat Nixon mention that her children had never had a dog, had sent a package to Union Station in Baltimore. "It was a little cocker spaniel, in a crate . . . black and white, spotted, and our little girl Tricia, the six-year-old, named it Checkers," Nixon said. "And you know, the kids, like all kids, love the dog, and I just want to say this, right now, that regardless of what they say about it, we're going to keep it." They did. Lyndon Johnson had a dog whose initials were LBJ: Little Beagle Johnson. The Reagans had a King Charles spaniel. The Obama household has a Portuguese water dog. In 1984 America learned that none could surpass Barbara Bush's golden-colored cocker spaniel C. Fred Bush for literacy.

Like her children, Mrs. Bush had grown up around and with dogs, aware that they divined qualities alien to the human condition. Dogs neither lied nor deceived nor complained of suffering. They were devoid of pretense, had a cold nose and a warm heart, and bespoke enduring love. C. Fred Bush was named after family friend C. Fred Chambers. Published by Doubleday, 1984's *C. Fred's Story: A Dog's Life*, by C. Fred Bush, "edited slightly by Barbara Bush," was a children's book about the Bush family told from her dog's "point of view." All proceeds benefited literacy charities. Mrs. Bush promoted it tirelessly, knowing that the spaniel breed was a favorite not only of hers but of America's. In a memorable World War II illustration, a soulful dog sits in a chair, shawl with a star covering an armrest, awaiting the GI's return. The dog inevitably was a C. Fred semi-look-alike. For a quarter century—1936–52 and 1983–90, according to the American Kennel Club—the cocker spaniel was America's most popular dog until overbreeding inevitably set in.

C. Fred's Story was a novel idea, artfully told, casting Mrs. Bush in a sympathetic, down-home, dog- and child-loving light. The book had a paw print on the cover page; photos of C. Fred with luminaries from Margaret Thatcher, Henry Kissinger, and Charlton Heston to astronauts Robert Crippen and John Young to President Reagan, Queen Beatrix, and Gene Hackman; and a breezy text by, you assume, C. Fred's Mistress of the Manor. *Story* was reprinted an enviable ten times, got excellent reviews, and led to even larger best-selling books. It also began a bond over the next third of a century between Mrs. Bush and America that was improbable, even phenomenal. Born in a manse, she became the girl next door, wearing pearls, yet seen as Main Street. Said son George W.: "She'll just let rip if she's got something on her mind."

On one hand, picture Mrs. Bush as Angela Lansbury's Jessica Fletcher, mannered, unflappable, inviting you for coffee at *Murder, She Wrote*'s fictional Cabot Cove, Maine, doubtless near Kennebunkport—that hourly whodunit, not coincidentally, the Bushes' favorite 1980s and '90s TV show. She had a great curiosity, tolerant mentality, and indiscriminate memory—the perfect host. On the other, Mrs. Bush could be redolent of Barbara Stanwyck in, say, *Cattle Queen of Montana*. One expected her to ford a stream, take the hill, or ward off the Indians till the cavalry came. Forceful, she was not coquettish; prideful, she was not immodest; she would persuade, but never profane, a listener. Politically, she narrowed the gulf between Poppy and the middle class.

George W. Bush praised his mother's "genius with the media," which I often saw after leaving the *Saturday Evening Post* in 1982 to return to Washington. I had missed the maelstrom of the capital. Moreover, President Reagan's belief in limited government, sane taxes and spending, in God we trust, and American nobility seemed worthy of the Founding Fathers then, and now. I was asked to write for three secretaries of the cabinet—Richard Schweiker and Margaret Heckler of Health and Human Services and Samuel Pierce of Housing and Urban Development—and often dealt with members of Bush's vice presidential office in the Eisenhower (née Old) Executive Office Building (EOB), next door to the West Wing.

The Bushies impressed me with their courtesy and quality—the class we seldom see any more, reflecting their boss's character. I also contributed, as speechwriters do, ideas and one-line phrases for the 1988 general campaign against Democrat Michael Dukakis, which led to my working for Bush as president. Let us retrieve the 1985–89 term that preceded Bush's presidency, in which Ronald Reagan showed why, as Sherwood Anderson wrote in *Winesburg, Ohio*, "at the same instant, and if the people of the town are his people, one loves life so intensely that tears come into the eyes."

In 1960 Vice President Nixon was glad to campaign as Eisenhower's successor, only to be hurt by recession, ballot box chicanery, and TV imagery in the first presidential debate. He lost, barely. In 1968 Lyndon Johnson, retiring, gave his vice president, Democratic nominee Hubert Humphrey, Vietnam, urban riot, and an America more torn apart than at any time since the Civil War. Humphrey lost, narrowly. Bush had studied both. "Nixon probably got more real votes in '60. And the other one [vice president] who tried was . . . Humphrey. And the very constituency that should have supported him the most was screaming outside the convention hall in Chicago because of the Vietnam War."

Bush meant to be, and was, exquisitely loyal to Ronald Reagan. If Reagan flagged, Bush would be a fatality. If not, he would gain from—no one was closer to—the man of whom *Time* magazine said in 1986: "Reagan is a sort of masterpiece of American magic, apparently one of the simplest creatures alive, yet a character of complexities that connect him with the myths and powers of his country in an unprecedented way." Democratic Speaker of the House Tip O'Neill would put it simpler: "I've been in politics half a century and have never seen a person as popular as you."

Reagan was called the Great Communicator for his likability, facility with the spoken word, reassuring voice, and rapport with American history and for being a rarity in Washington—a politician who was funny on purpose. He was proud of his craft, aware what it meant today: "There've been times," he told Michael Deaver, "that I've wondered how you could do the job if you *hadn't* been an actor." Reagan paid exceptional care to how a president should look and act. He dressed formally but not ostentatiously. He never took his suit coat off in the Oval Office, respecting it. Even when shot in 1981, he hitched up his pants to precisely meet his suit button when leaving the limousine to enter DC's George Washington Hospital. "He had this habit of making sure the pants and jacket fit just right," said Deaver. Ignoring a bullet lodged near his heart, Reagan "checks his pants, buttons his suit," then collapsed entering the revolving hospital door.

The Gipper had fine writers—Peggy Noonan, Tony Dolan, Ben Elliott, Ken Khachigian, Aram Bakshian, and Peter Robinson, among others—but they would tell you the staff's best writer delivered his speeches too. Reagan gave them the gift of knowing his own mind; they never had to guess. He called the Soviet Union "an evil empire"—raising hate and hubris at the *New York Times*. In Berlin the president uttered perhaps his most famous line: "Mr. Gorbachev, tear down this wall!" When the *Challenger* shuttle exploded, killing a crew of seven, he soothed grieving congregants: "We will never forget them . . . as they waved goodbye and 'slipped the surly bonds of earth' to 'touch the face of God.'" On the fortieth anniversary of D-day, Reagan spoke at the U.S. Ranger Monument at Normandy: "These are the boys of Pointe du Hoc. These are the men who took the cliffs." Why had they risked their lives—some no more than teens? "It was faith and belief; it was loyalty and love." Reagan's presidency played long-running verbal hits.

Once, he asked Nancy, "Where do we find such men?" The answer,

To the Brink—and Back

Reagan said, came almost as soon as the question: "Where we've always found them—on the farms, in the shops, the stores, and the offices." His oneness with their America evoked "a simpler place and a simpler time," said the PBS documentary *Reagan*—"small towns, patriotic values, family and community, an idealized America that no longer was, that perhaps never was," except that it *was* real for those who lived there. Reagan lived there, even as he bounced from one 1920s small town to another, Dad looking for work. Bush lived there, even as he tried to volunteer at seventeen to avenge Pearl Harbor. So did I, the verities of my boyhood town knitting race and class. Most Americans lived there, or hoped to from afar.

In July 1986 Reagan helped mark the centennial of the Statue of Liberty, given to America by France. It had been closed to the public, refurbished, and would be relit by the president, pushing a button to send a laser one mile to the statue in New York Harbor. Aboard the USS *John F. Kennedy*, Reagan hailed assimilation—out of many, one—what Lady Liberty had promised Slavs and Poles and Italians and Jews and, belatedly, blacks, for a century—all, said Emma Lazarus, "yearning to breathe free." The Gipper mused, "The things that unite us—America's past, of which we're so proud; our hopes and aspirations for the future of the world and this much-loved country—these things far outweigh what little divides us." Then: "Tonight we pledge ourselves to each other—and to the cause of human freedom—the cause that has given light to this land—and hope to the world."

Historian Robert Dallek called Reagan "brilliant at creating a rapport with the country, appealing to its better angels." No other president could have, or has, so "found the American sweet spot," wrote *Time*. Liberty Weekend 1986 caught the Gipper at high tide. If Bush could ride it, he would likely be the next U.S. president. Cautious—to use a favorite word, "prudent"—the boyhood angler at Walker's Point also knew the tide inevitably ran out.

Reagan was bent on not letting terrorism undo his presidency—easier said than done. In 1984 William F. Buckley, CIA station chief in Beirut, was kidnapped by the terrorist group Hezbollah, tortured for fifteen months, and probably died of a heart attack on June 3, 1985. A year later terrorists hijacked a plane and murdered an American passenger. The crisis was resolved but fueled Reagan's worry about seven other passengers held hostage in Beirut, kidnapped by fanatics of Iran's Ayatollah Khomeini, who had bedeviled Carter in 1979–81. This president vowed to spurn appeasement: "Let me make it plain to the assassins in Beirut and their accomplices, wherever they may be, that America will never make concessions to terrorism. To do so would only invite more terrorism." Invariably, Reagan knew what to say. The question was how closely he listened to himself.

At this point the Gipper did not know of Buckley's murder. He did know, as the then actor once wrote, that "my heart is a ham loaf." In 1985 his national security adviser, Robert "Bud" McFarlane, proposed a plan to improve relations with alleged moderates in Iran. As McFarlane explained the scheme, this might influence hostage takers in Beirut—and expedite Khomeini's fall. Reagan approved it, later saying he was unsure whether the plan included sending guns to anyone in Iran.

That November Reagan and Mikhail Gorbachev, the new Soviet general secretary, met in Geneva. Margaret Thatcher had said, "This is a man we can do business with." Reagan had opposed every arms treaty signed by each 1970s U.S. president but now hoped to do business on *his* terms with Communism's leader. In their first meeting, Reagan calmly but brutally lashed the Soviet system, yet somehow managed to ingratiate himself personally. "Reagan had something which was so dear to Gorbachev, and that was sincerity," the Soviet Foreign Ministry's Alexander Bessmertnykh said. Could sincerity neutralize Gorbachev's opposition to Reagan's desire to keep Polish Solidarity alive, boot the Soviets out of Afghanistan, and sustain the anti-Communist Contras in Nicaragua?

By then Congress had ended Contra funding, confirming Reagan's belief that liberal Democrats were weak on defense. Publicly, the president tied the Contras to the Founding Fathers and World War II's French Resistance. "All they need is proof that we care as much about the fight for freedom seven hundred miles from *our* shores," Reagan said, "as the Soviets care about the fight *against* freedom five thousand miles from *theirs*." Privately, he told McFarlane, "Bud, I want you to do all you have to do to help those people keep body and soul together." The aide's automatic pilot response would almost bring the administration down.

The Geneva summit touched more on disarmament than terrorism, Reagan and Gorbachev agreeing that "a nuclear war cannot be won and must never be fought." In October 1986 the reform Red, who preached glasnost and perestroika, had a smile said to hide teeth of iron, and knew that Reagan wished devoutly for his nation's demise, invited the old Cold Warrior to another summit, in Reykjavik, Iceland. What they almost achieved was enough to make each's aides gasp, and they did. "You've got the two leaders of these two powerful countries running way beyond their arms controllers and their defense ministries and their state departments in saying, 'Let's get rid of all nuclear weapons,'" Reagan biographer Lou Cannon told PBS.

At bottom Reagan's foreign policy rested largely on the notion that America could legitimately threaten to spend the Evil Empire into oblivion or irrelevance, whichever came first. Gorbachev could not afford arms competition and economic reform—guns and butter. Thus, he proposed to eliminate all nuclear weapons, contingent on the United States cashiering the Strategic Defense Initiative. Aware that America had no shield against incoming missiles, the Gipper said no, bringing the summit to a close.

"We were *that* close," said Reagan, putting his thumb and index finger less than an inch apart, "from eliminating all nuclear weapons." Instead, aping convention, Senate majority leader Bob Dole, sure to oppose Bush for the 1988 GOP nomination, scored Reagan for trading no-nuke peace for a high-tech toy unsure to even work. "I feel very comfortable with President Reagan's priorities," the veep countered without being asked. "He's lifted us up and restored our respect."

What happened next, Bush said later, was a "bigger downer" than being attack dog in 1984. That fall of 1986 a Middle East newspaper reported a guns-for-hostage swap. McFarlane had resigned a year earlier, succeeded by John Poindexter. Reagan denied the deal, then amended his denial. "We did not, repeat, did not trade weapons or anything else for hostages, nor will we," he said in a televised November 13, 1986, Oval Office address, insisting that better relations had caused the exchange. Whatever the reason, the trade violated administration policy.

Reagan could not explain why arms had been shipped just before Iran released each hostage. Confused and dissembling, he asked Attorney General Edwin Meese to investigate that weekend. Monday morning Meese told him of a probable diversion of funds from Iran to the Contras in Nicaragua—a violation of the law.

Reagan turned white. "What could have been going through their minds? How could they do this?" he said, forgetting his telling McFarlane to keep the Contras "body and soul together." He sent Meese to brief the press, which turned apoplectic.

Poindexter soon resigned. Reagan fired Oliver North, who ran the lunacy. To many, it seemed superfluous. "This Presidency is over," wrote columnist Charles Krauthammer. "Nineteen eighty-seven will be a Watergate year, and the following year an election year."

Reagan appointed an independent (former Senator John) Tower Commission, which found him guilty of lazy management and trading arms—for hostages. Shocked, the president belatedly agreed, giving another network TV address: "As the Tower Board reported, what began as a strategic opening to Iran for hostages deteriorated in its implementation into trading arms for hostages."

Reagan then apologized, hating to do it, knowing he had to and perhaps should have done it earlier: "There are reasons that this happened, but no excuses. It was a mistake." His apologia was accepted. Incrementally, the Gipper's luster reappeared.

In December 1987 Reagan and Gorbachev signed the Intermediate Nuclear Force (INF) Treaty, the first pact to cut the number, not merely limit the rise, of nuclear missiles. The Soviets accepted Reagan's zero option, once scorned by *Pravda* as a fascist fantasy. "It is a simple proposal," said Reagan in the East Room as Gorbachev stood nearby. "One might say disarmingly simple." It was also a startling

To the Brink—and Back

victory for the man Democratic grandee Clark Clifford once called an "amiable dunce."

The Bushes sat next to Nancy Reagan and the Gorbachevs in the front row, each pleased in a way they had not expected. Mrs. Reagan delighted in her spouse cast as a peacemaker. On taking office, Gorbachev had heard Reagan compared to Hitler. Unexpectedly, the Soviet found a peer he liked and respected. Theoretically, INF would let him focus on economic reform. The Bushes' joy was political. Reagan's popularity invariably augured Poppy's. "This was the best day for him," said Lee Atwater, "since election night of '84."

The Iran-Contra morass had flung Bush into limbo land. The secretaries of defense and state, Weinberger and George Schultz, respectively, said they had opposed the plan. As Texas governor Ann Richards, in another context, sneered at the 1988 Democratic Convention: "Where was George?" Had Poppy backed the Iran-Contra botch up? If so, he had broken the law. Had he even known? If not, why not? Bush's curriculum vitae flaunted foreign policy. That identity—also integrity—was now in doubt. Sophocles was said to "know the world steadily, and . . . know it whole." So was Bush. How could he be in the dark? Announcing for the GOP nomination, Alexander Haig asked, "Where was George Bush during this story? Was he the copilot in the cockpit, or . . . back in economy class?" If Bush couldn't reply convincingly, his campaign's raison d'être might collapse.

On October 12, 1987, Reagan's number two announced for number one. He said Poindexter had "compartmentalized" the plan; thus, Bush knew only some parts, "deliberately excluded" from others. The vice president claimed to have been "out of the loop"—in effect, ignorant or innocent. Polls showed the public not convinced about either or sure why Bush was running.

"If I were elected," he had told David Keene, a senior official in the 1980 campaign, "I'd bring in the best people."

"Fine, George," Keene would say, "but what are you going to tell them to *do*?"

If elected, would he veer left of Reagan? Build on his beginnings? Revert to the good government moderate liberalism of his dad? Reflect the mores and concerns of the Sunbelt, where the GOP's base and future lay? Bush's proudest achievement, he often said, was that his five children still came home. Few pols could say the same, but it wouldn't fit on a bumper sticker or stir a thirty-second ad.

Serve *whom*? was a question Bush answered only in his 1988 acceptance speech and in the general campaign pursuant. On the other hand, some of "the best people" had already arrived by late 1987: Atwater, tactics and organization; Bob Teeter, polling; Craig Fuller, campaign and government scheduling; and Roger Ailes, whose 1968 TV "Man in the Arena" brainstorm helped elect Nixon and who revived Reagan after 1984's first debate, later founded the Fox News channel, and as media guru, was now trying to remake Bush's persona on the tube.

"I speak Spanish to God, Italian to women, French to men, and German to my horse," said Charles V, Holy Roman Emperor. He left English to Bush, who could leave it mangled. If a president can't speak, he can't educate. If he can't educate, he can't lead. Ailes went to work, seeing Bush between twice and ten times a week, trying to slow his speed, which, in turn, deepened his voice. Smile; be calm; limit gestures; sit erect toward the front of the chair; lean forward; be polite but aggressive; use any question to springboard to your agenda. Stay on message; when necessary, parry and pirouette. To woo the voter, you must persuade. To persuade, you must articulate. *Take control.* Ailes had little time to waste.

"TV does something to George," Barbara Bush once said, wisely. It often shrunk him, made her husband seem shrill and gaunt, a schoolmarm, not a cowboy like the Gipper. His pleasant-in-person voice could turn high and tinny on the tube. Wearing eyeglasses, Bush looked older, less presidential than the athlete who left younger aides exhausted campaigning or "rec-reating," he laughed. Gestures often failed to correspond with words. Few viewers associated with prep-school Bushisms like "Tension City" or "deep doo-doo" or "I'm not going to wear a mini-skirt or have purple hair" to win. Trying to note his and Reagan's "setbacks," Bush malapropped, "we had sex." A reporter said he should be sued for malpractice of the tongue.

In October 1987 *Newsweek* had profiled Bush on the cover, calling a war hero, self-made oil man, and virtually goof-free vice president a "wimp." Reading, you would think Iran-Contra the totality of his career. It made Bush seethe—and Ailes thankful, since an angry Bush was a more effective Bush. Poppy became more determined than ever to erase "his pallor as a performing artist," said *Newsweek* later, "a visible unease [present] whenever he got in front of an audience or a camera." Fine. Bush would do what the expert told him. If doubt lingered, it dissolved January 25, 1988.

The CBS *Evening News* had already aired standard profiles of the eleven other presidential candidates. Richard Cohen, CBS News politics producer, now sought an interview with Bush for a similar "candidate profile," *Evening News* anchor Dan Rather questioning. Bush assumed it would be an honest interview—"He's a fair man," said the vice president, knowing Rather from Houston TV in the early 1960s. Dorothy Bush might have told him that people change.

As reporters revealed in the *Newsweek* book *The Quest for the Presidency*, aides warned that Rather had developed his own partisan story of Bush, the Ayatollah, and Contra *commandantes* and then requested the Bush interview. Their five-minute "profile" would be an edited setup job.

"Ab-so-lute-ly *no!*" Ailes bellowed at a staff meeting. "*Jesus*. No, no, no!"

Staffers at CBS had been "running around the network," the *Newsweek* book later read, "boasting that they would take Bush out of the race." After a Ferris wheel of debate, the Bushies countered any Rather interview must be live. Atwater was unconvinced: "I'd really watch that guy," he said when Bush phoned in the day of the January 25 telecast.

"He's a fair man," Bush repeated.

"All right," said Atwater, not believing a syllable.

Teeter had found that CBS planned to do the separate Iran-Contra piece first, then stage the interview. Confirming it, Ailes met the veep when Air Force Two landed at Andrews Air Force Base prior to the newscast. Even with a live interview, he told Bush, you are being set up.

"I've answered the [Iran-Contra] question five hundred times," Bush said in the limousine ride to Washington. "I don't see any big deal."

It was, Ailes said. "All they have to do is press you on dates and bullshit that you haven't had time to review, and you're gonna look like you don't know what you're talking about."

"No, no," Bush said. "Dan Rather is a good newsman. He won't do that."

"Hey," Ailes said, "his job tonight is ratings. His ass is on the line. He doesn't care about you. If he thought he could get away with it, he'd shoot you."

Slowly, Bush sensed the danger. Pleased, Ailes plowed on. "Don't accept *anything* Rather says to you," he said. "Don't accept the premise of any question—I don't even care if it's *right*. Stay on offense the whole time and wear him out." According to *The Quest*, Ailes had "studied Bush. The guy wouldn't fight unless he got mad, and what dependably would get him mad was the feeling that he was being treated unfairly."

Ailes told Bush to watch the Iran-Contra segment before his interview. "That'll get you up." Another story did too. Months earlier Rather, on location in Miami, had his newscast delayed by a tennis match. Peeved, he walked off the set to call CBS New York to complain. The match ended during Rather's absence. Ailes recalled that with nothing else to put on the air, CBS went to black—an empty screen—for six minutes.

"Look," Ailes said, "he's trying to judge your whole vice presidency by this stuff. That's like judging *his* whole career in broadcasting by six minutes when he acted like an asshole."

A rebroadcast of the interview a quarter century later makes Rather a poster child for the irrefutability of media bias. He impugns, badgers, accuses, interrupts in a way he would never do, never *did*, to liberals he interviewed—among them, Walter Mondale, Al Gore, and Bill and Hillary Clinton. This Ahab's Moby Dick was the

GOP, as Rather later showed in his dishonest coverage of George W. Bush's National Guard service, which more or less ended his network career.

In 2003 Rather guested on a series I hosted on then-CBS WHAM Radio in Rochester, New York. I said that *Time* columnist Hugh Sidey had called Richard Nixon the finest foreign policy president since FDR. Straightaway Rather began a two-minute soliloquy. His rancor was self-evident. More alarming was how Rather seemed unhinged. I once admired his judgment and courtly made-in-Texas mien. Nothing proved their erosion like his 1988 inquisition of Bush.

The CBS *Evening News* anchor resembled a district attorney: "[Many people] believe you're hiding something. . . . How could you? . . . You made us hypocrites in the face of the world."

Warned by Ailes, Bush replied, "[You] told me this was going to be a political profile," not a nine-minute "rehash into something that has been exhaustively looked into"—so different from CBS's other eleven "candidate profiles" as to resemble today's MSNBC.

Six times Bush said a variation of "I want to be judged on the whole record, and you're not giving me an opportunity."

Rather wasn't interested in the whole record, or in keeping CBS's word. Toward the end he said, "I don't want to be argumentative, Mr. Vice President."

"You do, Dan," said Bush.

"No . . . no, sir, I don't," Rather insisted.

". . . I don't think it's fair . . . to judge my whole career by a rehash on Iran," Bush said. At that point he used the coda Ailes had planted a few hours earlier. "How would you like it if I judged your career by those seven [*sic*] minutes when you walked off the set in New York [actually, Miami]?" he asked Rather.

"Well, Mister," said the CBS anchor, stunned.

"Would you like that?" Bush continued.

"Mr. Vice President," Rather stumbled.

"I have respect for you," Bush said, "but I don't have respect for what you're doing here tonight."

The sound heard was millions of Americans cheering. Save Spiro Agnew, no national Republican had so ably indicted media prejudice since Nixon's "last press conference" in 1962.

Bush's tour de force came two weeks before the first in the nation 1988 Iowa caucus. His chief rival seemed to be Bob Dole, sixty-four, from Russell, Kansas, a small-town boy who some feared had left it long ago. Like Bush, he was a World War II hero, but unlucky—in the war's final weeks, enemy fire had shredded his right arm and shoulder. It took him forever to insert a button, put on a coat, tie his tie. Nixon used his left hand to shake Dole's good hand—no other pol showed the sensitivity to think of it—bringing tears to Dole's eyes. He had come to DC in 1961, absorbed it, and become a Senate heavyweight. Dole talked in Beltway babble but liked to think he still identified with the Midwest's roughhewn life. The public wasn't sure. Had Dole changed? Was he still one of us?

Bush's second rival was John French "Jack" Kemp, former pro football quarterback, Buffalo area congressman since 1973, and apostle of supply-side economics. He had a wonderful tan, JFK-like blow-dried hair, kinetic energy, generous self-esteem, and a desire to talk dwarfing Hubert Humphrey's. Kemp was conservative, but mostly in a fiscal Johnny-one-note way. Asked about MTV, U2, the Rubik's Cube, or *Who Framed Roger Rabbit*, Kemp would answer supply side: It was his prologue and finis. He appealed to that sliver of the GOP whose Dead Sea Scrolls was the *Wall Street Journal* editorial page. It is not that Republicans disliked Kemp's agenda—only that one note would not suffice. Many vainly urged him to also talk of military strength and cultural decay—balance. Otherwise, Kemp might soon be benched, and was.

A wild card was the Right Reverend Pat Robertson, who had $10 million in the bank. On one hand, GOP solons feared the party was increasingly too much a theocracy. On the other, Robertson owned the Christian Broadcasting Network, hosted its *700 Club*, and represented, he said, the 65 to 70 million people who termed themselves evangelical—perhaps America's largest, if loosely affiliated, religious group. Robertson wouldn't hurt Dole, aides thought, since the Kansan was overtly secular. Bush might be different, since on occasion he mimed Reagan's prescription of Calvinist salvation and America as Beulah Land.

"In a two-man race, our votes would be split," one Des Moines minister said. "Robertson provides another option." There were many to divide. By 2004, according to a Pew Research Forum poll, 44 percent of the nation termed itself "born-again." Politically, these Christian, mostly Protestant, evangelicals were the Republicans' largest block: 35 percent of George W. Bush's entire vote. More "born-agains" voted than all blacks and union members combined. Moreover, their scorn of secularism, moral decline, and border insecurity tracked millions of Catholic, orthodox Jewish, and Protestant non-evangelicals'. W. coined the phrase "coalition of the *willing*." Born-agains and friends formed a GOP coalition of the *winning*.

Iowa presaged a key element of Bush *père*'s 1988 coalition: church groups and prayer meetings and Sunday socials across the state. Dole countered by speaking their cant about farming and factory work and being raised in such small towns as Alton and Audubon and Eldridge and Eagle Grove. Like them, he knew how to get things done, like living off the land. Like them, he hadn't had it easy. Here, if anywhere, Dole should have scored, and did: 37 percent to Robertson's 25 and Bush's 19. "The results are hard to read as anything but a repudiation of George Bush," read the *Des Moines Register*. Even a television evangelist had trounced the vice president of the United States.

A caucus is a closed affair, whereby you enroll, spend much of the day on local issues and trivia, then vote. The February 16 New Hampshire primary, eight days after Iowa, required only that you cast a ballot. Arriving, Barbara was told by Governor John Sununu, "Don't worry. He'll win. 'Mr. Fix-it' will see to it." Richard Wirthlin, Dole's pollster, thought it "90 percent certain" that his candidate's victory there would make him the GOP nominee. Two days after Iowa, his New Hampshire poll showed Dole five points behind Bush but gaining. "We're going to win this thing," Wirthlin told the senator. On preelection Friday the poll showed the Kansan five points ahead. Withdrawing, Al Haig endorsed Dole. Later, Bush confessed, "I stared into the abyss and decided something had to change."

Until then Bush had campaigned formally, almost regally, amid limousines and Secret Service agents, as if expecting to be knighted. (As our narrative shows, Queen Elizabeth finally got with the program, knighting him in 1993.) Grasping his near-death experience, in one day Bush traded his blue suit and red tie for a blue parka and Boston Red Sox cap, junked set-piece speeches, worked a forklift at a lumberyard, and took a spin on an eighteen-wheeler at Cuzzin Richie's Truck Stop. "Wait till you see the sky diving," said Sununu, eerily foretelling Bush's post-presidency. Populist and pugnacious, he guided Bush through five days of glad-handing, flesh pressing, and made-for-TV footage, "dominating every broadcast medium from drive-time radio to network," said *The Quest for the Presidency*.

Bush was behind, but still alive, when a friend, fellow outdoorsman, and second only to JFK in many polls as "most important New Englander of the twentieth century" appeared out of nowhere. He had flown his own plane from Florida to Boston's Logan Airport—whose idea is still a blur—then drove to New Hampshire, arriving backstage at a rally. When Bush arrived, he was atypically scolding an aide. As Rick Robinson wrote in *All Right Magazine*, "a figure larger than New England itself" then approached the candidate, saying, "Any problems, Mr. Vice-President?"

"Not now," said Bush, stunned, staring at Theodore Samuel Williams. "Everything's going to be fine now." Robinson titled his profile "How Ted Williams Changed the World."

Raised in Connecticut, Bush had early gravitated toward Ted's Red Sox. "The first game Dad took me to was the Polo Grounds," he said of the Giants' pre-1958 home across the Harlem River from Yankee Stadium, "but my favorite park was [Boston's] Fenway. It's nice to know some things don't change," including awe for someone who could hit, "something I never mastered at Yale." After moving to

To the Brink—and Back

Texas, Barbara carpooled players to Little League, giving umpires her mind. Eldest son George W. became Texas Rangers general managing partner before he entered politics. Most of pop's speeches after he left office in 1993 were paid, to help build his library. Gratis was 1994's keynote opening of the Ted Williams Museum and Hitters Hall of Fame—"a dear friend," Bush said, "and the greatest hitter who ever lived."

Articulate, profane, more handsome than Tyrone Power, Williams became a hero to my father, Woody Hayes, John Updike, and Bobby Knight. By 1988 I knew of no one so revered by men, say, over fifty. Bush felt him a hero too and was glad to tell you why. "The first reason is character. Ted couldn't stand what he termed 'politicians'—phonies. Teammates adored him. Rivals asked for batting tips"—wise, given Williams's six league titles, .344 career average, twice winning the Most Valuable Player award and the Triple Crown—"and Ted never turned them down." Finally, Sox owner Tom Yawkey had enough. "Ted, I know you're generous, but why are you helping the enemy?"

Real enemies, said Bush, spiked Korea and World War II. The Kid, aka Splendid Splinter, Thumper, and Teddy Ballgame, among other monikers, flew fifty-eight combat missions, never complaining about "losing five and a half seasons from the prime of his career," Bush jibed. Add them, said longtime Sox announcer Curt Gowdy, "and there'd be no room in the record books for anyone but Ted." Bush thought him an extraordinary batter, hunter, and fisherman— "also a conservationist before the phrase 'environment' existed. Ted raised millions of dollars for charity," especially the Jimmy Fund, New England's charity against childhood cancer. "He was a Point of Light before my administration coined the term."

The introduction of bit pols had begun at the 1988 New Hampshire rally, Rick Robinson wrote, when Williams, unannounced and unexpected, strode on stage, getting and needing no introduction. The crowd gasped, stared in disbelief, then stood and roared. The noise volleyed, rose, and crashed outside against the trees. Ted, still The Kid at seventy, introduced "a good friend of mine who's running for president." Applause greeted Bush, though not as deafening as number 9's. For several days they were inseparable: "Where thou goest," Ruth said to Naomi, "I goest, too"—a Laconia dogsled, a Manchester fishing show, the sidewalks of Currier and Ives towns—Williams mobbed; Bush joking that the candidate was hired help. Years later I asked Sununu what had pivoted the primary. Instantly, he roared, "The Kid!" The ex-governor then added diplomatically, "And Bush having his picture taken with fifty thousand people in the state."

Roger Ailes bought thirty minutes on virtually every TV station serving New Hampshire, including those based in Boston, for a Saturday evening special. The only thing missing was negative advertising to match Dole's. It is fair to characterize most politicians' attitudes as do unto others before they do unto you. By contrast, Bush loathed the negative ad, thought it mean and small, and was reticent to use it, even if behind.

On Friday afternoon Bush's aides were still pleading with him to air the ad "Straddle," attacking Dole on taxes. The Kansan was unfairly smearing him, they said. No one would blame Bush for setting the record straight.

"George," said Mrs. Bush, "I don't think it's so bad."

"Well," Bush succumbed, "you guys know more about the state."

The ad, calling Dole a waffler, ran all weekend. Polling moved toward Bush, who vowed, unlike Dole, never to raise taxes. Much later Bush recalled the last several days as personal, neighborly; as if having braved an outer-body experience, he was in a real sense *coming home*. He blitzed Dole, 38–28 percent. Kemp got 13, Pete du Pont 10, Robertson just 9. On election night NBC's Tom Brokaw prepared to quiz Dole as his interview with Bush was ending. Did Poppy, he asked, have anything to say to his rival?

"No," Bush said, gracious in victory, "just wish him well and meet him in the South"—each primary in Lee Atwater's bailiwick.

"And Senator Dole," Brokaw said, "is there anything you'd like to say to the vice president?"

"Yeah," Dole growled. "Stop lying about my record."

Yogi Berra famously said, "It ain't over till it's over." At that point the Republican contest for president was.

Dole trudged on, bruised and bitter, his window of opportunity closed. The Kansan won uncontested next door Minnesota and North Dakota. Next came Atwater's state, South Carolina, where Bush's strategist had organized in each county like a courthouse race. "We can break his back. We can finish him," he said of Dole, knowing that it would have a domino effect on seventeen-state Super Tuesday three days hence. Atwater busted Bush's TV budget, spending $750,000 to ensure Dole's demise. More than any GOP strategist since Nixon, who ran the 1960, 1968, and 1972 campaigns in his head, Atwater grasped what moved the middle class.

On March 5 Bush won all six South Carolina congressional districts, all thirty-seven delegates, and 49 percent of the vote. Dole and Robertson took 21 and 19 percent, respectively. In 1945 Japanese emperor Hirohito surrendered, saying, "We must endure the unendurable." On March 29 Dole surrendered, withdrawing from the race. Still, he would do "all I can for our nominee, George Bush." Dole then made a prearranged call to Poppy in his office—brief, civil, no reference to "lying about my record." Dole hoped vainly that Bush might name him vice president—thus, embraced good behavior. Meanwhile, Bush began musing what behavior might make him president.

The backdrop already made for pleasant reading. Economic growth was high, inflation low. The market had revived from the single-day 508-point plunge on October 19, 1987. Soviet troops began to leave Afghanistan. In May 1988 the Gipper spoke to Soviet dissidents at the U.S. embassy in Moscow and about religious freedom at the Danilov Monastery and intellectual freedom at Moscow State University. Reagan and Gorbachev walked through Red Square, apparently as close as Bogart and Bacall. Many would have endorsed Bush's vow at Reagan's 1991 library dedication: "Mr. President, we'll get you on Mount Rushmore yet." Poppy gained from how at seventy-seven—this was crucial—the incumbent could easily have won a third-straight term.

The Gipper had helped solidify America as a right-of-center country. Bush's unpleasant reading was that America did not yet see him as a right-of-center man. Moreover, his nomination had almost come too soon. Massachusetts governor Michael Dukakis used Jesse Jackson as a weekly foil to lure headlines and delegates and become the certain Democratic nominee. In June Bob Teeter showed him eighteen points ahead of Bush. In turn, Dick Wirthlin's survey showed Bush's approval rating lower than Gorbachev's—"like Ike's being lower in America," he said, "than Khrushchev's during the 1950s Cold War."

Reagan's foreign policy had aimed to build up (arms) to ultimately build down (then negotiate). Bush aides began to consider what the imminent Republican nominee had not: tearing down (Dukakis) might be easier than building up (Bush).

To the Brink—and Back

EIGHT

The Immaculate Election

In April–August 2012 Barack Obama spent an estimated $100 million on TV to caricature the prospective GOP presidential candidate as Gordon Gekko Jr.—a tax cheat, corporate raider at Bain Capital, even responsible for a woman's death from cancer. Mitt Romney, former Massachusetts governor, 2002 Olympics hero, and savior of firms like Staples, chose not to respond until the campaign's traditional autumn start—a fatal mistake, given how in politics a charge unanswered becomes a fact undenied. By the time Romney reacted, the U.S. jury was closed. In 1988 Bush too wanted to wait till September to go negative, and then lightly. Unlike Mitt, he had tenacious aides who saved Poppy from himself.

According to *Newsweek* magazine's *The Quest for the Presidency*, the general campaign hinged on pollster Bob Teeter's late spring interview of two groups of Reagan Democrats—specifically, middle-class Catholics, the 1988 election's decisive swing group—who had returned to the Democrat Dukakis. At Bush's June retreat with his high command in Kennebunkport, Teeter took two videotapes of voters from Paramus, New Jersey, and told the veep, "I think you should look at these." Bush did and left the screening sadder, wiser, and aware of his challenge's size.

Poppy's image with these Jerseyites was vague, tepid—*wimpy*. Worse, they preferred the liberal Dukakis to Bush, though the Democrat opposed the death penalty, had refused to sign a law mandating the Pledge of Allegiance in his state's public schools, had okayed a lenient prison furlough program, and belonged to the American Civil Liberties Union—the radical ACLU. "They don't know this guy's record," the vice president explained next day, startled. (That week Bush said for the first time that Dukakis represents "old-style '60s liberalism" from "Harvard Yard's boutique," leading the *New York Times*'s Maureen Dowd to ask, "Wasn't this a case of the pot calling the kettle elite?" Bush replied, "Yale's reputation is so diffuse, there isn't a symbol. Harvard boutique to me has the connotation of liberalism and elitism.") Teeter's groups even thought Dukakis would out-tough Bush on drugs.

Only one fact saved the vice president from despair. When the Reagan Democrats learned Dukakis's record, half returned to Bush. "They don't know enough about him," said the veep. As that omission changed, he thought, Dukakis's lead would fall. I watched in curiosity, having written for Reagan's cabinet since 1982. My first speaker, ex–Pennsylvania senator Richard Schweiker, had been Reagan's vice presidential pick before the 1976 GOP Convention, the Gipper vainly trying to loosen that state delegation's pro-Ford tilt. As Reagan's later head of Health and Human Services, Schweiker was an early politician to hype stopping disease *before* it struck—wellness. In addition, he liked to quote non-pols like longshoreman philosopher Eric Hoffer: America was "still the best country for the common man, black or white. If he can't make it here he can't make it anywhere else."

Unlike many politicians, Schweiker would intersperse humor through the body of a speech, recalling when "'Who lost China' meant a debate between political historians—not an argument over who misplaced Nancy's dinnerware," Mrs. Reagan having spent $200,000 for new White House china. An introduction was "overly immodest—but as a golfer, I'm always grateful for a good lie." Edward Kennedy had recently been rumored to have met with Reagan. "He promised to deliver Massachusetts—as a retirement home." Schweiker thought the one-line phrase a device not to dumb down an audience but to rouse and keep its interest—e.g., "My only special interest is America's." "The worst environment is to be cold, hungry, and unemployed"—for millions the nation Reagan inherited as president.

When Schweiker left to head the American Council of Life Insurers (née Insurance), liberal congresswoman Margaret Heckler of suburban Boston succeeded him. Bad news: she was petulant and superficial. Good: she liked to break an audience up. "Groucho Marx once said of a woman he knew, 'She got her good looks from her father— he's a plastic surgeon,'" Heckler said.

In 1984 I got my first look at the Department of Housing and Urban Development, headed by Samuel Pierce, the cabinet's sole black, a fellow New Yorker, smart, taciturn, and vastly underrated. His low profile frustrated political aides. Policy makers noted his Enterprise Zones, private-sector initiatives, and help for those at the margin of the home-buying marketplace.

Pierce spoke largely to business and minority groups, saying of Martin Luther King Jr., "He strove to ensure that as all were born equal in dignity before God, all could become equal in dignity before man." He quoted the twelfth-century Jewish philosopher Moses Ben Maimon, or Maimonides, to the American Jewish Heritage Committee, urging its members "to anticipate charity by preventing poverty; assist the reduced fellowman . . . so that he can earn an honest livelihood."

This, Pierce said, was "the highest step and the summit of charity's golden ladder." In July 1988 Dukakis climbed the golden ladder to his.

Officially nominated in Atlanta, the Democratic candidate for president chose Senator Lloyd Bentsen of Texas as vice president, evoking 1960's JFK-LBJ Boston-Austin axis. He entered the convention stage to Neil Diamond's "Coming to America," gave a rousing speech that tended the different clients of his party, and ended it, polls said, having reestablished a seventeen-point lead over Bush. "It doesn't get any better than this," Dukakis said to no one in particular. Later, he would rue the irony of being right.

Bush had to pick his vice president before or at the GOP Convention in New Orleans. Dukakis had auditioned his candidates at rallies, embarrassing those not picked. The spectacle offended Poppy. He would choose his veep privately, no one except the contenders knowing. Bob Dole was one; politics' Gary Cooper never said a word when a nod would do. Another, Jack Kemp, could be rude, loudly coughing at meetings when he wanted to be heard. Other candidates may or may not have included Elizabeth Dole, Attorney General Dick Thornburgh, and Senators Alan Simpson, Pete Domenici, and John Danforth. Bush didn't really want to pick any of the above. What he wanted was to surprise. "Watch my vice presidential choice," he said. "That will tell all."

His vice presidential surprise was J. Danforth Quayle, forty-one, Indiana's junior senator, a Robert Redford look-alike, and Bush thought, GOP entrée to the baby boom generation. Praising Quayle, John McCain looked skin deep, not deep down: "I can't believe a guy that handsome wouldn't have some impact." Instead, the media accented Quayle's National Guard service, as if it were a lark; affluent background, as if it differed from most of theirs; and ideology, as if the first national boomer candidate had to be a liberal. Picking Quayle was Bush's first decision as presidential nominee, and the media less analyzed than ravaged him. You could accuse it of a feeding frenzy, except that would be unfair to animals.

Bush didn't ask, but I would have picked another surprise: Supreme Court Justice Antonin Scalia, Italian, Catholic, then fifty-two. He had nine children, liked classical music and rhetoric, and was the ultimate strict constructionist. He could have lanced Dukakis, was a recognizable heavyweight, and was probably too brilliant for the job. George H. W. Bush's job was now to give the best—surely, most widely watched—address of his life: the GOP acceptance speech at the convention, striving to fill center stage after two decades in the wings.

Bush assigned the speech to celebrity Reagan writer Peggy Noonan, who enlisted a talented free-lance humor writer from California. Doug Gamble had left Canada in 1980 because "I had had it up to here with [then–prime minister] Pierre Trudeau's socialist paradise." Arriving in Los Angeles, Gamble happened to write a piece of political satire that famed commentator Paul Harvey read on the air. Someone heard it at the White House, called Doug, and asked him to submit material. To Gamble's shock, soon he was writing regularly for the Gipper. After Reagan's forty-nine-state blowout, director of speechwriting Ben Elliott wrote Gamble a thank-you note citing his favorite line: "They [Democrats] dream of an America where every day is April 15th. We dream of an America where every day is the 4th of July."

In 1987 Noonan and Gamble began writing for Bush. In the 1988 acceptance, they aptly cast him as a quiet man, "but I hear the quiet people others don't. The ones who raise the family, pay the taxes, meet the mortgage. I hear them and I am moved, and their concerns are mine." This is America, Bush said: "The Knights of Columbus, the Grange, Hadassah, the Disabled American Veterans, the Order of AHEPA, the Business and Professional Women of America, the union hall, the Bible study group, LULAC [League of United Latin American Citizens], 'Holy Name'—a brilliant diversity spread like stars, like a thousand Points of Light in a broad and peaceful sky"— voluntary individuals and groups who knew, as the French nobleman Alexis de Tocqueville said in 1828, that liberty could not be created without morality, nor morality without faith.

The acceptance speech shone a spotlight on Bush's perceived infelicities, as Reagan had by accenting his age. Poppy didn't fear glamorous rivals, he explained: "I'll try to be fair to the other side. I'll try to hold my charisma in check." Bush spoke to those who said he didn't "always communicate in the clearest, most concise way. . . . I dare them to keep it up. Go ahead, make my twenty-four-hour time period." He was plainspoken, seeing "life in terms of missions— missions defined and missions completed," from torpedo bomber to the Texas plains. "I may not be the most eloquent, but I learned early that eloquence won't draw oil from the ground."

Bush's overall mission was continuity: "After two great terms, a switch will be made. But when you have to change horses in midstream, doesn't it make sense to switch to the one who's going the same way?" Its foundation was record jobs, businesses, and income and low inflation, unemployment, and interest rates. "[Democrats] call it a Swiss cheese economy. Well, that's the way it may look to the three blind mice. But when they were in charge, it was all holes and no cheese." Bush named other issues, like school prayer, gun ownership, the death penalty, and the Pledge of Allegiance, on which he was uniformly to Dukakis's right. "We must change from abortion—to adoption," he said, emotionally. "Barbara and I have an adopted granddaughter. The day of her christening, we wept with joy. I thank God that her parents chose life."

The speech lasted forty-nine minutes, was interrupted eighty times, and changed the election. Some recall Bush's attack on Dukakis's furloughing murderers and vetoing the Pledge, which worked because it affirmed the Democrats' rift with Middle America. Others remember self-deprecation, which worked because it was natural. At the Democratic Convention, Ann Richards had barbed that Bush was "born with a silver foot in his mouth." In New Orleans he said, "Once Barbara asked . . . what I was doing. I said, 'I'm working hard,' and she said, 'Oh, dear, don't worry. Relax, sit back, take off your shoes, and put up your silver foot.'" Many recall another pledge. "My opponent now says he'll raise [taxes] as a last resort, or a third resort. When a politician talks like that, you know that's one resort he'll be checking into." Then, unforgettably: "The Congress will push me to raise taxes, and I'll say no, and they'll push, and I'll say no, and they'll push again, and I'll say to them, 'Read my lips. No new taxes.'"

Later, drawing an unfortunate distinction between speaking and governing, Bush did not treat each speech as president as fully or carefully as the material or event may have merited. By contrast, Poppy *owned* this speech, giving it with inflection and rhythm and energy and heart. More than any event, it made him president. Before the address Dukakis had led by 10 percentage points. After it Bush led by 7. Before the acceptance Bush had never led Dukakis one-on-one. Afterward, he almost never trailed.

Traditionally, Labor Day started the general presidential election. For the Bush campaign, headquartered on Fifteenth Street in Washing-

The Immaculate Election

ton, each day had been Labor Day since July. In his acceptance Bush had vowed a "kinder, gentler" America. His campaign's aim was to equate Dukakis with the suspect and alien. By August the governor's pollster, Ed Reilly, said the Bushies had recast the campaign as Fred MacMurray vs. Robert De Niro. Bush had not seen the Democratic Convention, which trashed him nightly and unseemly as Reagan's spoon-fed valet. Returning home, he was convinced by aides that the Democrats had played dirty, gone nuclear first. Furious, Bush set out, like any gentleman, to reclaim his name. Looking back, a more innocuous convention would have served Dukakis better.

On the stump Bush began to even the score. What kind of man would oppose a mandatory Pledge? Why had "this card-carrying member of the ACLU" furloughed—released—"a hardened first-degree killer who hadn't even served enough time to be eligible for parole"? Bush, in his acceptance speech, was referring to convicted murderer Willie Horton, who then committed a rape and assault in Maryland. Horton became the poster child for Dukakis caring more about hoods than victims. Bush was an outdoorsman—"a Teddy Roosevelt Republican," he said. Why had Dukakis let corporate greed dirty Boston Harbor? The campaign paired attack with Bush's crusade for conservation, family, and a more ennobling culture. Usually the challenger controls the agenda. Here the incumbent—Bush, as Reagan's surrogate—did. In his acceptance Dukakis tried to flee his record by saying, "This is an election about competence, not ideology." By late August Bush led in both.

That month I joined an ad hoc group of about a dozen people from within and outside the Reagan administration to plot speech ideas, propose scheduling events, and write one-line phrases for the campaign. We met or spoke by phone after office hours—no cheating the taxpayer—once a week with ex–Nixon and Connally scheduler David Parker, Bush speechwriter Bob Grady and policy expert Jim Pinkerton, and other writers, consultants, and analysts. Some material was used; most probably not. I am not sure how much it helped. I do think it helped me become a speechwriter to Bush. I sent numerous memoranda to Parker, Grady, Pinkerton, and other aides. Those excerpted here recall the photographs and memories—above all, the general state—of the campaign.

On September 15 I warned that with Bush peaking; "the press may say 'he has run out of gas.'" To avoid his being tarred for preferring superficiality to substance, I urged that he repeat Nixon's 1968 use of nighttime network radio: ten speeches, each thirty minutes, addressing issues from drug abuse and health policy to spending and the work ethic, given successive nights October 25–November 3, on CBS's then 220-outlet network. In addition, Bush could discuss 1990s national defense and traditional values germane to Billy Graham Democrats in the South and Richard Daley Democrats in the North. Speeches might include "American Values" to the Catholic Youth Organization; "Foreign Policy," Council on Foreign Relations; "The Perils of Appeasement," Ford Library; and "Our Judeo-Christian Tradition: America's Timeless Treasure," University of Notre Dame.

The national media would despise this tactic; Reagan Democrats, love it. The memorandum said, "In summary, we must keep the press from claiming: 'The Force now lies with Dukakis. The Bush campaign has stalled.'" Bush's Gallup and Harris lead had stabilized at 5–7 percent. The veep held a large lead in the South—an estimated 150 electoral votes of the 270 needed. My memo urged Bush to appear on *The Grand Ole Opry* in Nashville. Cynics had mocked the Yalie's genuine love of country music, Dukakis needed a mid-South upset somewhere, and the Opry's WSM radio and TV network reached millions. "To us, the Opry means America," Bush could say. "There are those—my rival and his friends in the Harvard-Cambridge crowd—who deride its values. I am proud to uphold them. As president, I will act on their behalf."

Inevitably, attention turned to the first presidential debate, September 25 in Winston-Salem. His campaign still at sea, Dukakis increasingly focused on America's drug epidemic—and the veep's inability to stem it as head of the White House anti-drug task force. Drugs were the sole social issue on which Democrats held a polling edge, so I urged that during the debate Bush say that if elected he would name 1984 Summer Olympics head Peter Ueberroth to a new

The Immaculate Election

cabinet position of drug czar. Ueberroth had assailed drug traffickers, was famously tough-minded, and boasted the highest favorable rating in the history of California's Field Poll. The announcement would have left Dukakis groping to respond.

Bush never made the proposal—grandstanding, he doubtless thought. Instead, the first debate left a viewer schizophrenic. Which registered? Dukakis's "solid content" or "stolid persona . . . not just cool and detached but smug and smirky"? asked Charles Krauthammer. Or, in the words of John Buckley, "George Bush's genuine humanity, goofy as he can sometimes be," his "Everyman quality that creates empathy"? Dukakis provided what Gerald Ford dubbed "a smart-alecky manner." Bush could treat English like a high schooler totaling his car. Someone dubbed the debate "the Ice Man" vs. "the Nice Man." The Nice Man thought he had let his team down: "I didn't do very well tonight," Bush said. His aides left the debate smiling. It lasted till Dan Quayle compared himself with another once U.S. senator.

An October 4 memorandum critiqued the next night's Quayle-Bentsen vice presidential debate. "Quayle must be calm, poised, above all, Presidential," I wrote. "If so, since expectations are so low, the Hoosier can't help but score." By the time Quayle had finished further lowering expectations, Justice Scalia looked like Oliver Wendell Holmes.

Coherent if robotic, Quayle was holding his own in the debate when he did what aides had warned against. "I have as much experience in the Congress," he began, "as Jack Kennedy did when he sought the presidency."

Bentsen, sixty-seven, adopted the look of a sad father about to ground a hapless son. "Senator," he fixed Quayle, "I served with Jack Kennedy. Jack Kennedy was a friend of mine. Senator, you're no Jack Kennedy."

Quayle looked frozen. "That was really uncalled for, Senator," he said.

"You're the one who was making the comparison, Senator," snapped Bentsen. The debate finally ended with Quayle having increased the number of those who thought him not ready for prime time or the presidency.

On October 12 Bush and Jim Baker went to Dodger Stadium in Los Angeles to see the home-team Dodgers win the National League pennant, blanking the New York Mets, 6–0. Next night the veep hoped to seal his own deal in the final TV joust—the horse race now competitive (Poppy up four to six points, depending on the poll) but the Electoral College a semi-lock (320 to 410 votes). On a pre-debate stage tour, the Nice Man, seeing Dukakis and aide Bob Squier, comically waved to them at Ailes's urging. Unnerved, the Ice Man glared. Bush's campaign, which began with the candidate's getting Bob Dole to snarl, "Stop lying about my record," ended with his getting inside his *other* main rival's head. Woody Allen said famously that 90 percent of success was just showing up. Mind control had become 90 percent of politics.

More than two decades later, interviewing Dukakis at length for a book, I found him a literate, knowledgeable, and thoroughly engaging person. In 1988 he entered the last debate inexplicably having been unable to use issues like Quayle, AIDS, the homeless, or the national debt doubling since 1981 to $2.6 trillion to dent the GOP. He was still reeling from a recent *Republican* TV spot which used a *Democratic* photo op to balloon Bush's already huge polling lead in national defense. Desperate to show Dukakis hadn't fallen off a turnip truck, his campaign had put the Korean War veteran in an M1 Abrams tank outside a General Dynamics plant in Sterling Heights, Michigan. The Republican ad used footage showing Dukakis helmeted, standing in one of the tank's hatches, smiling, and waving to the crowd. "Dukakis in the Tank" became almost as ridiculed as Quayle.

Braving the flu, Dukakis spent much of the last debate's day in bed. More painful was his divided staff. Smile. Don't smile. Be strong. Be likeable. Be a next-door neighbor. Don't be too common. Be yourself. Please don't. Moderator Bernard Shaw of CNN asked the opening question—whether Dukakis would still oppose the death penalty if his own wife were raped and murdered. The governor might have mentioned that his own brother had been killed by a hit-and-run driver or that his father had been mugged at the age of seventy-seven in his office. Instead, emotion gone, he answered like a student trying to pass the bar, even omitting wife Kitty's name. By the time Dukakis finished, some in his headquarters on Chauncey Street in Boston were likely planning a post-debate wake in a different kind of bar.

Shaw tried a similar ploy with Bush, asking a hypothetical question about Quayle becoming president upon his death. Bush interrupted with a mock one-word reply—"Bernie!"—conveying natural reluctance to address his own mortality. Dukakis did not tell one story in ninety minutes, fixed on fact like a CPA on numbers. Bush told many, leaving his first debate's fondness for numbers back at the hotel. Ahead, he was gracious. Asked if he could find something to praise about Dukakis, Poppy smiled: "Listen, you're stealing my close. I had something very nice to say in that." Behind, trying to be warm—"I think I'm a little more loveable these days than I used to be back in my youth"—Dukakis must have found Bush like punching at a pillow. After the first debate, a *Time* poll showed that voters thought Dukakis had won but that by 44 to 38 percent Bush was more likeable. The last debate turned perception into steel.

Six days before the election, James Baker, said *Newsweek*, held a senior staff meeting. "We need to be very careful. This [negative] thing has been pushed right to the limit." He was right, but so was Atwater: you dance with the one who brung you, and us vs. them had brought Bush to the brink. Hating negative campaigning, Bush hated losing even more. In late October Dukakis, rising from the crypt, began using the *L* for *Liberal* word, appeared on every TV show but Emeril Lagasse's, and nearly caught Bush in Bob Teeter's polls. Was Mr. Smooth's fall a blip or trend? The former, as it occurred.

Dukakis's only hope was what aides called an eighteen-state strategy—focus on the states where Bush's late lead was not "insurmountable," including California, New York, Pennsylvania, Maryland, Minnesota, Massachusetts, Wisconsin, and Washington. The Democrats had to win each, drawing what Atwater dubbed "an inside straight"—more hope than game plan, foretelling Mitt Romney vs. Barack Obama in 2012. Dukakis's problem was Bush's more than two hundred electoral vote firewall: the 155-vote Confederacy, farm and Rocky Mountain states, and likely the California to which *Grapes of Wrath* Okies had trekked, where Nixon and Reagan had evangelized, and of the Orange County birthplace of Goldwaterism. To them Bush would add New Jersey, Missouri, Ohio, Pennsylvania, Connecticut, and Michigan, among others.

On one hand, the Republican "presidential electoral lock"—former LBJ aide Horace Busby coined the term—was so strong at this time that "Mother Goose could have beaten Dukakis," said a Democratic aide, hyperbolically. On the other, Bush's image had been so defaced—it was only a year since *Newsweek*'s "wimp" cover—that the mere possibility of victory amazed. That magazine now hailed "a brilliant achievement—owed . . . in . . . part . . . to his paid handlers, the cosmeticians who had made a mild man look hard and the armorers who had made a genteel man sound like a schoolyard bully." No "recent President had been, or been presented as, so completely an artifact of packaging and promotion."

If the artifact was more electable than the man, the man was more presidential than the artifact. We now return to both as the campaign ended and a presidency in waiting began.

In October 1988 Bush had told Ailes, "I want to get back on the issues, and quit talking about *him*"—Dukakis. That fall Congress debated the federal seven-day waiting period before someone could buy a handgun, a provision backed by many police officers. "I wish the police chiefs and the gun owners could figure out a compromise," Bush said. "I'm for both sides"—the Second Amendment and the rule of law.

Increasingly, people grew to like a person who viewed politics less cynically than bemusedly. Once Poppy termed Dukakis an excellent debater, adding, "I'm lowering expectations." He began a speech by asking as an aside, "Is this the time we unleash our one-liners?" Calling from a phone bank to benefit photographers, he told a startled listener, "I'm just doing a little show-biz phoning here." A friend recalled how Bush walked across Yale's campus in 1948 to be inducted into Phi

Beta Kappa, humbly noting that he was not a real intellectual. Perspective made Bush a pragmatist, a problem solver. What mattered was honor, right and wrong, and at every juncture, how things worked.

In 1988 what worked was to make the election a referendum on Dukakis's liberalism. Bush said that the approach was political, not personal. Lloyd Bentsen attacked him as "all hat and no cattle." Other insults were meaner. Bush did not respond. Another fellow Texan, House majority leader Jim Wright, was under investigation for financial hanky-panky. Bush barely touched it—too busy ballyhooing that his and not Dukakis's ideology worked. In the end Poppy won a handsome if not quite Gipper-size landslide: 53.4 to 46.6 percent of the popular vote and 426 to 112 Electoral College vote. Dukakis won Massachusetts, next-door New York, Rhode Island, West Virginia, Hawaii, Oregon, Washington, and Wisconsin, Iowa, and Minnesota's Middle America outlier—a mere ten states and Washington DC.

I was at the Houstonian Hotel on election night as Bush, having lost in the past and knowing Dukakis's pain, phoned his rival. He then came down to the ballroom to thank the crowd and, over television, share an outcome that had seemed improbable less than four months before. Few had expected such a pasting of Dukakis even twenty-four hours earlier. Bush won the election, paraphrasing the Beatles, getting by with a lot of help from his friend. For tens of millions, he came as close as they could get to reelecting the Gipper.

More than 85 percent of voters who approved of Reagan, thought he had made them better off, and liked his course supported Bush. According to NBC News, Bush also got 46 percent of the blue-collar vote, equal to Reagan in 1980. He narrowed the gender gap to four points vs. Reagan's ten in 1984 and took a majority of women in the South. On the other hand, he won men by ten points vs. the Gipper's twenty-five. Bush won rural America, 58–42 percent, and suburbia, 54–46, 43 percent of the electorate. Dukakis won the cities, 57–43; Catholics, 52–48; and blacks and Hispanics easily. Poppy narrowly won baby boomers, retirees, and white-collar workers, 51–49; professionals and managers, 56–44; and crucially, independents, 58–42. The better educated and more affluent, the more decisively Bush won.

Other polling suggested Bush as safe and experienced—an agent of "cautious change." In the South, said political scientist Earl Black, Willie Horton and the Pledge made Dukakis "seem someone who isn't 'one of us.'" Elsewhere, the federal deficit, drug abuse, and programs for the middle class were more discussed. Bush led among people wanting competence, experience, strength, and trustworthiness in a crisis. Dukakis led among those interested in domestic issues. In the NBC poll, a 50–44 percent majority said yes to the question, "Does the country want change?" Bush won overwhelmingly among the 44 percent wanting no change—and narrowly among an additional 18 percent wanting minor change. Ideologically, he may have been the ideal Republican to follow the Gipper.

Looking back, Bush's victory was seminal, though it cannot be said that many realized it then. He was the last Republican to win each of ten states today known as "blue," voting Democratic for president: Vermont, Maine, Connecticut, New Jersey, Delaware, Maryland, Pennsylvania, Michigan, Illinois, and California—152 electoral votes in 2012. No candidate in either party has equaled his 1988 electoral or percentage vote total. On election night Bush spoke of telling Dukakis that he wanted to be president of all the people, including those who had not supported him.

"When I said I wanted a kinder and gentler nation, I meant it—I mean it. My hand is out to you and I want to be your president too." A campaign is a disagreement, he continued, "and disagreements divide. But an election is a decision. And decisions clear the way for harmony and peace." He must have felt as Dukakis, winning the nomination, said: "It doesn't get any better than this."

Not everyone felt Poppy's bliss. According to *Time*, "For Bush it was a victory without drum rolls, a majority without a meaningful mandate. The promise of a Bush Administration lies in the hope that the new President will soon forget the manner in which he won." Conceding Democratic ineptitude, Walter Shapiro put greater onus on

"Bush's angry scripts as he launched fusillades of demeaning attitudes against the hapless Michael Dukakis."

In such a fever swamp, many expected liberals from Bill Moyers to Mario Cuomo to try to discredit Poppy's legitimacy before Bush took the oath. There would be no honeymoon until Democrats respected—*feared*—the president-elect's potency and resolve. In 1949–50, bitter over Thomas Dewey's 1948 debacle, the congressional GOP placed its feet—"Korea, Communism, and Corruption"— squarely on Harry Truman's throatlatch. If permitted, Democrats would do the same. Furious at Dukakis, incredulous at blowing a sure thing, they blamed the Duke, voter naiveté, Willie Horton, the Pledge, or the turpitude of the GOP Right—anything but the ideology Bush campaigned against.

In a landmark book, *Presidential Power*, historian Richard E. Neustadt concluded that the public's opinion of a chief executive "takes shape for most executives no later than the time they first perceive him as being President (a different thing than seeing him as President)." Bush had vowed to be an activist president, sustain Reagan's legacy, and make his presidency matter. This demanded he be streetwise and aggressive, acting quickly against forces determined to disembowel him. It also meant he must affirm the three themes of the electorate that had chosen him: economic opportunity, a strong defense, and traditional values.

As we shall see, in 1992 independent candidate H. Ross Perot was backed by nearly one in five Americans—traditional in outlook, raised on American preeminence, and taken from Bush's base. In election week 1988, not knowing of Perot, I submitted a memo, as many colleagues did, I hoped, to fuel the diversity of opinion every administration needs.

My memo focused on how the new administration might tie Bush and the Silent Majority, eliminate any need for a third party, and secure a second term. Following is a sampling:

1. Billy Graham had been the Bushes' close friend for the past thirty years. He and wife Ruth had even vacationed in Kennebunkport

since the 1970s. The memo suggested that they jointly attend church post-election Sunday, November 13. On Inauguration Day Graham might grace the Bush family box; New York Archbishop Cardinal John Joseph O'Connor, deliver an invocation; a Jewish prelate, the benediction; a black evangelist, a prayer about the indigent. In America, ecumenicalism is smart—and right. "I don't care what religion a man has," Bush quoted Eisenhower saying, "as long as he has one. Without that none of this makes any sense."

2. As this account has shown, like the average American male, Ike loved college football—ruggedly individual, wholesome in a swelling-of-the-heart Norman Rockwell way—and nothing wed its heroism and amber waves of grain like the Army-Navy game. It was a day of pageantry and epitome of who we are: "duty, honor, country." In 1961 John F. Kennedy, a World War II Navy hero, sat on the Army side in the first half, crossing the field at halftime. The entire Navy section rose to cheer. A chant erupted: "Welcome home! Welcome home!" The thirty-fifth president beamed.

As Bush grew up, only the World Series matched the Army-Navy game as America's midcentury divertissement. One Fall Classic highlight film observed, "Each autumn comes a day in this great land of ours when the wheels of industry turn a little slower . . . the white-collar worker takes a little more time [at] lunch . . . when almost everyone is stricken with WORLD SERIES fever." Especially in World War II, service-academy football, wrote Robert Mayer, seemed "America's sporting equivalent of war." In 1944 Gen. Douglas MacArthur wired victorious West Point coach Red Blaik: "We stopped the war [in the Pacific] to celebrate your magnificent success."

To Bush and Reagan, people like Blaik and MacArthur were figures from Olympus. If the Secret Service agreed, I urged, have the president and president-elect travel to the Army-Navy game in early December in Philadelphia. In the first half, the Gipper could sit amid midshipmen; Bush, the cadets. At halftime they would meet at midfield, shake hands, and each proceed to the other side of the field—Bush doubtless hearing, "Welcome home!" The symbolism would resound: continuity, football, and the military meshing.

3. The 1988 campaign clearly implied that values would form the boot of the Bush administration. Yet it was plain that foreign policy would be the buckle. Polling showed that most Americans expected Bush, like JFK and Nixon, to be a foreign-policy president. It linked his skill and interest. Even better, less fettered by Congress, a president had greater latitude abroad than at home. Bush could act decisively, showing himself a leader.

Bush grasped that his best interest required reacquainting foreign leaders with his familiarity with world events, building on the UN, China, the CIA, and many trips abroad as vice president. This approach would swell his presidential cachet, underline his legitimacy as Leader of the Free World, and use Bush's turf to strengthen him domestically so that Congress would hesitate to block his agenda. Such combinations are hard to find.

One example was Margaret Thatcher's November 1988 state visit. The prime minister and Bush liked one another. I suggested each would benefit from Bush holding a dinner for Mrs. Thatcher at the veep's residence, where the past and present cream of the foreign policy elite could laud the Anglo-American alliance. Bush could invite Clark Clifford, Dean Rusk, and George Ball, making this anchor of U.S. policy inclusive. Solicitude, Bush's forte, would aid the bipartisan foreign policy his own dad admired.

In the Old West, whose movies Bush loved as a good-guy prism and progenitor, the outlaw tried to stay a step ahead of the sheriff. In the interregnum between the election and inaugural, Bush tried to stay ahead of a posse determined, as this narrative has noted, to delegitimize his victory. What came naturally to Bush made strategic sense: consensus. Let Democrats throw the first stone, as they shortly would; then, tut-tutting, Bushies could say, "They're not interested in the national interest—only in guerrilla war."

4. On November 2, 1988, the *Washington Post* had published a "No Endorsement" editorial. Opening the door, I wrote, Bush might

send a letter to board chairman Katharine Graham, saying, "Once this election is history, and both of us have the chance to catch our breath, perhaps we can meet at a time of your convenience to discuss, in a more personal vein, our years ahead as public people and as citizens."

After such a meeting, the *Post*, perhaps, would have treated President Bush less acidly, which is not to say sycophantically; perhaps not (I suspect not). No matter. It cost nothing to extend an open hand. The political goal was to create a preemptive public record. A larger goal—which, growing to know Bush, I found he deeply felt—was to communicate across a no-man's land in which liberal and conservative talked *at*, not *with*, each other, as stick figure, not human being.

5. In the past a president-elect had shown this perspective in what JFK dubbed his cabinet's and senior staff's "ministry of talent," officials announced irregularly, one by one, or all at once. I proposed that each Saturday morning from mid-November to mid-December Bush announce two or three cabinet and senior staff officials, starting with, say, the secretary of commerce, and concluding, before Christmas, with the secretaries of defense, state, and treasury.

Saturday brunch with Bush might have ensured, to the greatest possible degree post-election, the attention of his country. Postscript: In the end Bush announced his cabinet "irregularly." He was receptive to advice, but trusted his instincts and followed his own timetable. After all, as he often asked aides, "If you're so smart, why aren't you president?" To my knowledge, no one yet has given an adequate response.

NINE

Hopeful at the Creation

More often than not, presidents hire personnel whose qualities offset, not duplicate, their own vulnerabilities. For example, just as Lyndon Johnson, roughhewn and coarse, lured such soft-spoken loyalists as George Christian and Horace Busby; just as Richard Nixon, constitutionally unable to brook personal confrontation, required H. R. Haldeman as his Official Son of a Bitch; just as Gerald Ford, open and amiable, needed Robert Hartmann to ward off outsiders; just as Ronald Reagan, a delegator unschooled in Washington, needed street-smart Chief of Staff James A. Baker—so, I wrote in early 1989, would George Bush, gentle, civil, a conciliator by nature, require White House appointees who were tough and tough-minded, facile and assertive, fiercely loyal to the new president's person and policies, and even brutal in their execution. In short, the forty-first president would need people who mirrored Nixon's praise, circa 1972, of George Herbert Walker Bush: "He'll do anything for the cause."

There are exceptions to every rule, but Democrats themselves best expressed what Bush faced, becoming president. "He may get a fifteen-minute honeymoon after he takes his hand off the Bible," said Representative Richard Durbin of Illinois. California representative Robert Matsui was less charitable, bragging, "This guy's not going to have any honeymoon at all." To confront academics, foundations, and Hill Democrats; fight the special interests vs. general;

and go above a hostile media to reach and move America, Bush did not need nice guys. He was decent enough for an entire staff.

The 1988 campaign showed brilliantly that this patient, generous, and kindhearted man could paint political pitchfork-populist art when linked, arm in arm, with aides who loved their country, hated what extremists had done to it, and did not dislike rolling up their sleeves, extending elbows, and using what they deemed necessary means to reach their end. To help the Bush presidency enrich 1990s America so that America could enrich the world, he and they, I believed, must be no less combative now.

In early 1989 I was hired as a speechwriter to Bush 41. The FBI did its usual indefatigable job probing every crevice of a nominee's life, knowing, for example, the name of my childhood dog, who was sadly unable to testify, having died when she was ten. My time at Gannett, at the *Saturday Evening Post*, and in the Reagan cabinet helped. As we have seen, a fall 1988 ad hoc media campaign group introduced me to people who joined the administration. Raymond Price again wrote on my behalf to Bush's new communications director, David Demarest, a moderate New Jersey Republican and public affairs official in Reagan's Labor Department.

Demarest knew, as historian Arthur Schlesinger's son Robert wrote in *White House Ghosts: Presidents and Their Speechwriters*, a history of modern presidential speechwriting since its birth in the early 1920s, that "Bush and his top advisors did not attach the same value to speechmaking that Reagan had." Demarest thought that Reagan's writers had too high a profile, were too self-absorbed, and resembled radio's 1940s serial *The Bickersons*. Instead, the communications director wanted team writers who played nice, were loyal, and checked ego at the door.

With luck, a varied staff might also serve Bush and the two occasionally harmonic but often warring wings of the GOP. The Main Street wing supplied most of the party's votes: a Silent still-Majority trying to save, buy a home, and educate their children. It touted sane tax and spend, limited government, the Bible as moral compass, and America as freedom's beacon. The Wall Street wing supplied most of the party's money. It touted globalism, increasing secularism, free if not necessarily fair trade, outsourcing, and a conciliatory or me-too political ideology, depending on your definition. The wings seldom overlapped.

Eisenhower fused them in 1952 and 1956; having dispatched Hitler, he left political quibbling to mortals. Nixon embodied Main Street and groveled for Wall Street's largesse. In 1976 and at first in 1980, Wall Street thought Reagan a troglodyte. A decade later, prosperity all around, he seemed almost as good as Milton Friedman. In 1988 Wall Street financiers forgave Poppy's impression of Grant Wood's *American Gothic*; Prescott Bush's son didn't—couldn't—mean it. White House writers might reduce the gulf.

In particular, Demarest, with a fine sense of humor, wanted Bush to get audiences to laugh. David had a late-night comedic attitude. Alas, as this book notes (see the "Author's Note" re: Aretha Franklin's song "R-E-S-P-E-C-T"), Bush was not a late-night kind of guy. We compensated by using humor writer Doug Gamble, key to Bush's 1988 acceptance speech, and adopting the president's cultural milieu, which considered "hipness" another word for as transient as the wind. My humor ran toward black comedy, forged as a child by the 1960 election and the Boston Red Sox. A ballad goes, "Being Irish means laughing at life knowing that in the end life will break your heart." What counted was Bush's humor. We would learn by trial and error.

In the book *President Kennedy*, Richard Reeves writes that JFK "came to power at the end of an old era or the beginning of a new, which was important because his words and actions were recorded in new ways. The pulse of communications speeded up in his time." So did Bush 41. At the beginning of his term, we had electric typewriters, fax machines, and primitive computers, which the technology challenged—e.g., me—did not know how to use. We had to learn quickly on the job. E-mail did not exist; neither did a social media that later tied "iPod" and "hashtag" and "iPad" and "tweet." As these new technologies grew, they helped the Democrats win four of six presidential elections from 1992 to 2012. In 1989 I was absorbed by words like "save," "search," and "shift"—and above all, the Indian saw "you can only know someone by putting your feet in their moccasins."

Our great adventure began January 20, 1989, George Bush giving the inaugural address that from his 1960s and '70s wilderness, even as recently as the 1988 Democratic Convention, must have seemed as distant as the green light to Jay Gatsby at the end of Tom and Daisy Buchanan's dock. Writer Peggy Noonan cast the site as "democracy's front porch." Bush's "first act as president" was a prayer. He then began a theme—"a new breeze is blowing"—freedom. "We know what works," he said. "Freedom works." The new president paraphrased from Saint Augustine: "In crucial things, unity; in important things, diversity; in all things, generosity."

Government could help, but only people could inspire. "[Together we could] make kinder the face of the Nation and gentler the face of the world." To 41, the bully pulpit meant example. Example meant bipartisanship. Goodwill begat goodwill. At one point Bush turned from the lectern and extended his hand to Speaker of the House Jim Wright and Senate majority leader George Mitchell. "For this is the thing," Bush said. "This is the age of the offered hand." Too late he sensed that Democrats wanted his head, not hand. For the moment, drugs inflamed him most. "Take my word for it: This scourge will stop." The speech ended with a fifth use of "breeze." Noonan then left speechwriting to pen a *Wall Street Journal* column and write books, including *What I Saw at the Revolution: A Political Life in the Reagan Era*, the Gipper's presidency in vivid prose.

Directly I officially began as speechwriter to the president. My office was room 120 on the first floor of the Eisenhower EOB, the former State, War, and Navy Building across West Executive Avenue from the West Wing door. It was large with a high ceiling and looked out on traffic on Seventeenth Street. The huge pillared and porticoed building looked like a skeleton from Victorian London. I liked it because it was historic and idiosyncratic and you could be in the Oval Office in less than five minutes. Since 1969 writers had been housed in the Old EOB—their corridor known as "Writers' Row" or

"Kings' Row," Theodore White wrote of the Nixon presidency, since Nixon had a first-floor EOB office hideaway. Under Bush, writers occupied offices to my right and left.

One was Dan McGroarty, a foreign policy specialist, having crafted speeches for Secretaries of Defense Caspar Weinberger and Frank Carlucci and worked at Voice of America. Another, Mark Davis, had written speeches for RNC head Frank Fahrenkopf. Mark Lange joined us from the Transportation Department, having worked for Secretaries Ann McLaughlin and Elizabeth Dole. Mary Kate Grant (later Cary) wrote magazine articles, then speeches, for Bush. Ed McNally had been a federal prosecutor in New York. Beth Hinchliffe was a lyric Boston magazine writer. I and several others served all four years of the Bush administration. Until 1992, when, paraphrasing Yeats, its center no longer held, most served at least two.

Bush's speech team resembled each president's since the 1960s, numbering five or six writers at a time, each assigned a research aide to cull local story, fact-check, and mediate with local people. Some writers served as alter ego, policy aide, or personal assistant. Some were a speechwriter before entering the White House, with a field of concentration: foreign policy, domestic policy, values and philosophy. Writing could be by committee and sound it. Most presidents agree: one writer, one speech works best. Bush worked with a single writer on a speech, assigned by Demarest from the West Wing, a floor above the president, and speech editor Chriss Winston, housed on Writers' Row.

For a major speech—State of the Union, UN address, network missive—you might have twenty days to visit aides, policy experts, and the president by phone, later e-mail, or in person and then write a draft. You tried not to abuse your stay; the president's plate was always full. Ultimately, for most speeches—fund-raiser here, Rose Garden greeting there—you knew your principal so well you could write without consulting him. My Gannett past helped me write on deadline. Especially in an election year, I might arrive at 6:30 a.m., get a phone call at 7, and hear, "The president needs a speech. No hurry. Get us a draft by 11"—11 *a.m.* I then remembered Reagan terming himself the king of the so-called B-movies: "A B-movie is one they didn't necessarily want good. They wanted them Tuesday."

A former aide to liberal Iowa representative Jim Leach, Winston primarily edited more than wrote. Receiving a writer's draft, she performed varying degrees of surgery, then sent the product to pertinent policy and political aides—the "staffing" process—each of whom played Broadway critic. Some suggested helpful prose and programmatic thoughts. Others strove to be a pain in the patootie—and succeeded. All returned changes to Chriss's office, where we tried to reconcile the oft irreconcilable—the "reconciliation" process. After that the speech reached "POTUS" (for president of the United States), who may or may not have been previously involved.

If Bush liked the speech, happy days were here again. It was printed in bold twenty-four-point type so that he could deliver it without glasses—hopefully, but not always, practiced. By contrast, since only POTUS's vote counted, if he disliked the final draft, it entered, as Reagan said of Communism, *your* ash heap of history. Scrap your weekend, turn on the computer, and as a great writer, Red Smith, said, "open your veins, and watch the blood come out." Mercifully, I had to start from scratch only once or twice—so the Red Cross was never called.

On January 21, 1989, Bush—surprisingly taller (six foot two) than Reagan, less angular and more handsome than on television, lithe, still an athlete—entered the Roosevelt Room to tell writers what he liked and disliked about speechwriting and giving. The first rule was to avoid the word *I*. Such modesty was thought to be unprecedented for a politician—the result of mother Dorothy's lifelong circumspection. "Fine, George, but what about the *team*?" she would say as he detailed a boyhood home run. Like River City, ditching *I* caused capital *T*, which stood for trouble. Try writing a third-person speech.

Bush's second rule was to be direct, voiding emotion. "If you give me a ten, I'm going to send it back and say, 'Give me an eight,'" he said. "And you'll be lucky if I deliver a six." A voter once compared two candidates: "Think of them as a violin. When one talks, you hear every squeak of the box. When the other talks, you hear his soul." To Bush, the squeak was safer.

Bush's third rule stemmed from grasping what he was and wasn't. "I am not Ronald Reagan," he told us. "I couldn't be if I wanted to." The spoken word had *been* Reagan's presidency. By design it was one aspect—like policy or personnel—of Bush's. James Agee wrote, "Let us now praise famous men." Bush's famous man said, "You can observe a lot by watching." As observed, Reagan liked to quote Jefferson. No matter an audience's age, race, sex, or education, Bush quoted Yogi Berra. With certain people—Sinatra, Streisand—only the surname counts. Others flaunt first name or initial: Ellen, W. No name is like the Yog's.

Born to Italian immigrants, Berra grew up on St. Louis's "Dago Hill." Once the squat, jug-eared teen and a friend saw a theater travelogue about India. The film included a yogi, likened to Berra by his pal. Like gold, the nickname stuck. Yogi learned a salute to the flag, catch in the throat, tear in the eye Americanism. Best friend and future broadcaster Joe Garagiola lived "a pickoff away." One day Berra took ill. "You look terrible," said Garagiola. "Why don't you go home?" Yogi shrugged: "If a guy can't get sick on a cold, miserable day like this, he ain't healthy."

Such logic endeared him to America, where by the early twenty-first century Yogi passed Shakespeare as the figure most quoted by U.S. public speakers. Yet Baseball Hall of Fame Class of '72 was more than "Yogi thinking funny," said Garagiola, "and speaking what he thinks." Like Bush, Berra braved World War II as a teenager. Back home he became what the ex-Yale captain termed "baseball's greatest catcher"—three-time Most Valuable Player, 358 homers, and the position's most runs batted in—showing that "baseball is 90 percent mental," said Berra. "The other half is physical."

"If you can't imitate him, don't copy him," Yogi said, as Bush said of Reagan. No one could copy baseball's most lethal bad-ball hitter. Number 8 also rolled seven behind the plate. Once Berra fielded a bunt and tagged the hitter and runner coming toward the plate, saying, "I just tagged everybody, including the ump." Yogi leads in all-time World Series games (75), hits (71), played (14), and won (10). If Berra were a movie, it would be *The Quiet Man* meets *Mr. Lucky*.

Yogi and wife Carmen were wed from 1949 till her death in 2014. The bowling alley Berra and ex-Yankee Phil Rizzuto opened rolled a financial 300; Yogi's Yoo-hoo drink became a hit; Aflac ads remain a classic—Berra, in barber chair; barber and duck, agape. In 2008 Yogi helped close the original Yankee Stadium. About this time, he said, "Always go to other people's funerals. Otherwise they won't come to yours." Mercifully, baseball's extraordinary Ordinary Man's funeral seemed more than a short pop fly away.

Ultimately, I found that Bush knew more Berraisms than I did. "Nobody goes to that restaurant anymore. It's too crowded." A woman cooed, "Yogi, you look cool in that suit." Berra smiled: "Thanks. You don't look so hot yourself." In 2009 Bush intern–turned–counselor Julie Harry Heiden invited me to keynote the Fairfax County, Virginia, Bar Association. Speech like "It's déjà vu all over again" dotted my address. Part-time college waiters left the kitchen to hear Berraisms they'd never heard. This is not uncommon. When it came to quotation, George Bush was far ahead of the curve.

For his first few months, finding my way around, I wrote about the environment, law enforcement, the growing savings and loan crisis, and the role of government. At American University Bush quoted Bernard Baruch to define his philosophy of pragmatism: "Government is not a *substitute* for people, but simply the *instrument* through which they act." At Ford Aerospace in Palo Alto, Bush said, "The *genius* of America has forged the *greatness* of America." In New York he defined justice at the United Negro College Fund dinner, recalling how at Yale Bush helped its drive while trying to captain the varsity and steady his grades. "I observed what Churchill said, 'Personally, I am always ready to learn, though I do not always enjoy being taught.'"

For a long time, Bush could boast of prosperity without inflation and prosperity without war. One-line phrases reflected his, as it had been Reagan's, forte. "A strong economy is the surest guarantee of lasting social justice." Abroad, from his first full month Bush renewed acquaintances and alliances from his globe-hopping time as veep in Canada, China, and South Korea. In Japan for Emperor Hirohito's state funeral, he met French president François Mitterrand, recalling Lafayette's "What impresses me is that in America all of the citizens are brethren." Bush swore in, among others, James Baker at State, Dick Cheney at Defense, William Bennett at Education, Elizabeth Dole at Transportation, and John Sununu as chief of staff. When possible, writers watched and listened, tried to measure Bush's voice and cadence, and adjusted ourselves to him, and he perhaps to us.

That spring, presenting Volunteer Awards, Bush spurned "what I can do for myself" for "what I can do by myself for others." The greatest gift, he said during Captive Nations Week, was freedom: "The totalitarian era is passing, its old ideas blown away like leaves from an ancient, lifeless tree." In 1942 Gen. James A. Doolittle led a squadron of planes off a U.S. aircraft carrier to bomb Japan—"Thirty Seconds over Tokyo"—pivoting World War II morale. In June 1989 Bush gave the Medal of Freedom, America's highest civilian award, to Doolittle for having "shown that ours would not be the land of the free if it were not also the home of the brave." By contrast, that month he addressed members of the Memorial Advisory Board about the Korean War Memorial—a postcard summer day. As noted, Ted Williams was a close friend. Bush knew his nickname—Teddy Ballgame— yet called him Ballgame Teddy, having not read the speech to know it—or know how the words would sound.

"He [Bush] just didn't buy into that," Demarest told Robert Schlesinger of a belief that success demanded eloquence. "It wasn't in his DNA." He rarely practiced reading speeches out loud, the exception a major address: a UN, prime-time, or Oval Office message. Noonan sent me a note, saying, "Bush, as you know, is skeptical of sweeping rhetoric. He likes it low-key. But that means you guys can't show what you've got and soar! And then you get knocked for not soaring!" Some higher-ups added insult by "de-Reaganizing" our staff— the Gipper's, they felt, too big for their britches—revoking White

House mess privileges and curbing West Wing access. We largely ignored or outmaneuvered such barbs. What hurt was the lack of more dialogue, even disagreement, among writers and between us and higher members of the White House staff through memoranda designed to make all of us, as Lincoln said, "think anew."

Such memoranda were invaluable to the 1980 Connally campaign, fall 1988 Bush Fifteenth Street ad hoc effort, and virtually every presidential speech outreach since FDR's. They spur contention, yes. They can be untidy. They can also adjust the political game plan when the original plan dissolves, as Bush's did in late 1991 and early 1992. I traded memos with Sununu, policy expert Jim Pinkerton, and then–Dan Quayle chief of staff Bill Kristol, now the *Weekly Standard* publisher. Other writers doubtless conversed with policy sources of their own. Missing was the spirit of invitation whereby we were urged to contribute cerebrally and emotionally to the larger picture of reelecting George Bush.

Eddie Gomez, who played bass with pianist Billy Evans, termed the jazz musician's aim "to make music that balanced passion and intellect." That should be a speechwriter's aim, exactly. Any administration needs to recall who elected it; address its constituents' priorities; and galvanize its base. Bush had been taught to hide his good Episcopalian soul. Without doing damage or an extreme makeover, our office tried to show it.

Totalitarianism was passing, Bush had predicted in early 1989. The Polish government agreed to hold free elections, Mikhail Gorbachev refusing to intervene. As Reagan prophesied, the rest of Europe fell. Hungary began dismantling the fences along its Austrian border. The Soviet Union held its first multicandidate election. In late May Mark Davis wrote a fine speech on Germany that detailed America's emerging Eastern European strategy: the Cold War would end "only when Europe is whole, and free." Freedom was in the air, Bush said, again prescient. In early July he revisited Europe, a rousing speech by Ed McNally scoring at the Polish shipyard in Gdansk.

Hopeful at the Creation

Bush then flew to Budapest, where several hundreds of thousands gathered in Kossuth Square, his text reading "liberty can light the globe." It recalled Lajos Kossuth, a patriot who arrived in America in 1852 to salute "the principle of self-government" after Hungary's Revolution of 1848 had temporarily been lost. In New York Harbor, an armada of ships sounded horns to hail his arrival. "Perhaps no visitor since Lafayette had been greeted so emotionally."

My assistant, Stephanie Blessey, found a fact with which Bush's text ended. More than five centuries earlier, Hungary's János Hunyadi had stopped a would-be Turkish invasion. In his honor the pope ordered each Catholic church to ring a bell at the time of day the battle had ended. Since then Catholic and other Christian church bells all over the world have rung precisely at midday. "Together," Bush was to conclude, "let us raise what Kossuth called 'the morning star of liberty.'"

His audience might have, except that Budapest had been pelted all day by torrential rain—a fact of which we were unaware in Washington in that pre–cell phone, iPod, and even largely cable-TV age. We were in the speech office, listening by squawk box—an intercom link with the speech site—no picture, explanation, or above all, context. Hungarian president Bruno Straub gave a stolid fifteen-minute introduction. Bush then began to speak, saying, "I'm going to take this speech and I'm going to tear it up. You've been out here long enough."

Hungarians roared as Bush ripped the speech cards—*my* cards—and held them above his head. Blessey's head hit the table. I tried to mask surprise, wondering what we'd done to deserve such a public flogging. Next day, word filtered back about Bush's ad-libbing, then waving the crowd home. Translated, the text would have lasted forty minutes in the rain; Bush was being kind. Later he sent me a Reuters photo that graced papers around the world: 41, in trench coat, smiling gleefully, holding half of each card in one hand and half in the other. "It's raining in Budapest," he wrote. "I'll wing it." Bush winged little about foreign policy, as his administration showed.

In his inaugural Bush had referenced the need to move beyond Vietnam: "That war cleaves us still." In November 1989 he dedicated the Texas Vietnam Veterans Memorial in Dallas. In *White House Ghosts*, Schlesinger wrote that I "specialized in speeches that appealed to the conservative base of the GOP—rallying-type addresses that touched on values issues and conservative philosophy." Actually, the speeches that meant most to me were those that touched Bush viscerally, because they showed an extraordinary human being. In Dallas Bush related a mother who had four children, each of whom had a dream. Two of her sons were killed in Vietnam. The daughter's dream had been to shake an American president's hand. Said Bush, voice breaking, "It is I who am honored to shake your hands."

That week Communist guards allowed passage through the Berlin Wall, ending twenty-eight years of a divided city. At Bush's 1942 prep school graduation, Secretary of War Henry Stimson had said the U.S. soldier should be "self-confident without boasting." The president now struck that balance. Press secretary Marlin Fitzwater wanted him to make a statement to the press. "Listen, Marlin," Bush said. "I'm not going to dance on the Berlin Wall. The last thing I want to do is brag about winning the Cold War, or bringing the wall down. It won't help us in Eastern Europe to be bragging about this." That day a reporter said, "Why don't you show the emotion we feel?" Unsaid: You don't insult potential colleagues. "I wanted the Soviets' help," Bush said. He never said "The Cold War is over" until Germany reunited on October 3, 1990.

In late November 1989 Bush added authenticity to humility as he traveled to the historic Mediterranean island of Malta for his first meeting as president with Gorbachev. My office, like many in the EOB, had a sofa, which I used awaiting the response of "staffing" to late-night speech drafts. After reconciling their changes, I sent Bush his draft. He then began his handiwork, writing "self-typed" notes. The president's sole speech of the summit was to the five thousand sailors on USS *Forrestal*. My draft included allusions to current entertainment. "Please re-do," typed Bush, who unlike most pols refused to say anything he felt even slightly phony. "I don't understand some of the humor. I'd [also] prefer to leave out most of the references to my own Naval experience." Bush's view was hard to miss. In the margin next to that paragraph, he wrote, "Too [much] ego."

My first draft to reach Bush ended with a prayer Franklin Roosevelt spoke, on D-day, over a nationwide radio network. Instead, Bush asked for his presidential frame of reference—and his December 1 remarks concluded so:

> Let me close with a moment you're too young to remember—but which wrote a glorious page in American history. It occurred on D-day as Dwight Eisenhower addressed the sailors, soldiers, and airmen of the Allied Expeditionary Force.
>
> "You are about to embark," he told them, "upon a great crusade. . . . The eyes of the world are upon you. The hopes and prayers of liberty-loving people everywhere march with you." Then Ike spoke this moving prayer: "Let us all beseech the blessing of Almighty God, upon this great and noble undertaking."
>
> Like the men of D-day, you, too, are the hope of "liberty-loving people everywhere." As the Navy has been in wartime—and in peacetime—keeping our hearts alight—and our faith unyielding. Sacrificing time away from *your* homes so that other Americans can sleep safely in *theirs*.

Voice wavering, the president observed, "Thank you for writing still-new pages in the history of America and her Navy. God bless you and our 'great and noble undertaking.' And God bless the United States of America."

Listening, I thought of my parents, who rejoiced when Ike was elected, and my grandparents, who cried when he died, and my hometown, which supported him, and Ike's hometown, which molded him—and of how only FDR, I believe, eclipses him as a pillar of Henry Luce's American Century. Later Bush marveled, "It's amazing what occurred in a blink of history's eye." He meant 1989–91 but could have meant World War I or II or Korea or Vietnam—all wars Ike either served in or observed.

On December 19, three weeks later, Bush asked his speechwriters to the residence for drinks, where his breeding masked a poker-faced heart. His grandkids were all over him. The family's English springer spaniel, Millie, licked my hand. Bush showed us the Lincoln Bedroom, noting that there Lincoln had signed the Emancipation Proclamation. He observed a painting of Lincoln and his generals—*The Peacemakers*—on the wall, saying that he constantly drew strength from Lincoln's example. I thought again that at heart Bush was a deeply religious man. We spoke for an hour, Bush several times drawn to the doorway to speak with aides—even so, a president at seeming ease with the world. At 7 p.m. we rose, Bush leaving to host a media Christmas party. Seated to his left, I was the only one close enough to hear him say, "I feel a thousand years old"— understandable, I thought, for any Republican president having to mingle with the press.

At about 2 a.m., unable to sleep, I turned on the television to see Marlin Fitzwater reveal America's invasion of Panama to snare drug kingpin Manuel Noriega. Earlier that week Noriega had declared war on America, Panamanian soldiers killing unarmed U.S. marines. Bush ordered the invasion—Operation Just Cause—to restore democracy and jail Noriega on drug-related charges. Meeting, we had no idea that Bush had already approved the gravest decision of his presidency. As Robert Schlesinger wrote in his book, "Smith thought that Bush must be the coolest customer in the world. The whole time that he had been entertaining the speechwriters, he had known that the [24,000] troops were on their way in." You would want him on your side playing blind-man's bluff.

Bush: the sunshine of his smile. As 1989 ended, the president addressed the Catholic University of America annual dinner for the second time in three years. "Tonight I'm back again," he told the audience. "Even though I know this isn't what you have in mind when you preach about the Second Coming." More than a thousand people had packed Washington's Pension Building. "For those of you in the back of the room, I'll try to speak up," Bush said. "Cardinal Hickey warned me that the agnostics in this room are very bad." Bush touted religious

Hopeful at the Creation

belief, service, devotion to higher learning, and fidelity to freedom, concluding, "God can live without man, but man cannot live without God." The crowd popped a cork. Later that week Chriss Winston said that the president wanted to see me. I went to the small anteroom off the Oval Office where he crafted his "self-typed" letters. Bush thanked me for the Catholic University speech—"the kind of speech I like," he said. "Anecdotes, humor, structure." I paused. "It's funny. You're Episcopalian, I'm Presbyterian, and the audience was Catholic." Bush laughed. "Well, we're all on the same side," he said.

Bush: stormy weather. Early that year I wrote an eyes-only—for mine—memo for the express purpose of blowing off steam. Its title: "Who Won the Election, Anyway?" Shortly after Bush's inaugural, his defense secretary nominee, former Texas senator John Tower, began being pilloried for private impropriety—namely, that he liked to drink, not unlike other politicians, including his late fellow Texan and president Lyndon Johnson. Washington hypocrisy made only Tower a risk to national security. Instead of bashing Tower's opposition, Bush praised the Senate for "looking at the allegations very carefully," adding, "If somebody comes up with [new anti-Tower] facts, I hope I'm not narrow-minded enough that I wouldn't take a look." In my view, the perception that Bush wouldn't fight led Democrats to believe that they could outface the GOP in the Budget Crisis of 1990, to which we will shortly turn.

Bush had been elected in 1988 on a conservative little guy vs. big guy plank. He felt it more real, I think, than sham. To him, Willie Horton was entirely legitimate—a metaphor for Democrats favoring criminal rights vs. victim rights. Disturbingly, some in our administration felt the issue bogus. Not quislings, exactly, they simply liked a me-too creed that hadn't—*couldn't*—elect a GOP president in our lifetime, before or since. Liking to win, Bush in 1988 showed with whom he stood. In 1989 he unveiled Reagan's official portrait, saying, "For years our opponents were hoping to see President Reagan's back against the wall here in the White House. But I don't think that this is what they had in mind." Bush also presented the National Academy of Engineering Awards, quoting Einstein: "Everything that is really great and inspiring is created by individuals who labor in freedom." He promised brevity to the National Religious Broadcasters: "I know there's a mention in the Bible about the Burning Bush, but I also know I'm not that hot a speaker." Bush was stroking his 1988 base: creators, homeschoolers, small-business people, retirees.

In February 1990 the Sandinistas were voted out of power in free elections in Nicaragua. In Czechoslovakia workers risked imprisonment by passing faded copies of playwright-turned-politician Václav Havel's manuscripts from one reader to another. In China students handed out handbills printed on mimeograph machines detailing the murder in Tiananmen Square. In October 1781 the British band at Yorktown had played "The World Turned Upside Down." In less than two years, Bush had helped invert his world. In the Market Opinion Research poll, Poppy's first four months registered 70 percent approval vs. Nixon's 61, Reagan's 67, and Ike's 74. By mid-1990 his mid-60s monthly approval average swung between 52 and 76 percent. Gallup, ABC News / *Washington Post*, *USA Today*, and NBC News / *Wall Street Journal* showed like results. "Kinder, gentler" seemed to be wearing well.

On March 22, 1990, Bush showed a comic streak to shame Henny Youngman. At a news conference on the South Grounds of the White House, he confirmed a reported ban on broccoli aboard Air Force One, saying, with fists clenched and voice rising, "I do not like broccoli. And I haven't liked it since I was a little kid, and my mother made me eat it. And I'm president of the United States, and I'm not going to eat any more broccoli!" This opened a national dialogue on Bush's teenage eating habits—beef jerky, nachos, tacos, hamburgers, hot dogs, popcorn, ice cream, chili, pork rinds, refried beans, barbecued ribs, and cake—all gobbled like an excavator gulps dirt. Mrs. Bush remained a broccoli holdout, the president said—indeed, a "total totalitarian," threatening to serve him a meal of broccoli soup and salad, a broccoli main course, and as the First Lady said, "finish with a little broccoli ice cream."

That summer Bush taped a Fourth of July TV special from Ford's Theatre, telling a story that President Lincoln loved. Two ladies were debating the merits of Honest Abe and Jefferson Davis, the president of the Confederacy. The first said, "I think Jefferson will succeed because he is a praying man." Second: "But so is Abraham." First: "Yes, but the Lord will think Abraham is joking." By turn, Bush launched Fitness Month on the South Lawn, quoting a fine golfer who often dieted but seldom exercised, Jackie Gleason: "a little traveling music." He addressed the Red Cross, glad to serve as honorary chair, a reason "being that if my speech is a disaster, relief is close at hand." He gloried that Barbara had already become the most popular First Lady, depending on your age, since Jacqueline Kennedy or Eleanor Roosevelt—"Everybody's mother," she said to explain her appeal. Increasingly, Bush feared he might have to *repeal* the pledge that helped make him president.

"Read my lips! No new taxes!" had been Bush's campaign cry—and risk. In 1985 Congress passed the Gramm-Rudman-Hollings Act, mandating a zero federal budget deficit by 1991. Since his inaugural Bush had inherited a huge deficit, Congress had become even more wastrel, and budget deficit estimates for fiscal year 1991 had soared from $111 billion to $171 billion. That year began October 1, 1990. Unless Bush cut the deficit to at least $64 billion, Gramm-Rudman would slash every entry in the federal budget by a draconian 40 percent—defense, farming, education, the elderly. Bush was trapped. Growth had stalled, largely owing to Federal Reserve Chairman Alan Greenspan's refusal to cut interest rates till the deficit shrank. Yet Poppy had vowed not to raise taxes. At the same time, Democrats refused to cut spending—moreover, could override Bush's veto pen, and had. As 1950s television's Chester A. Riley bayed, "What a revoltin' development *this* is!"

In April 1990 Bush and Democratic leaders agreed to new revenue for the 1990 budget. "I mean to live by what I've said: no new taxes," 41 said, publicly. His diary read differently: "If we handle it wrong, our troops will rebel on taxes." Then ABC White House correspondent Brit Hume asked about taxes. "Well, I'd like it [the vow] to be more than a first-year pledge," Bush said, tentatively. On June 25 he, Sununu, budget director Richard Darman, Treasury Secretary

Brady, and Democratic dons met in closed session at Andrews Air Force Base—their aim, broader talks, with other members of each party. House Speaker Tom Foley, replacing Jim Wright, made Bush an offer: entitlement and budget reform, defense and domestic discretionary spending cuts—and new taxes—or risk Gramm-Rudman and continued deadlock. "The more he [Poppy] sat in on the meetings," said Marlin Fitzwater, "the more he decided that regardless of the politics, regardless of the consequences, that he had to raise more money through taxation."

Bush could have gone over Congress to the public, explaining his change of heart. Instead, he trusted the Democrat elite—we'll cover you politically. "He did it out of good motives trying to get something done, as he said, to govern," said Brit Hume. Finally, Bush said, "Okay, if I can say you agreed." Foley and Senate leader Mitchell said fine; Democrats were almost always for new taxes anyway. Bush hoped a pact including new taxes would sire short- and long-term stability. Too late did he grasp the tax reversal's effect on his credibility. In 1517 Martin Luther is said to have nailed his Ninety-Five Theses to the door of All Saints' Church in Wittenberg, Germany, sparking the Reformation. In 1928 Calvin Coolidge announced on the White House bulletin board that he would not seek reelection: "I do not choose to run." Darman wrote a two-sentence statement that Sununu edited, gave to Fitzwater, and had him put on the press office bulletin board—no cause or context about why overnight the White House was crying uncle.

For a time, breaking "No New Taxes" meant chaos. "The budget plan was successful in achieving a non-partisan [adverse] public reaction," said GOP pollster Bob Teeter. "The President's perceived handling of the budget crisis has caused much more disapproval than approval." Later, it became a low-grade fever for much of 1991, dwarfed by Bush's global élan. In 1992 the virus returned to help Ross Perot, making 41 seem just another pol. In 1990 I wrote as many as four fundamentally different drafts of the same budget speech in an afternoon. We were glad to have axed the pledge. We weren't glad, but had been forced to do it. We would never do it again. (This pleased conservatives, not trusting Dems to cut spending.) We just wanted the damn thing done. For Bush's writers, the broken pledge made the 1990 campaign more Kafkaesque than Reaganesque.

At a Detroit fund-raiser, Bush minimized progress toward an agreement. In Iowa the president said he had negotiated for eight months. "The American people didn't send me here [*sic*] to play politics. They sent me here to govern. So I put it all on the table—and I took the heat." In California he called his tax reversal "a serious response to a serious deficit"—and it might have been seen as such had he stayed on message, telling how the act decreed two dollars in spending cuts for each dollar in new taxes. (Ultimately, it didn't happen.) Bush wrote me, "On tonight's speech to political audience, better to not polarize until talks are over for better or worse." He composed this text: "You know how much I want to get a real deficit package. I have composed etc. etc. but now is not the time for partisan rhetoric. Now is the time to get the job done etc. etc." The etc. etc. would have been to inform people how a lower deficit could fuel prosperity—here, till America's longest post–World War II recession began in 2007.

A budget agreement was announced September 30, 1990, raising the top federal individual income tax rate from 28 to 31 percent—a relatively minor, not major, hike. (Today's top rate is 39.6 percent.) Some liberals opposed its spending cuts. As Bush feared, "the [conservative] troops rebelled," having largely been ignored. On October 2 he gave a rare Oval Office speech on network television, saying, "This is the first time in my presidency that I've made an appeal like this to you." Conditions had changed since 1988, Poppy said, a smaller deficit now a prerequisite for growth. Then House minority whip Newt Gingrich had changed as well. At Andrews he backed the deal. Now he pivoted, blasting it and taking most of the GOP House—for Bush, betrayal. "It was stunning to see how many fellow Republicans shot old George out of the saddle," former Senate minority whip Alan Simpson told Bush writer–turned–*U.S. News* columnist Mary Kate Cary in 2014. "[It] brings tears to your eyes." Gingrich Inc. wanted Democrats to further cut spending, deeming "No New Taxes" less political than theological. Only 32 of 168 Republicans backed the final package. It passed because 218 of 246 Democrats voted yes, liking what they saw.

That month I tried bipartisanship too, giving liberal *New York Post* columnist Phil Mushnick and his two young daughters a tour of the White House. Both girls sent thank-you notes, including Laura, age eight: "Dear Mr. Smith: Thank you for the wonderful tour. My sister enjoyed it, too. My father says you are a nice man for a Republican." For months the cliché that the nice man in the Oval Office was more interested in foreign than domestic affairs had become consensus. The administration denied it, except that the cliché was true. Bush himself agreed in his diary on October 6: "There's a story in one of the papers saying that I am more comfortable with foreign affairs, and that is absolutely true. Because I don't like the deficiencies of the domestic, political scene. I hate the posturing on both sides." Having broken the "taxes" pledge, Bush found their speeches no-win to give.

Other speeches were easier, even that summer's Nixon Library dedication at Yorba Linda, California. On one hand, Nixon's once protégé felt betrayed by the 1972 Watergate burglary of Democratic Party headquarters—then, far worse, a cover-up by Nixon officials to protect those party to the crime. On the other, Bush felt gratitude for Nixon's past loyalty and shared his belief that "Americans elect a president for foreign policy," enormously respecting the thirty-seventh president's. Admiring Nixon yet appreciating Bush's attitude, I requested and got the speech. In the Oval Office, we discussed it. "This is sensitive," he said. "I owe Nixon an awful lot, but he lied to me. Try to be gracious, not obsequious." Back at the computer, I squared a circle as I walked Bush's line.

On July 19, 1990, more than seventy-five thousand people sat under a cerulean blue sky: union members, other blue-collar workers, small-business owners, housewives, retirees, farmers—all grandly unhip and unboutique. Nixon had grown up among them, as had I. Presidents Ford and Reagan spoke woodenly and wonderfully, respectively. Bush then rose to introduce Nixon, whereupon John Sununu,

Hopeful at the Creation

sitting in front of me, turned and jibed, deadpan, "Smith, he had better be good."

Bush observed that next-day visitors would be the first to enter America's tenth presidential library. "They will note that only FDR ran as many times as Richard Nixon—five—for national office, each winning four elections, and that [at that time] more people [had] voted for Richard Nixon as president than any other man in history. They will hear of Horatio Alger and Alger Hiss; of the book *Six Crises* and the seventh crisis, Watergate"—Bush's was the only of the day's four presidents to mention it. "They will think of Checkers, Millie's role model. And, yes, Mr. President, they will hear again your answer to my 'vision thing'—'Let me make this perfectly clear.'"

Bush segued to Nixon's family—"Think of his mother, a gentle Quaker"—and Nixon's intellectual complexity—"Knowing how you feel about some intellectuals, Mr. President, I don't mean to offend you." He noted how Nixon "'came from the heart of America'—not geographically, perhaps, but culturally"—then cited RN's domestic policy from ending the draft via revenue sharing to the Environmental Protection Agency.

Above all, said Bush, a visitor would recall Nixon "dedicating his life to the greatest cause offered any president"—peace among nations. In Moscow "Richard Nixon signed the first agreement to limit strategic nuclear arms." In the Middle East, "he planted the first fragile seeds of peace." In Vietnam he pursued "a quest for peace with honor."

"Even now, memories resound of President Nixon's trip to China—the week that revolutionized the world," said one sinophile of another. "No American president had ever stood on the soil of the People's Republic of China. As President Nixon stepped from Air Force One and extended his hand to Zhou Enlai, his vision ended more than two decades of isolation.

"'Being president,' he often said, 'is nothing compared with what you can do as president,'" Bush concluded. "Mr. President, you worked . . . to help achieve a *generation* of peace." As democracy's tide swept the globe, Nixon could take pride that history would say, "Here was a true *architect* of peace."

That night ABC TV's *Nightline* gathered several commentators to dissect the ceremony. Critiquing the speeches, *New York Times* columnist William Safire proclaimed Bush's "the best. It touched every base." Presumably Sununu was pleased.

Fourteen days later—Thursday, August 2—Iraq's Saddam Hussein invaded next-door Kuwait and dubbed it his nation's nineteenth province. In 1940, when Churchill became prime minister with the Nazis at Britain's door, he wrote, "I felt as if . . . all my past life had been but a preparation for this hour and for this trial." Bush must have felt so now—and that a bully had kicked sand in freedom's face. He reacted quickly, his instinct more sure than in the budget process. As if Providence were in Aspen, Colorado, to write a coda, Margaret Thatcher was with Bush at a conference there. "Now, George," she said, famously, "this is no time to go wobbly."

On August 8 Bush delivered an unwobbly speech, written by Mark Lange, in the Oval Office. "In the life of a nation, we're called upon to define who we are and what we believe. Sometimes these choices are not easy," Bush said. "But today as president, I ask for your support in a decision I've made to stand up for what's right and condemn what's wrong, all in the cause of peace." At his behest elements of World War II's famed Eighty-Second Airborne Division and key units of the U.S. Air Force were taking up defensive positions in Saudi Arabia. Iraq proposed a deal to keep half of Kuwait. Bush rejected it, forging a UN armada—Operation Desert Shield. Iraq must withdraw "completely, immediately, and without condition"; its "aggression must not stand."

On Monday, August 20, Bush traveled to Baltimore to address the Veterans of Foreign Wars (VFW) and review the lessons of the last eighteen days "that speak to America and to the world." First, aggression must, and would, be checked—so we had sent U.S. forces to the Middle East reluctantly but decisively. Second, by itself America could do much. With friends and allies, America could do more—so Bush was forging the armada to oppose unprovoked aggression. The third lesson, said Bush, "as veterans won't surprise you: the stead-

Hopeful at the Creation

1. George H. W. Bush, thirteen, in 1937 at Phillips Academy in Andover, Massachusetts. As president, returning in 1989, he said, "I loved this school, this place." GEORGE BUSH PRESIDENTIAL LIBRARY AND MUSEUM

2. Bush (bottom), with unidentified seaman, moments after being rescued by the submarine USS *Finback*, September 2, 1944. Bush was shot down, and two crewmates killed, when the Japanese attacked their plane near Chichi Jima. GEORGE BUSH PRESIDENTIAL LIBRARY AND MUSEUM

3. Babe Ruth (left), dying of throat cancer, presents a manuscript copy of the book *The Babe Ruth Story* to Bush, captain of Yale University's varsity team, before a 1948 game at Yale Field. OFFICIAL WHITE HOUSE PHOTO

4. U.S. senator Prescott Bush and wife Dorothy supplemented each other's strengths. He taught son George self-reliance. She taught him a becoming modesty. Each taught faith, tenacity, and honor. GEORGE BUSH PRESIDENTIAL LIBRARY AND MUSEUM

5. In 1948 Bush left Connecticut to become an independent oil man in Texas. Here he is shown examining equipment on an oil rig with a worker. He entered politics only when financially self-sufficient. GEORGE BUSH PRESIDENTIAL LIBRARY AND MUSEUM

6. Richard Nixon was Bush's first mentor, campaigning for him for Congress and U.S. Senate. In 1971 Bush became the president's UN ambassador—the first step in his impressive foreign policy education. GEORGE BUSH PRESIDENTIAL LIBRARY AND MUSEUM

7. In 1971 Democrat, ex-Texas governor, and Bush rival John Connally became Nixon's secretary of the treasury. Here Connally, to Bush's right, makes a point aboard Air Force One. Nixon listens to rear. RICHARD NIXON PRESIDENTIAL LIBRARY AND MUSEUM

8. In 1980 Ronald Reagan won the GOP presidential nomination, chose Bush as vice president, and
became a beloved and historic president. As veep
Bush earned the Gipper's trust, crucial to his own
presidential election victory in 1988. GEORGE BUSH
PRESIDENTIAL LIBRARY AND MUSEUM

9. After being sworn in as president, Bush delivered his January 20, 1989, inaugural address. The new president paraphrased from Saint Augustine: "In crucial things, unity; in important things, diversity; in all things, generosity." GEORGE BUSH PRESIDENTIAL LIBRARY AND MUSEUM

10. Amid rain in Budapest, Bush tore up author's speech and briefly ad-libbed on July 11, 1989. Listening by intercom in DC, Curt Smith did not know the reason for his public flogging. Back home, Bush sent him this photo, signed, "It's raining in Budapest, I'll wing it, George Bush." REUTERS

11. George and Barbara Bush with English springer spaniel Millie on August 8, 1989, at Walker's Point, estate and home bought and built in the early twentieth century by Bush's family in Kennebunkport, Maine. It became Bush's Summer White House. GEORGE BUSH PRESIDENTIAL LIBRARY AND MUSEUM

12. The author, on first floor of the Eisenhower Executive Office Building (née Old EOB). Next to the White House, it is noted for extremely high ceilings. Since 1969 the writers' corridor in this former State, War, and Navy Building has been called Writers' Row. COURTESY OF AUTHOR

13. On December 1, 1989, Bush held his first meeting as president with Soviet Union general secretary Mikhail Gorbachev on USS *Forrestal* off Malta. Bush also spoke to five thousand sailors, quoting Gen. Dwight D. Eisenhower's D-day address. GEORGE BUSH PRESIDENTIAL LIBRARY AND MUSEUM

14. In late 1989 Smith was summoned to Bush's office to discuss the response to his speech at the Catholic University of America dinner. It had concluded, "God can live without man, but man cannot live without God."

15. On December 19, 1989, no one knew when the president hosted speechwriters in his residence that he had already sent forces to capture Panama's drug duce Manuel Noriega. Only the author, to Bush's left, heard him say, "I feel a thousand years old."

16. When Saddam Hussein invaded Kuwait in
August 1990, Margaret Thatcher told Bush, "Now,
George, this is no time to go wobbly." In March
1991 he gave her the Medal of Freedom, America's
highest civilian award. Smith (left) wrote Bush's
speech about "the greengrocer's daughter."

1O DOWNING STREET
LONDON SW1A 2AA

THE PRIME MINISTER   26 November 1990

Dear Mr. Smith

I received your very kind message on behalf of the White House speech writers, and would just say how much I have admired your marvellously professional work over the last two years. You have produced some splendid speeches which have been a tremendous encouragement to those of us who believe in a free society, and in a leading world role for the United States.

With many thanks and best wishes,

Kind regards.

Yours sincerely

Margaret Thatcher

17. In November 1990 Mrs. Thatcher was ousted from power by a coup d'etat by her Conservative Party. That week the author got her response to a letter he had written with several other writers vowing support for the Iron Lady, who had shaped a nation to her will. COURTESY OF THE THATCHER FOUNDATION

18. At Thanksgiving 1990 President and Mrs. Bush flew to Saudi Arabia to meet with troops of the greatest allied armada since World War II. Their mission: to drive Saddam Hussein from Kuwait. Bush told them, "This aggression will not stand." GEORGE BUSH PRESIDENTIAL LIBRARY AND MUSEUM

19. On March 6, 1991, Operation Desert Storm complete, Bush addressed a joint session of Congress. The president stood, as Edmund Burke once said of a peer, at "the summit. . . . He may live long. He may do much. But he can never exceed what he does this day." GEORGE BUSH PRESIDENTIAL LIBRARY AND MUSEUM

20. The president boarding Marine One, the presidential helicopter. In March 1991 he left the White House for a weekend at the presidential getaway at Camp David. Aides held signs saying "91," meaning Gallup's historic high 91 percent approval rating. GEORGE BUSH PRESIDENTIAL LIBRARY AND MUSEUM

21. In spring 1991 President Bush gathered speechwriters and other aides in the Oval Office to discuss what the administration should do next. The quest for a "domestic Desert Storm" proved elusive as legislative proposals and the economy stalled. OFFICIAL WHITE HOUSE PHOTO

22. On June 8, 1991, the commander in chief was saluted by the armed services which that year helped free a nation. The parade to hail the victorious Gulf War was held on Constitution Avenue in Washington and attracted a half a million spectators. GEORGE BUSH PRESIDENTIAL LIBRARY AND MUSEUM

23. Bush hated politics' incivility. What he liked was on display on July 4, 1991, at Mount Rushmore, showing how four nation builders—Washington, Jefferson, Lincoln, and TR—their likenesses completed half a century earlier, embodied America's core. GEORGE BUSH PRESIDENTIAL LIBRARY AND MUSEUM

24. The 1992 campaign hung over a November 1991 luncheon of Bush with presidential speechwriters. "We need a formulation for placing the blame on Congress for the economy without losing their support," the president said. It was like squaring a circle. OFFICIAL WHITE HOUSE PHOTO

25. (*Opposite top*) Friends of Bush died at Pearl Harbor in 1941. Half a century later, he gave perhaps his presidency's most emotional speech there. "Every fifteen seconds a drop of oil still rises from the [sunken] *Arizona* and drifts to the surface," he said, voice breaking. "It is as though God Himself were crying." GEORGE BUSH PRESIDENTIAL LIBRARY AND MUSEUM

26. (*Opposite bottom*) Christmas at the White House was magical. In 1992, 120,000 visitors saw decorations that included thirty trees with icicles, tinsel, and white lights; needlepoint; toy trains; eleven-foot-tall toy nutcracker soldiers; and a gingerbread house turned Santa's Village. OFFICIAL WHITE HOUSE PHOTO

27. (*Above*) Improbably, Bush lost the 1992 election, getting only 37.5 percent of the vote. On October 19 he debated victorious Democratic nominee Bill Clinton (center) and third-party candidate H. Ross Perot. Perot lured 18.9 percent of the vote, most of it from Bush. GEORGE BUSH PRESIDENTIAL LIBRARY AND MUSEUM

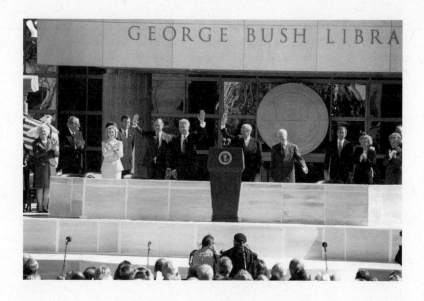

28. (*Above*) Five U.S. presidents—the current (Clinton), three past (Bush, Carter, and Ford), and one future (George W. Bush)—shared November 1997's dedication of the George Bush Presidential Library and Museum at Texas A&M University at College Station, Texas. GEORGE BUSH PRESIDENTIAL LIBRARY AND MUSEUM

29. (*Opposite top*) On June 12, 2009, to honor two crewmates killed when the Japanese destroyed their Avenger plane in 1944, Bush did a tandem parachute jump in Kennebunkport with the U.S. Army Golden Knights to mark his eighty-fifth birthday. Amazingly, he encored at ninety in 2014. GEORGE BUSH PRESIDENTIAL LIBRARY AND MUSEUM

30. (*Opposite bottom*) The former First Couple at the Bush Presidential Library and Museum in 2002. In 2013 President Obama invited them back to the White House for the five thousandth daily Point of Light Award, an honor given by the famed volunteer program begun by Bush. GEORGE BUSH PRESIDENTIAL LIBRARY FOUNDATION. Chandler Arden, photographer

GEORGE BUSH

March 14, 2001

Dear Olivia,

Just a few weeks ago, you arrived in your new home, Rochester, New York in the United States of America. Welcome!

Already you are a lucky little girl -- luckier than most -- for you have a mother and dad who love you so much.

And you have friends, too. I want to be your friend. I used to be President of the United States. Now, though, I am a happy, private citizen; but I know something true. Family and friends are what really count. Your mother and father are my friends. Your dad, a very talented writer, worked with me in the White House long before you were born, and we all love him – and your mom, too.

All the best to you, Olivia. I hope your exciting life ahead in your new homeland is full of happiness, and I hope you spend all of it living in a world at peace.

Sincerely,

GB

Miss Olivia Smith
Two Woodbriar Lane
Rochester, New York 14624

P. O. BOX 79798 · HOUSTON, TEXAS 77279-9798
PHONE (713) 686-1188 · FAX (713) 683-0801

31. In 2001 Bush learned that the author and his wife were about to adopt two very young children from Ukraine, a country that the president, helped by others here and abroad, had helped to liberate. Unsolicited, he wrote each child a letter that they received upon arriving in America. COURTESY OF PRESIDENT GEORGE H. W. BUSH

fast character of the American will. Look at the sands of Saudi Arabia and the waters offshore—where brave Americans are doing their duty—just as *you* did at Inchon, Remagen, and Hamburger Hill."

A fourth lesson concerned the future size of the U.S. armed forces: smaller because "the threat to our security is changing," said Bush, with American defense capacity greater—"a lean, mean fighting machine." When it comes to national defense, "finishing *second* means finishing *last*," he argued, noting that more than half of all VFW members fought in World War II. "Half a century ago, the world had the chance to stop an aggressor, and missed it," the president said. "I pledge to you: Unlike isolationists here and abroad, *we will not make that mistake again*."

This was the first speech in which Bush likened Hussein to Hitler. It wasn't easy. Bush's writers, like the president, tried to include the comparison, prompting the National Security Council to erase it, at which point writers reinstated it. In this speech, I put it in, the NSC took it out, then Bush ad-libbed it—all in the name of exquisitely named *reconciliation*. Next month he spoke to Congress, setting four immediate goals: "Iraq must leave Kuwait . . . Kuwait's legitimate government must be restored. The security and stability of the Persian Gulf must be assured. And American citizens abroad must be protected." Bush also foresaw a new world order. More tangibly, Congress okayed the use of military force.

For 166 days Bush tried to peacefully remove Hussein from Kuwait. The president knew what he meant to say and said it. I often arrived at the White House, checked my mailbox, and found page after page of text "self-typed" by him the previous night. I retyped it; fixed grammar, spelling, and punctuation; used the president's text as the first draft; and seldom deviated from its spine. Bush was involved at every level of Gulf War speech preparation. By contrast, his explanation of the budget process in the 1990 midterm campaign was considerably less thorough. "The budget agreement was as good as we could get," he said. "It would have been better with a GOP Congress." Looking back, it would have been best if Congress didn't treat fiscal discipline like malaria or beriberi.

With the election over—essentially a wash in each house—the president turned wholly to foreign policy, i.e., the Persian Gulf. He flew in Air Force One with Mrs. Bush and General Norman Schwarzkopf, head of U.S. Central Command, escorted by F-15 Eagle fighter jets, to spend Thanksgiving Day with U.S. troops stationed in Saudi Arabia. As *White House Ghosts* relates, Bush found the day's remarks, written movingly by McNally, too personal. "Dave," he asked Demarest, "what are you trying to do to me?"—he was afraid he would break down. The communications head began to delete text. Bush joined him. Next day editing continued. Finally, Marines encircling Bush, Demarest saw the light: "The power of him [Bush] being with the troops really was the message." Less *was* more.

Bush returned to an America less of war fever than the sheer intention to see war through—January 15, 1991, was the UN-set deadline for Hussein to withdraw his troops from Kuwait. "No one wanted war less than I, but we will see it through," Bush wrote in his diary. On Sunday, January 13, he added, "It is my decision—my decision to send these kids into battle, my decision that may affect the lives of innocence [*sic*]. . . . It is my intention to step back and let the sanctions work. Or to move forward. . . . I know what I have to do. . . . This man is evil, and let him win and we rise again to fight tomorrow," as after Munich, appeasement bred World War II.

"There is no way to describe the pressure," said the man who, almost killed at twenty, knew war perhaps as well as any U.S. president. The bombing would begin at 7 p.m. on January 16. The president would address the nation two hours later. Dan McGroarty wrote two initial drafts. Bush—saying, "I want to write this speech myself"—did, referencing parts of McGroarty's text. The president's draft asked the question, "Why act now?"

He answered, "While the world waited, Saddam Hussein systematically raped, pillaged, and plundered a tiny nation, no threat to his own. . . . While the world waited, Saddam sought to add to the chemical weapons arsenal he now possesses, an infinitely more dangerous weapon of mass destruction—a nuclear weapon. And while the world waited, while the world talked peace and withdrawal, Saddam Hussein dug in and moved massive forces into Kuwait."

Five months earlier Hussein had started this "cruel war against Kuwait," Bush said. "Tonight, the battle has been joined."

At 10:45 that night, Bush again wrote in his diary: "I am about to go to bed. I didn't feel nervous about it at all. . . . I knew what I wanted to say, and I said it. And I hope it resonates."

Victory would ensure it did.

TEN

Bush at the Summit

On January 17, 1991, Operation Desert Shield turned Desert Storm. The first attack included more than four thousand bombing runs by coalition aircraft against Saddam Hussein's forces and locales. For the next five weeks, CNN TV showed the first high-tech war, mesmerizing viewers raised on *Mission Impossible*, *Star Trek*, and Luke Sykwalker in an America that had stormed Normandy, split the atom, and beat the Ruskies to the moon. Night after night we witnessed smart bombs and Scuds and Patriot missiles. It was captivating—also distant, therefore safe. Though no troops were in combat, some in Congress, plucking a figure from the air, prophesied 100,000 "body bags." Ignoring Hussein's brutality, Bush's own presiding bishop said force would be immoral. Said the *New York Times*, "War never leaves . . . a President where it found him." Yellow ribbons dotted America. Church attendance spiraled. At the National Hockey League All-Star Game at Chicago Stadium, the crowd sang the National Anthem so wildly as to give "the roof came off" new connotation.

At a time like this, it is not unusual for a president to try to crush his opposition. In a 1936 speech, Franklin Roosevelt said of businessmen, "They are united in their hatred of me—and I welcome their hatred." The reaction at Madison Square Garden was primal, almost atavistic. In 1969 Richard Nixon's Silent Majority speech demonized elite hostility. In 2012 Barack Obama, aiming to shred conservatism, said, "We're gonna punish our enemies and we're gonna reward our friends." Bush's response to the Gulf War was antipodal. At the peak of his career, he respected his critics enough to tell them how, and why, he had reached his decision to use force. Bush didn't need to. In January 1991 his opposition was as strong as Charles Atlas's ninety-eight-pound weakling. He did it anyway—a sublimely civil gesture by a supremely civil man.

Clerics, educators, and policy experts debated what constitutes a "just war"—how could force be used and "still uphold," as our text said, "moral values like tolerance, compassion, faith, and courage"? Delivered January 28 in Washington, the address quoted the clergyman Richard Cecil: "There are two classes of the wise: the men who serve God because they have found Him, and the men who seek Him because they have not found Him yet." Bush's task, he said, was to "serve and seek wisely"—e.g., Saddam Hussein vs. the world. Hussein had "tried to cast this conflict as a religious war—but it has nothing to do with religion per se." It had "*everything* to do with what religion *embodies*," said Bush. "Good versus evil. Right versus wrong. Human dignity and freedom versus tyranny and oppression." The Gulf War was "not a Christian war or a Jewish war—or a Muslim war. It is a Just War—and it is a war in which good will prevail."

The principles of a "just war" originated with classical Greek and Roman philosophers like Plato and Cicero, later expounded by such Christian theologians as Ambrose, Augustine, and Thomas Aquinas, I wrote. Their first principle, Bush said, was that it support a just cause. To Bush, the Gulf War was ennobling. It would free Kuwait, end Iraq's brutal occupation, and ensure that "naked aggression will not be rewarded." A just war must also be declared by legitimate authority—here, by nonpareil UN solidarity; the principle of collective self-defense; twelve Security Council resolutions; and twenty-eight nations from six continents united—resolute. "We're not going it alone," Bush said of America, "but believe me, we *are* going to see it through."

A just war, he continued, was fought for right reasons—moral, not selfish. Bush told of a family whose two sons, eighteen and nineteen, reportedly refused to lower the Kuwaiti flag in front of their home.

"For this crime, they were executed by the Iraqis. Then, unbeliev-ably, their parents were asked to pay the price of the bullets used to kill them." Was it moral for force to stop such slaughter? Said Bush: "It would be immoral *not* to use force." A fourth principle was that a just war would be a last resort when all else had failed. Seeking peace, James Baker had more than two hundred meetings with for-eign dignitaries, ten diplomatic missions, six congressional appear-ances, and more than 103,000 miles traveled to talk with, among others, members of the UN, Arab League, and European commu-nity. Hussein "made this Just War an *inevitable* war."

Finally, if war must be fought, the fifth principle was to conduct it in proportion to the threat, making "every effort possible to keep casualties to a minimum." We would try to avoid harming the inno-cent, not bomb civilian areas, yet have "total commitment to a suc-cessful outcome." The Gulf War would not be "another Vietnam." Bush knew that "some disagree with the course that I have taken. I have no bitterness in my heart about that, no anger. I am convinced that we are doing the right thing—and tolerance is a virtue, not a vice." Abraham Lincoln was once asked if he thought the Lord was on his side. He said, "My concern is not whether God is on *our* side, but whether *we* are on *God's* side." More than ever, Bush closed, he could not imagine being president without trust in Him.

One year earlier Bush had sent a "self-typed" note for a speech introducing a lecture on Lincoln and the presidency, asking me to "work in" that "I have been President for less than a year, but I am ["personally," written by hand] more convinced than ever that one cannot be President of this country without believing in God, with-out a belief in prayer. . . . Lincoln talked about spending times on one's knees. Though not tested as Lincoln was tested, I know now how true those words were."

The Gulf War was Bush's test. Among the most telling pictures shows the First Couple, eyes closed, deep in prayer, at a service in the chapel at Camp David two days before Bush announced the air war. He had always worried about showing tears in public—"the emo-tion." Now, tears streaming down his cheeks, George Bush thought more about "those young men and women overseas." Looking up, Poppy saw his home minister—Claude Payne of St. Martin's Episcopal Church in Houston—"smiling back. And I no longer worried about how I looked to others."

Bush gave the "just war" speech to provide a moral framework for his decision almost a month before UN ground forces invaded Kuwait on February 24. The Allies broke Iraqi lines, moved toward Kuwait City, and in the country's western part, intercepted Hussein's retreating army—Saddam's Mother of Battles soon his Orphan of Defeats. Israel so trusted Bush that it abided Iraqi bombing sans response, preserving UN and Arab solidarity against Hussein. On February 27 Bush addressed the nation to report that the United States and its allies would "suspend" combat operations after only one hundred hours. The president acted to minimize U.S. casualties— also because he had spectacularly fulfilled the UN mandate to boot the bully from Kuwait.

At the time carpers knocked Bush for not pursuing Hussein back to Baghdad, removing him from power. Bush replied, "We would have incurred incalculable human and political costs. We would have been forced to occupy Baghdad and, in effect, rule Iraq." Many disagreed. They—I among them—were wrong. In a twist worthy of Dostoyevsky, President George W. Bush declared war in 2003 against the very leader that Bush *père* had demolished a decade earlier. "You break it. You own it," said Colin Powell, Bush 41's chair of the Joint Chiefs of Staff and Bush 43's secretary of state. W. invaded Iraq, removed Hussein, and became the occupier. To many it took the son's risk to redeem the father's caution.

In February 1991 Bush taped an eightieth birthday salute to Ronald Reagan, whom he said defined "what you described as the American song: 'Hopeful, big-hearted, idealistic, daring, decent, and fair.'" Even here Bush's mind was on his mission, adding to my draft: "I join all Americans in rejoicing at the high level of technical advantage that we enjoy in our war with Iraq." The video included his self-typed "When I think of the accuracy of our missiles and the superb performance of our planes, I think of your passionate conviction that no American should be asked to fight unless equipped with the very best. Your fighting for strong defense budgets over the eight years you were President is paying off now for every man and woman fighting for our country half-way around the world." Margaret Thatcher would be at the dinner, Bush adding, "May God bless PM [Prime Minister] Thatcher and those courageous men and women of the UK who are fighting shoulder to shoulder with our brave troops."

Comedian Dana Carvey once called Bush's mot "wouldn't be prudent" the president's third middle name. Freeze early 1991: for once, the Prudent Man had jumped over the moon. "By God," he said, "we've licked the Vietnam syndrome once and for all!" On March 6 Poppy addressed a joint session of Congress, saying, "I come to this House to speak about the world—the world after war." As they met, "Saddam walks amidst ruin. His war machine is crushed." From division Bush saw "a new world coming into view," quoting Churchill, a new world order in which "the principles of justice and fair play protect the weak against the strong." On June 8 Operation Desert Storm commanders saluted Bush during the victory parade on Washington's Constitution Avenue; half a million watched. The president stood, as Edmund Burke once described a peer, "at the summit. He may live long, he may do much. But . . . he can never exceed what he does this day."

Hussein's demolition put the Arab-Israeli peace process back in play. That July Bush and Gorbachev signed the Strategic Arms Reduction Treaty (START I)—the first major arms pact since 1987's INF Treaty. Lech Wałęsa received the Medal of Freedom as "the first democratically elected president [of Poland]," said Bush, having "forged a solidarity of spirit which has held millions of Poles to gather in steel mills and shipyards and tenements and towns. They knew that some would die in the crusade against aggression. Yet they cheered as they sang to you, 'Sto lat.'—May he live one hundred years! *Our* task is to help freedom live still longer." *New York Times* columnist Russell Baker wrote that Bush had gained "a popularity and stature almost inconceivable for any president in his third year in office."

Another *Times* columnist, Abe Rosenthal, told me, "He is giving America the best leadership abroad this nation has ever seen." A *USA Today* poll read, "Bush: 91 percent approval"—Gallup's historic high. In March he had left for a weekend at the presidential getaway at Camp David. Staff members and families congregated on the South Lawn to say good-bye. It was surreal and couldn't last. Hand-lettered signs read, "The Great Liberator" and "91." How could Bush top the topper? The question lingers, even now.

On February 27 Bush spoke to the American Society of Association Executives about education, opportunity, and crime—"part of our domestic Desert Storm," said its writer, Mary Kate Grant. The audience response rivaled "one hand clapping. Maybe they weren't ready to move on [from the war]." In his March 6 Persian Gulf victory speech, the president asked Congress "to move forward aggressively on our domestic front." Bush noted the already enacted: a historic Clean Air Act; child-care legislation; the landmark Americans with Disabilities Act; the Immigration Act of 1990, increasing legal entrée to the United States by 40 percent. Now, he urged Capitol Hill to pass pending administration programs, first in crime and transportation, then civil rights and energy. "If our forces could win the ground war in a hundred hours," he said, "then surely the Congress can pass this legislation in a hundred days."

Bush knew that foreign policy rarely elects a president. An exception had been Nixon's forty-nine-state 1972 landslide, tying his trip to China, arms treaty with the Soviet Union, and winnowing of the war. Even its foundation had been "the United States in the midst of a new economic boom," artificially helped by 1971–73 wage and price controls, said the *New York Times*. Bush often said, "We know what works. Freedom works." If the economy worked, among other things, Poppy could return to foreign affairs. As we have seen, Bush inherited a huge federal deficit from Reagan: three times 1980's. Raising taxes to curb it pleased the Left at the cost of a conservative revolt. To Sununu, that rebellion cost the GOP a chance to own the 1990s recovery. "That budget agreement was much more significant than people recognize," he said in 2014, noting that the deficit fell and economy rose in what would have been Bush's second term.

For the moment, the economy fell further. A mild recession had begun in 1990. As unemployment rose, Bush added benefits for jobless workers. Downsizing cost many largely Republican and independent white-collar jobs. In 1991 Bush convened about twenty political aides, went around the table, and asked each for advice. Almost all urged him to pump-prime the economy—now. Bush refused. He had named Fred Malek, former Marriott Hotels president, as 1992 campaign manager, working with Teeter and fund-raiser Robert Mosbacher. Malek now told the president that he needed above all to insulate himself from the recession. Eighteen months before Election Day, Bush answered that he had already done all that was needed to win a second term, citing low inflation and interest rates. Inexplicably, economists had convinced the Yale '48 economics major that in 1992 America would be recession-proof.

That being—at least seeming—true, some wanted to restore exemptions for high-income taxpayers and reduce marginal tax rates. Many wanted Bush to make good on his 1988 campaign: voluntary prayer in school; a less coarse culture; teach, not torch, American history. Others wanted him to forcefully enunciate a Reaganesque approach to government: keep taxes and spending low and liberties unencumbered. Bush was sympathetic, I think, to each view. Inevitably, though, the president returned to foreign policy, like an old tune or first love.

No ally was a greater friend of late twentieth century America than, as Bush said, another recipient of the Medal of Freedom— "the greengrocer's daughter who shaped a nation to her will." As the reader has seen, in August 1990 Margaret Thatcher was at a conference with Bush when Hussein invaded Kuwait. "Now, George, this is no time to go wobbly" was her advice he recited in the months ahead. That November Thatcher was removed from office by a coup d'etat of her own Tory party—a cabal she would have called the "wets"— Britain's answer to U.S. RINOS.

In 1981 Thatcher was the first official guest of the newly inaugurated President Reagan. In 1988 she was his last White House guest before the Gipper left office. She died in 2013, at eighty-seven, nine years after Reagan "left this beachhead for another," as he once said of American and Allied D-day fatalities. Shakespeare could have been describing Britain's only female prime minister: "[We] shall not look upon [her] like again."

First elected in 1979, she found Britain economically on her knees—so Thatcher decreased what government must do and increased what the individual may do. She axed inflation, slashed price controls, and privatized public housing so that the poor could own their homes.

Thatcher found her island nation unsure of its mythic past—so that when Argentina threatened Britain's Falkland Islands, she formed an armada to defend their rights, as had elsewhere Lord Nelson and the Duke of Wellington and her hero, Winston Churchill.

Under her the special relationship between America and the United Kingdom became even more unbreakable—so that when Hussein began the Gulf War, the two partners plotted policy in tandem. Churchill wrote Britain's finest hour; Thatcher perhaps democracy's finest era.

Thatcher, relishing the sobriquet, was called the Iron Lady. Once a clique of Tories urged her to U-turn a policy. "Turn if *you* like," she admonished them. "The Lady is not for turning." Her strength came from a need to work and belief in tradition, sovereignty, family, and British—by extension, American—exceptionalism. It produced a pitch-perfect affinity with both nations' middle-class instincts and intuitions.

In 1991 I was asked to write Bush's speech giving Thatcher the Medal of Freedom. Jotting notes, I thought of how her upright upbringing—the family lived above her father's store—evoked the character of sublime World War II films like *Mrs. Miniver*. Her background produced the woman whose picture can be found in thousands of homes in Eastern Europe, where she showed, as was said of

Charles de Gaulle, that "greatness knows no national boundaries." The Iron Curtain was no match for the Iron Lady.

My last memory of Thatcher was her scalding and brilliant November 22, 1990, Question Time farewell in Parliament upon her leaving office. "[For those opposing her policies] it's all compromise . . . it's sweep it under the carpet, leave it for another day, it might sort out and sort itself, in the hope that the people . . . would not notice," she said, hecklers crushed, the ancient hall roaring in approbation.

I recall a tale of the London cabbie, hearing Thatcher's speech by radio, laughing and crying so hard he had to pull off the road. *"Just listen to her!"* he said. "Maggie's leaving"—her heart breaking—"and she's givin' 'em hell. What a woman! God, we're going to miss her." We have and do. Thatcher left, a lioness in winter. The Rockies would crumble before this great Briton did.

Coda. In mid-1990 I began to talk informally with several Tory members of the British parliament about the possibility of writing for Prime Minister Thatcher for a short period through a leave of absence or secondment from the White House. Thatcher, it seemed, might be well inclined. Jonathan Aitken, a conservative member of Parliament (MP), wrote Peter Morrison, Mrs. Thatcher's parliamentary private secretary, who contacted Aitken and me just before she was deposed by the conservative coup. "I have been in touch with him," Morrison then wrote Aitken of me, "but sadly, the need does not now arise." On November 22, as Thatcher led her final Question Time, a loyalist shouted, "You can wipe the floor with those people!" That week Thatcher graciously replied to a letter our speech staff had mailed to London.

Dear Mr. Smith:

I received your very kind message on behalf of the White House speech writers, and would just say how much I have admired your marvellously professional work over the last two years. You have produced some splendid speeches which have been a tremendous encouragement to those of us who believe in a free society, and in a leading world role for the United States.

With many thanks and best wishes.

Kind regards.

Yours sincerely,

Margaret Thatcher

Like Franklin Roosevelt, Harry Truman, Ike, Kennedy, Reagan, and Bill Clinton, among many others, Bush treasured the "special relationship." In 1939 King George VI of England visited Washington. Presenting the singer Kate Smith to His Majesty, FDR said, "This *is* America." He also knew what Great Britain was: a nation joined to ours by heritage and culture, civilization and law.

A song that year vowed "There'll always be an England." In 1940 the Nazi blitz sowed doubt about whether even the country's capital would survive. After being spared, Buckingham Palace, like the rest of London, was bombed. "Finally, we can look the [battered blue-collar] East Side in the face," said the future Queen Mother, Elizabeth, feeling that England's stiff upper lip and stiffer spine would gain American sympathy, then aid.

In 1991 her daughter, Queen Elizabeth II, visited Washington for the first time since 1976, when, as she said, "with a gallant disregard for history, we shared wholeheartedly in the celebrations of the two hundredth anniversary of the founding of this great nation." I was honored to write each of Bush's five speeches honoring Her Majesty, starting with her May 14 arrival on the South Lawn. Terming her "freedom's friend," Bush noted that at eighteen she had fought in World War II "against fascism." America "began to know you as one of us, summoning . . . our values and our dreams.

"For nearly four hundred years," said the president, "the histories of Britain and America have been inseparable"—from Jamestown and Plymouth Rock to "the sands and seas of the Persian Gulf. Years from now [men and women] will talk of the First Infantry Division and the Desert Rats and of the finest sons and daughters any nation could ever have."

Bush then quoted from Elizabeth, twenty-one, in 1947's wake of World War II, over radio to the British people: "My whole life, whether it be long or short, shall be devoted to your service and the service of our family to which we all belong." She concluded, "But I shall not have strength to carry out the resolution alone unless you join it with me." By twenty-six Queen Elizabeth II had braved her father's death, become monarch, and begun a reign to rival Victoria's.

Bush said, "Your example helped inspire a nation—and helped your nation inspire the world." On behalf of America, "which reveres [its] mother country," he introduced the queen. Memorably, event staff had placed the podium too high for her, so Her Majesty's hat peered from behind the mike. She recalled that "it is forty years since our first visit to this country, when Mr. Truman was president. It made such a deep impression that I can hardly believe that so many years have slipped past in the meanwhile."

Now, she said, "I fully understand what Winston Churchill meant when he spoke of the inspiration and renewed vitality he found every time he came here. In her third as in her first century, the United States represents an ideal, an emblem, and an example: an ideal of freedom under the law, an emblem of democracy, and an example of constant striving for the betterment of the people."

Two hours later Bush received the Winston Churchill Award for "the leadership you have shown to the world in recent months," said the queen in the Rose Garden. Accepting, Bush was to say, "Like Gladstone, Churchill forged a fidelity to honor. Like Disraeli, he rallied others to that cause. We can never reinvent him—but we must never forget him. So we are here to recall what he meant, and what he was.

"Churchill provided hope when the free world had abandoned it," the president's text continued. "He was likened to the bull dog—but to the enemy he was a pit bull. When Britain was under attack by the godless, it was sustained by a leader whom God must have bestowed at its time of greatest peril." Bush's peril was 100 percent humidity. "I have prepared here about a forty-five-minute speech, but if I gave it, we would all melt," he said, the crowd laughing. Bush thanked the queen, ended the event, and at least didn't tear up my cards.

Ten minutes later, back on the South Lawn, Bush recalled how in 1937 FDR "celebrat[ed] the British-American family by praising

Bush at the Summit

a friend," planting two "small-leaf linden trees . . . in honor of your father, King George the Sixth's coronation. For decades they stood erect and proud, like the ties that bind our nations." In September 1990 a storm in the Washington area had destroyed one of the lindens. Bush could think "of no better way to show our friendship . . . than to plant a new linden tree."

It was Bush's honor "now to dedicate this tree to a truly great and good man, King George the Sixth," who reigned until his death in 1952, whereupon Elizabeth succeeded him. In 2011 an Oscar-winning film, *The King's Speech*, showed King George's courage in combating stuttering. Like Queen Elizabeth's visit to Washington, it exuded class.

Class is not a term Democrats would instantly apply to Lee Atwater—rather, profane, populist, incendiary, a 33 1/3 RPM record played at 78 speed, and win at all costs, which he did. Some would say racist—wrongly, I think—in his early incarnation. Others might say bright, shrewd, knowing "the depth, the draught of water of every one of [his candidates, districts, and constituents]," paraphrasing Emerson. They might even call Atwater the Roy Hobbs of campaign strategists: if not the best there ever was, the best of the GOP's.

In 1988 the native Georgian piloted Connecticut Yankee George Bush to the presidency; the two formed an irrepressible combination of the pauper and patrician. Had Atwater lived, I feel almost sure that Bush would have been reelected handsomely in 1992. *National Journal*'s Tom DeFrank tentatively disagrees. "Atwater might have forced Bush to focus on the 'out of touch' charge then beginning," he said. "His trouble was that Americans had basically decided that twelve years of Reagan were enough." Meanwhile, millions, flocking to Ross Perot, became estranged because Bush hadn't been *enough* like Reagan. "So you had an internal contradiction in what Atwater would have had to do."

DeFrank cites a late 1991 Bush note to doubt whether he would have even run. "'It's going to be an ugly year,' Bush said. I wonder if he ever had the fire in the belly." Atwater, who did, was named GOP national chairman in 1989, developed cancer in 1990, and died in 1991, having known Middle America like the scale on his guitar. In 1940 Republicans mocked FDR's third-term campaign of indispensability, as if only he could combat "Hitlerism." Roosevelt was indispensable. Atwater was indispensable, politically. Since his death, with the possible exception of Bush 43's Karl Rove, no Republican has approached Atwater's grasp of tactic, history, and strategy—witness a GOP unhorsed by Bill Clinton and Barack Obama. In the Bush 41 White House, John Sununu was closest, though it surprises how few grasped that at the time.

Sununu was born in Havana, was raised in the Big Apple borough of Queens, got his doctorate in mechanical engineering at the Massachusetts Institute of Technology, and later became a three-term New Hampshire governor and father of eight sons. He was conservative in dress and policy. He fathomed who elected Bush in 1988 and why. He could be barbed, making *Time*'s May 21, 1990, cover—"Bush's Bad Cop." He was often *literally* the smartest person in the room. If you backed down or were a blowhard, Sununu had little use for you. If you stood up to him and weren't, you generally got along fine.

In early 1991 Chriss Winston left the White House to free-lance and spend more time with her pre-kindergarten son. Sununu quickly picked Tony Snow to replace her as speech editor and also to become chief writer. He was thirty-five, a Davidson graduate, editorial page editor of the rightist *Washington Times*, and more conservative than Winston or Demarest, whom Sununu ignored in Snow's hiring. Tony quickly began regular speech meetings, encouraging a locker-room give-and-take on how Bush could aggressively convey a more conservative air.

As in 1988, I wanted Bush to run on foreign policy and cultural conservatism. After all, it beat Dukakis. (The same amalgam also won in 1968, 1972, 1980, and 1984.) Some wanted him to become the environmental president. In 1992 Bush rightly gave many green speeches. Others wanted to accent economic growth; at this point there wasn't much. Some fixated on proving the GOP wasn't as mean as Dems insisted—inane then and now. Speech meetings also discussed wearability—key amid 24/7 coverage. In 2012 Queen Elizabeth observed her Diamond Jubilee. No newsstand snubbed her. That summer 220 million Americans made the London Olympics our most-watched-ever event. Each wore well. After eight years America hadn't tired of Reagan. After three, had it tired of Bush?

Arriving, Snow got Bush to use the 1991 commencement speech at the University of Michigan to lash speech codes erasing language "hateful"—often, simply unpopular—to the left-wing sensibility. In totalitarian countries, secret police crush freedom of expression. Today, Bush told the crowd, academe's political correctness does. "Ironically, on the two hundredth anniversary of our Bill of Rights, we find free speech under assault throughout the United States, including on some college campuses," Bush said. "The notion of political correctness has ignited controversy across the land. . . . What began as a crusade for civility has soured into a cause of conflict and even censorship. Disputants treat sheer force—getting their foes punished or expelled, for instance—as a substitute for the power of ideas."

Bush's broadside was prescient. I think he would have tried in a second term to lessen PC's assault on unfettered speech. In one speech he hailed "a government of the extended hand—not closed mind and self-indulgent heart." Bush wished he could move as swiftly on domestic issues as on foreign policy—"Let me deny I plan to meet with the world's most venerable remaining Communist leader [U.S. Communist Party leader], Gus Hall," he joked—but couldn't. "The president can propose—but only Congress can legislate." Bush bristled as unemployment rose, Democrats revived, and tales grew of him being "out of touch." By fall Bush said, "Last March 6, I challenged Congress to pass crime and transportation bills. It's 225 days later, and Congress is still in mental recess." Humor was an antidote: "Driving over here, I heard Randy Travis singing, 'It's just a matter of time.' What a relief to hear a song expressing confidence in my ultimate ability to catch a fish."

Increasingly, even the judiciary showed what Bush called "the deficiencies of the domestic political scene," why he "hate[d] the posturing on both sides." In 1990 Supreme Court nominee David Souter, proposed to Sununu by liberal New Hampshire U.S. senator Warren Rudman, was approved by the Senate, only to promptly "turn on us"—the same phrase Thomas Dewey had used about Earl Warren four decades earlier in Ike's administration—each an alleged conservative who became a radical judicial wrecker. In September 1991, not about to err again, Bush nominated African-American Clarence Thomas, the real thing, to Sununu's right. With reelection near, the president did what he hadn't with John Tower in 1989: put his prestige on the line. It worked. Thomas was narrowly confirmed. For a quarter century, Thomas and Antonin Scalia have been ballasts of strict constructionism.

Thomas "gave a powerful captivating opening statement to Congress," Bush wrote in his diary. "I am proud of the job he did. There was not a dry eye in the place"—nor soon a dispassionate voice as ex-intern Anita Hill used pornographic prose to accuse Thomas of sexual harassment. Campaigning, Bush told a crowd, "Republican control of Congress would avoid the vicious character assassination to great Americans like Clarence Thomas. With the support of special interest groups, Congress has replaced the process of advise and consent with the politics of revise and attack." Finding it hard to hate people, Bush hated such incivility. The politics he liked illumined the Fourth of July 1991 at Mount Rushmore, South Dakota, Poppy showing how four nation builders, their likenesses completed by brave men half a century earlier, embodied America's core. Washington forged independence. Jefferson stirred democracy. Lincoln demanded equality. Theodore Roosevelt—TR—preserved what Bush called "the very wonder of the environment."

The president began with the father of our country. Ben Franklin, then American minister to France, attended a diplomatic dinner in Paris during the War for Independence. "First a French official rose, toasting Louis XVI and comparing him to the moon," said Bush. "The British ambassador then toasted *his* monarch, George III, likening him to the sun." Finally, the aging Franklin stood to speak: "I cannot give you the sun nor the moon, but I give you George Washington . . . who, like Joshua of old, commanded both the sun and the moon to stand still, and both obeyed."

Jefferson, Bush resumed, obeyed his endless curiosity, knowing "how self-determination could unleash the full flower of the individual American." Traveling, "Jefferson stopped in an inn and began conversation with a stranger. They talked of mechanics, and the stranger decided the newcomer must be an *engineer*," said the president. "When the talk shifted to agriculture, it seemed Jefferson must be a *farmer*. More talk led the stranger to think Jefferson must be a *lawyer*, then a *physician*, then a *clergyman*. The following day, when Jefferson left, the stranger learned that he was merely *president*."

All of us learned from Lincoln. He preserved the Union, abolished slavery, and said, "As I would not be a slave, so I would not be a master." Bush felt that Abe would also want him to tell a story. "A stranger found him on the street with two of his sons. Both of them were sobbing uncontrollably. 'Whatever is the matter with the boys, Mr. Lincoln?' the stranger asked. Lincoln sighed, then said: 'Just what's the matter with the world. I've got three walnuts, and each wants two.'"

Like each face on Mount Rushmore, Lincoln was pulled in countless directions, living in a time of extraordinary peril. Yet each acted extraordinarily, like the monument's final face, Teddy Roosevelt, grasping "that to widely *use* we must wisely *serve* our national and cultural resources," said Bush. "To preserve them, we must protect them. TR expanded the size of the National Forest by 40 million acres. He created five National Parks and sixteen monuments, including the Grand Canyon. Above all, he used the bully pulpit—to TR, the essence of the presidency."

By mid-1991 did Bush's essence resonate as it had even a few months earlier? That spring the *New York Times*'s Maureen Dowd had written, "This President relaxes by wearing the others out." Surprisingly, Poppy then lost fifteen pounds in six weeks. (The ultimate diagnosis was Graves' disease, which causes an overactive thyroid.) In May the seemingly preternaturally young Bush, sixty-six, was hospitalized for two days, for atrial fibrillation, an irregular heartbeat discovered while the president was jogging. The incidents bruised Bush's persona and convinced some that he was no longer up to the job. A few felt him old-timey, not in sync with a postmodern culture. Like Churchill, Bush had been an exquisite war leader. A people's peace priorities can differ, as the Brits showed in 1945.

At one end Bush's Gallup approval still topped 70 percent, easily besting any 1992 Democratic contender. At the other his intensity level trailed the Gipper's, who had a lower overall approval at the same time in his own first term. Moderate Democrats like Georgia's Sam Nunn and Missouri's Richard Gephardt had "scrambled to show they'd backed Bush's Gulf policy," Hugh Sidey told me of early 1991, "when in fact they'd opposed it—rats trying to reboard the ship. Now they were edging back toward their party." What surprised is that regular White House communications meetings fixed almost exclusively on the president's approval rating and reaction from the hustings.

Seldom did we use Bush's post–Gulf War prestige to advance a domestic program—too busy applauding popularity for its own sake—nor did polling affect Bush's position on any issue, which must strike today's reader as ennobling or crazed. Bush wanted politics to end at the water's edge. It even ended largely *inside* his White House as the calendar turned toward 1992.

For a long time after taking office, George Bush was helped by the fact that he was the most nonpartisan president, I would argue, since Dwight Eisenhower. The past quarter century had been nothing if not partisan—sharply, even recklessly. For many, possibly a clear majority of Americans, Bush was culturally a welcome time-out. He seemed a model husband, father, and grandfather. He loved real dogs of every type. As we have seen, he liked to fish, hunt, run, play golf and tennis, and drive his cigarette boat, *Fidelity*, at Walker's Point. He installed a horseshoe pit on the White House lawn. He played to win but, unlike Bill Clinton on the links, didn't claim a mulligan. He liked people, generally, telling and hearing stories, and Nashville's love of country. He was religious, but not off-putting; dignified, but not starchy; humorous, but never made a fool of himself. He was a bona fide war hero whose gallantry, like that of most of broadcaster Tom Brokaw's *The Greatest Generation*, you had to hear about from others. A distinguished other was the U.S. Navy Foundation, which gave Bush its 1991 Lone Sailor Award for naval and government service.

All of these knit, as I have written, Bush's upper-class Connecticut lineage and this nation's vast middle-class lilt. Together they formed a mix vital to his political success—president, but a regular guy. Another denominator was a game so American that in World War II Japanese warriors charged U.S. GIs chanting, "To hell with Babe Ruth!" Billy Joel sang *A New York State of Mind*. For Bush's and my younger generation's, baseball's state of mind imbued our growing up.

Joseph Alsop wrote, "If I feel that there were giants in the Roosevelt years, I claim the right to say so." To Bush, Lou Gehrig was a giant. His coming of baseball age included Babe Ruth and Jimmie Foxx, then Stan Musial and Enos Slaughter, with Graham McNamee and Red Barber behind the mike. Mine tied Henry Aaron, Roberto Clemente, Vin Scully, and Willie, Mickey, and the Duke (Snider). All were the welcome beckoner of a thousand afternoons.

"To express the game you have to follow it from childhood," said Mel Allen, the 1939–64 Yankees announcer whose voice *meant* baseball to Bush and me. Among his reverie: a 1942 game at Yankee Stadium. Like Bush, New York's Tommy Henrich was about to go to war.

"Ladies and gentlemen," the PA announcer said, "this is the last time that you will see Tommy Henrich in a Yankee uniform for the duration."

The crowd burst a lung. Detroit's Dizzy Trout stepped off the pitching rubber. Henrich stepped into the batter's box, yelling, "Come on, Dizzy, throw the ball."

Trout cupped his hands: "Stand there and listen to it, you SOB. You'll remember it as long as you live." He was expressing something on his baseball mind.

The player most on Bush's mind was "the greatest hitter who ever lived"—the man whom he and John Sununu credited with helping to pivot the 1988 New Hampshire primary. They had a lot of company. In 1974 Brendan C. Boyd and Fred C. Harris wrote *The Great American Card Flipping, Trading, and Bubble Gum Book*, saying, "In 1955, there were 77,263,127 male American human beings, and every one of them in his heart of hearts would have given two arms, a leg, and his collection of Davey Crockett iron-ons to be Teddy Ballgame."

In 1959 a pinched nerve caused Ted Williams to bat a career-low .254. In response, Ted wouldn't sign a new contract till Red Sox owner Tom Yawkey *cut* his salary. The Kid then hit .316 in 1960. That September 28, Williams exited as only a deity could—homering, number 521, in his last at bat, and declining, as Ted always did, to tip his cap. John Updike explained why in a classic *New Yorker* article: "God does not answer letters."

Williams retired, made the Hall of Fame, gave what many deem its best-ever acceptance speech, and became, said *Sports Illustrated*, "the patron saint of Cooperstown." Three decades later George H. W. Bush plotted a designation of his own.

In 1990 Bush wanted to give Williams the Medal of Freedom. As Leigh Montville writes in his fine book, *Ted Williams: The Biography of an American Hero*, The Kid originally declined. Startled, Chief of Staff Sununu called to learn why.

"No, thanks," Williams said.

"No, thanks?" said Sununu.

Teddy Ballgame: "I don't want to do it."

Sununu called a longtime Bush family friend to ask Ted to change his mind. Baseball commissioner Fay Vincent found that Williams didn't want to wear a tuxedo. In turn, "Sununu said he didn't have to wear a tuxedo, but did have to wear a tie," wrote Montville. In the past Ted had likened a necktie to a noose.

Surgery then delayed Ted's honor, starting a year of speculation— "like waiting for Godot," said a West Wing aide, "except that Godot couldn't hit." It ended with Number 9 getting the Medal of Freedom that Lucille Ball, Omar Bradley, Warren Buffett, Martin Luther

King, Edward R. Murrow, and six U.S. presidents, including Bush, have also received.

In July 1991 Bush and Sununu concocted another event. One day the chief of staff called not to discuss a UN speech, Oval Office talk, or birthday message for the Dalai Lama. *This* was important: a fiftieth anniversary tribute to Ted's and Joe DiMaggio's 1941 magic daybook—the Yankee Clipper's fifty-six-game hitting streak and Williams's colossal .406 average.

"The president wants to celebrate them," Sununu told me, "and we've come up with a way." I was to write Bush's speech and text for each's "President's Award."

"*President's* Award?" I said, having never heard of it. "When was it last given?"

"Never!" Sununu bayed, nor has it been given since.

Next week I joined other middle-aged teeny/Teddy-boppers in the Rose Garden. Bush praised DiMag's "grace and modesty," asked Williams's "help with my press relations," and recited his ninth-inning homer to help the American League beat the Nationals, 7–5, in the 1941 All-Star Game. He then introduced The Kid, whose presence domineered the event.

"I've always realized what a lucky guy I've been in my life," Williams said, humbled. "I was born in America. I was a Marine and I served my country, and I'm very, very proud of that. I got to play baseball and have a chance to hit. I owe so very, very much to the game that I love so much. I want to thank you, Mr. President. I think you're doing a tremendous job. And I want you to know you're looking at one of the greatest supporters you'll ever have."

Joe D. followed. "Thank you, Mr. President, ladies and gentleman. I'm honored. Thank you. And to you LSU players [Louisiana State University, NCAA title–winning team, in the audience], congratulations on your championship. I know the feeling. I've been in one or two myself. [His Yankees won nine World Series.] It's nice to be here with you. And thank you again."

Bush then asked Maj. David Bonwitt, Marine Cops aide to the president, to read each citation.

"JOE DIMAGGIO. Graceful afield and sterling at bat, Joe DiMaggio bespoke excellence as few athletes ever have. In 1941 'Joltin' Joe' electrified America by hitting safely in a record fifty-six straight games. A writer once said, 'Watching Joe DiMaggio play baseball was like listening to Jascha Heifetz play the violin.' Today, the nation still turns its eyes to you—Number 5, the Yankee Clipper."

"TED WILLIAMS. He was called The Kid, the Splendid Splinter, and in New England, simply Himself. He was an iconoclast and rebel who, half a century ago, batted .406—last hitter to eclipse .400. His feat was especially redoubtable since, as Number 9 has said, 'hitting a baseball is the hardest task in sports.' Teddy Ballgame remains John Wayne in baseball woolies—perhaps the greatest hitter of all time."

Numbers 41, 9, and 5—Bush, Williams, and DiMaggio, respectively—then took Air Force One to a "summit" in Toronto with Canadian prime minister Brian Mulroney, arranged hurriedly so that Bush and company could see that night's All-Star Game. "The idea behind the whole thing," Sununu told Montville, "was that we could ride on the plane for an hour and a half and have these two guys to ourselves and listen to them talk. It was wonderful."

Someday some administration may like baseball more than Bush 41's, though it is hard to imagine how. In July 1989, marking the fiftieth anniversary of Little League Baseball before five thousand players, officials, and coaches gathered on the South Lawn, the president decided to use *The Encyclopedia of Baseball* as a source. "At this point," he wrote me, "I will take out my handy baseball ref. book and read a couple of lines on both Stan [Musial] and Yaz [Carl Yastrzemski]. 'Let me consult my handy dandy pocket size book of statistics . . . Musial, Stan . . . Yastrzemski, Carl.'" At the event he told Little Leaguers, "Wanna know about Yaz? You gotta have this book!"

One year I helped Bush write the Official World Series program cover story, "Memories in the Fall," Poppy saying, "You never forget your first love. For me, that was, and is, Barbara. But a runner-up is baseball." Yearly, he welcomed the World Series titlist to the Rose Garden; from 1989 to 1992, Oakland, Cincinnati, Minnesota, and Toronto respectively. "Usually when I'm told of a meeting with some heavy hitters, it turns out to be the congressional leadership," the president told one team. "Today it's you." A year later he advised another, "When I talk to Mr. Gorbachev about reducing offensive weaponry, I'm going to tell him your bats are not negotiable."

In 1990 I should have, but didn't, ask for a special baseball card produced by the Topps Baseball Card Company. The idea originated with Doug Gamble, who prepared a joke for use in welcoming Oakland, Bush saying, "One of my grandkids told me he wanted to be a baseball player, not a politician, because politicians never get their picture on bubble gum cards." Gamble made it up, verbal license key to comedy. Topps took it seriously, producing an exclusive edition of a hundred cards with a picture of Bush, twenty-four, in his 1948 Yale baseball uniform. The president was given the card set. *Newsweek* later printed a photo. By 2013 a card in good condition and clearly coated sold for $3,367.

On January 20, 1993, his last day in office, Bush was kind enough to have his secretary ask if I'd like a ball autographed by the Miami (née Florida) Marlins. Nineteen years later, speaking at the Baseball Hall of Fame, I noted that the former president was liberally mentioned in my new book on Fenway Park—for Bush, going back to the future attending games there as a boy.

A member of the audience observed that the date, June 12, was Poppy's eighty-eighth birthday. Within seconds each person in the Hall's Bullpen Theater was singing "Happy Birthday" to Bush, hundreds of miles away in Maine. Williams had died in 2002. Were Ted still alive, he would have said that the Mormon Tabernacle Choir never sounded better.

On April 4, 1991, Bush's season of Gulf War triumph, Pennsylvania senator John Heinz, a Republican, died in a plane crash, leaving his U.S. Senate seat open. Governor Bob Casey offered the vacancy to auto executive Lee Iacocca, who declined. Harris Wofford, former special assistant to President Kennedy on civil rights, then accepted, taking office May 9. That fall a special election matched the Democrat against the GOP's heavily favored former Pennsylvania governor and U.S. attorney general Dick Thornburgh. Future Bill Clinton aides Paul Begala and James Carville piloted Wofford to a ten-point victory, using health care and the flagging economy. The election staggered the Bush White House, already unsure of how to seek reelection. Clearly, with unemployment at midyear 7.8 percent, it couldn't tout Reagan's "Morning in America." Still, Democrats like Gephardt and Nunn had declined to run. In Albany, New York governor Mario Cuomo sat in a plane, preparing to fly to New Hampshire to file for its primary when he read a John Zogby poll showing him losing his home state to Bush, 42–36 percent. The plane never left. Cuomo didn't run. Inflation and interest rates were still low, Bush was personally popular, and even many Democrats thought him a seminal foreign policy president. In January 1991 Media Opinion Research gave Bush a 62–31 percent approval/disapproval rating. (A year later his average was 43–53 negative.) Plus, his wife was Barbara Bush Superstar.

She had debuted on a populist note, reviving the first open-house inaugural reception since William Howard Taft. On the morning after Bush's swearing-in, people who had waited through the night were greeted by the new First Couple and escorted through the mansion. Early in the administration, Mrs. Bush founded the Barbara Bush Foundation for Family Literacy, a private group seeking grants from public and private institutions, today chaired by children Jeb Bush and Doro Bush Koch. "I'm talking about the big, bouncy kind [of family], the single parent, extended families, divorced, homeless, and migrant," she said, giving the term "inclusive" new depth. By and by she appeared on the *Oprah Winfrey Show*. Moreover, she began *Mrs. Bush's Story Time*, a national radio program about reading aloud to children.

Barbara accented synergism—how failure to comprehend what you read could devastate each chapter of a life—education, work, parenthood, travel. At the same time, Mrs. Bush opposed any law making English America's official language owing to "racial overtones." It let her discuss problems like AIDS, teen pregnancy, and homelessness sans baggage—visiting the inner-city organization Martha's Table, which provided food for the poor and homeless; noting the need of unmarried mothers for help with children; at Grandma's House, a pediatric AIDS care center, holding a baby infected with the virus and posing for photographers to contradict the then impression that this act could spread the disease.

The first First Lady to have a black press secretary, Anna Perez, lobbied her husband to sign the Hate Crimes Statistics Act. The *Washington Post*'s David Broder credited her for the president naming Health and Human Services Secretary Louis Sullivan, the administration's sole black cabinet member. Improbably, her energy matched her peripatetic spouse's. She worked to renew the White House Preservation Fund, renaming it the White House Endowment Trust, of the White House Historical Association, and met her $25 million endowment goal. In 1990, invited to speak at all-women's Wellesley College in suburban Boston, Mrs. Bush was criticized by students for defining herself through the president, not her résumé. Adeptly, she calmed a student backlash. "I was twenty myself," she quipped, addressing their potential to have a family and career and saying in a speech written by Ed McNally that perhaps one day a member of the audience might follow her path—"and I wish *him* well!"

One day she revealed that Millie had given birth to puppies, an event that made *Life* magazine's cover. In 1990 *Millie's Book: As Dictated to Barbara Bush* became the *New York Times*'s number-one nonfiction best seller. Routinely, in sneakers and jeans or slippers and housecoat, Mrs. Bush walked Millie in Maine and across the White House lawn. Like Poppy and Millie, she was diagnosed with Graves' disease, often telling about coping with an overactive thyroid. Three cases in one household led the Secret Service to vainly test the water at the White House, Camp David, the vice president's residence, and Walker's Point for lithium and iodine, thought to be culpable. The first First Lady who knew how to score a baseball game since Bess Truman also became the first to throw out a ball to open the season. Barbara lacked pretense, shunned politics, and curbed her proclivity to "vent very well," said son W. Still, "You don't have to guess if something's on her mind."

Could all of this—Bush's wisdom, the respect foreign leaders accorded him, his wife's wide appeal, the belief that they were the kind of people you *wanted* to represent America—compensate for Bush's perceived lack of a domestic map? On November 4, 1991, he helped dedicate the Ronald Reagan Presidential Library in Simi Valley, California. At that moment I thought Reagan a good, even great, president, not sensing that nearly a quarter century later America would add *historic*—according to a 2012 Gallup Poll, the greatest president in U.S. history—partly *because* he had such a map. Bush's allusions to "We'll get you on Mount Rushmore yet!" show this appreciation of the Gipper's niche. Bush often changed policy, leaving voters unsure, say, about the budget, but rarely changed values, or what he thought about certain people. Why was Reagan an exception?

From 1981, when they began to know each other, Bush developed for Reagan not envy but respect, even awe, for his ability to communicate—thus, persuade. He liked—I think, because he shared—Reagan's decency, kindness, and reluctance to hurt. Both were unfailingly humble—an unusual trait in politics' narcissism. Both had a long-standing marriage key to their success—wives not stronger but tougher than they were, quicker to spot phonies, aides with their own agenda, strays who might harm the Boss. The two presidents differed in chronology: Reagan was a true believer who later learned how to get things done; Bush was a pragmatist who later came to conservatism. Personally, each conducted himself as a president should.

A record five presidents—Bush, Reagan, Carter, Ford, and Nixon—heard the forty-first begin by telling Carter, "I feel badly that you haven't met a Democratic president yet, but please don't do anything about that." Bush then noted that "today we honor an American Life—which is the title of his autobiography. We also honor an American Original. Ronald Reagan was born on February 6th—but his heart is pure Fourth of July." Reagan was humorous extempore and with a script. He was also, said Bush, "a visionary, a crusader, and prophet in his time."

Reagan was "a political prophet—leading the tide toward conservatism." He was also a "Main Street prophet. Politics can be cruel, uncivil. . . . Reagan was strong and gentle." For eight years Bush "saw a man who was thoughtful and sentimental, sending money to strangers whose stories touched him, writing letters on yellow legal paper." Reagan then asked that they be retyped—because he wanted to make it easier for the recipients to read.

"Not even a bullet from the gun of a would-be assassin could stay his spirit. On that terrible day in March 1981, he looked at the doctors in the emergency room and said, 'I hope you're all Republicans.'" As president, Reagan "was unmoved by the vagaries of intellectual fashion. He treasured values that endure. I speak of patriotism and civility and generosity—values etched in the American character. Once, asked whom he most admired in history, he simply responded, 'The Man from Galilee.'"

Next, Reagan was a national prophet. "Ronald Reagan believed in returning power to the people. So he helped the private sector create more than 16 million new jobs. He sought to enlarge opportunity, not government. So Ronald Reagan lowered taxes and spending, cut inflation, and helped create the longest peacetime boom in American history. How ironic that the oldest president of the United States would prove as young as the American spirit."

Finally, Reagan was a global prophet. "Today, the world is safer because he believed that we who are free to *live our dreams*, have a duty to support those who *dream of living free*. Ronald Reagan predicted that communism would land in the ash heap of history—and history proved him right. . . . He practiced what he preached, supporting a strong military and pioneering the Strategic Defense Initiative. His vision paid off for every American in the sea and sands of the Gulf," said Bush, the man who perhaps knew best.

"Our friend—the Iron Lady—as usual, said it best. I speak of Margaret Thatcher—your fellow liegeman of liberty. Recently, she spoke of how great leaders are summed up in a sentence. 'Ronald Reagan,' she said, 'won the Cold War without firing a shot. He had a little help—at least that's what he tells me.' Looking here at men and women of the presidencies of the last three decades, it occurs to me that help came largely from the American people and you."

Bush concluded: "Here's part of what historians will say of Ronald Reagan. He was the Great Communicator and also the Great Liberator. From Normandy to Moscow, from Berlin to the Oval Office, no leader since Churchill used words so effectively to help freedom unchain our world. You know America. And you have blessed America as few men ever have"—Reagan's voice as lilting as any musical, crying *gotcha* to the soul.

Bush scrapped one library dedication story for fear he would break down telling it about Reagan, weak from being shot, wiping spilled water from the hospital floor to keep nurses out of trouble. He told it in his 2004 eulogy for the Gipper. By then he had absorbed Reagan's counsel that every time a speaker practices an emotional story, "you drain your emotion but not its impact on the crowd," explained Bush. "So you better own the material." That said, his voice cracked in another sentence; for Bush, the eulogy was exceedingly difficult to give.

No one had to tell Bush why the Gipper had a January 1989 63 percent approval—Gallup's highest upon leaving office since Ike. No one should have had to tell any policy or political aide either. In 1988 Poppy had brought a dazzling curriculum vitae to the electorate. Under Atwater's tutelage, he ran an electric campaign. Yet as Bush said at the 1990 Nixon Presidential Library dedication, "I know how I got here"—Reagan's benediction. *Newsweek*'s "Conventional-Wisdom Watch" indelicately put it well: "Reagan: '87 CW: another failed president. '88 CW: so great he even elected Bush." Poppy was the closest candidate on the ballot to a third Reagan term.

Therefore, it surprised me to see several aides slight the Gipper in the Bush speechwriting "staffing" process, which was described earlier. This let administration officials critique speeches—e.g., an economist on a farm address or political expert on a fund-raiser—before they reached the president. Some comments about the man who in

1984 won forty-nine states included "Sounds too much like Reagan," "Reaganesque—take out," or "too extreme, like Reagan." Most snubs were rejected in the "reconciliation" process—thus, never reached the president. Had Bush seen them, he would have been appalled.

Bush said, accurately, "I am not Ronald Reagan. I couldn't be if I wanted to." Unlike Bush, such aides—a decided minority of the staff—showed ingratitude, not grasping that sans Reagan's record they would have needed a visitors' tour to see the Oval Office. They were also ignorant of how a president today gains, as Reagan showed, by linking prose and popular culture. In addition, some disliked the tone of Bush's 1988 campaign, preferring that social issues, like Reaganism, vanish from the GOP. *Newsweek* had praised "Bush's transformation from pragmatist to ideologue." The aides who wrote "Reaganesque—take out" apparently would have liked Bush to run a pragmatist's 1988 campaign—and lose.

Like liberal Republicanism generally, these aides often also loathed many of the people who elected Reagan and Bush—people trying to teach their children work, faith, and family, less ideological than traditional—Middle America, the Silent Majority, their overlapping social and cultural conservatism vital to the GOP. Before 1968 losing nominees ignored or belittled social and value issues. In 1968 and 1972, Nixon added social rightism to fiscal and foreign policy—and won. In 1980 Reagan used "welfare queens"; 1988, Bush, Willie Horton; 2004, George W. Bush, gay marriage. Each won. In 1996, 2008, and 2012, Bob Dole, John McCain, and Mitt Romney, respectively, snubbed social conservatism—and lost.

According to the 2004 Pew Research Forum poll, 90 percent of the nation backed vigilant border security; 87, religious symbols on public property; and 80, voluntary school prayer. Aides scrawling "Sounds too much like Reagan" found such attitudes puerile. They would roll their eyes at how the Gipper had a Fundamentalist mother, asked at ten to be baptized, dated a minister's daughter, graduated from a religious college, and ended his 1980 acceptance speech with a moment of silent prayer.

Reagan never forgot who sent him to Washington—and why. "In

Dixon, [we] may have had little in material terms, but we were emotionally wealthy beyond imagination," he said in his library speech. "I grew up in a town where everyone cared about one another because everyone knew one another." Reagan's childhood vantage animated the 1980, 1984, and 1988 campaigns. Most Americans shared it. Bush had vowed to continue it. Aides trashing Reagan on speech drafts helped to betray it, ignoring social policies without which the GOP has been deader than the dodo bird.

Blinded by bias, they often let ideology trump fact. For example, the Bush White House included the Gay GOP Office—their national presence then slight—and the Evangelical Outreach Office—as we have seen, the Republicans' largest bloc. Neither should have had to justify its existence, but one did—to some, improbably, the latter. In the end apostles of the Big Tent Party can be the biggest unpragmatists of all.

Every meeting of the president is catalogued by a notetaker. A November 20, 1991, luncheon with presidential speechwriters and researchers was held against a backdrop of political angst. Bush spurned his usual casual fast-food cuisine for chicken salad or tuna salad, with cottage cheese on lettuce encircled by fruit. Cappuccino frozen yogurt with cream and shaved cinnamon on top topped the menu. The president put Tabasco sauce on his tuna and mixed sweetener and thyroid medicine into his coffee. The lunch looked ahead to the campaign, Bush starting with a plaudit: the speechwriters might not know how much he appreciated us, but we were doing a great job.

"We need a formulation for placing the blame on Congress for the economy without losing their support," read the notes of the late Robert Simon, a fine speechwriting researcher. The economy had been flagging, Bush charged with obsessing on foreign policy. "In the next few weeks," Simon continued, "POTUS wants to let the people know he is concerned, he cares, and is in touch with the American people." To Bush, the message was key. At Yale he had taken a psychology class, in which in selling repetition was taught as crucial. Thomas Dewey said that you had to say something four times before the audience remembered it. Billy Graham said, "Repeat, repeat, repeat—tell the audience what you're going to tell it, tell it, then tell it what you told it."

Bush was determined to be natural—"not to undermine what you are and what you believe." John F. Kennedy "got away with a lot of intellectual stuff; potus doesn't feel comfortable doing that," Simon wrote. He wanted speeches that were short and humorous and shunned "high-flying" rhetoric which would undercut how Bush usually appeared. Similarly, he believed in the Bible, noting God in the "just war" speech and those to the Catholic cardinals and religious broadcasters, but didn't "want to over-do Bible references." His religion was in the heart, not on the sleeve. Bush was comfortable with family values but not with discussing abortion. "We made our view clear, and we stand with our decision." Pro-life since 1980, Bush had favored abortion rights before then.

Bush spoke for a time about speaking skill. He admired Reagan's ability to "separate the words from his heart"—he cited the Gipper's Pointe du Hoc D-day speech—but said that he could not. "You can blame it on the genes." The president blamed his dropping polls on the economy—"a recession," he now conceded—noting that Reagan's approval rating in November 1983 before the 1984 election matched his now; the difference, Bush's mid-50s percent was falling, Reagan's rising. Another goper, Pat Buchanan, was posing a primary challenge. Bush asked us to be charitable so that Pat would endorse him once Buchanan was eliminated. "He's out there on a weird platform," Poppy shook his head. He then talked about his "personal interests." Bush loved country music, naming two "personal favorites—Reba and Crystal," McEntire and Gayle, respectively—by first name. He also played golf to escape reporters, "the only thing I can do to relax."

Golf ran deeply through his clan. Bush's grandfather George Herbert Walker founded the famed amateur Walker Cup, between the United States and UK. Bush once asked me to write about it for his then-eighty-seven-year-old uncle, Louis Walker, representing the family at the cup matches at Nairn, Scotland. "One point you might make is that with all this golf heritage, we [Americans] have never come up in recent years with much [amateur] golf talent," Bush wrote, "also perhaps something about the wonder of the Walker Cup itself and the joy of pure amateur competition." Bush was inducted into the World Golf Hall of Fame, once addressed America's Ryder Cup team, and loved golf's history, élan, and grace. He said he liked sports in general—"the sportsmanship, the analogies, the winning, the losing."

The next day, November 21, Gallup started a three-day poll that found Bush's approval rating at barely 51 percent—the last time he got majority approval in the poll until January 1993, his last month on the job.

In our visit with Bush, the president discussed his December 7, 1991, address in Honolulu to World War II veterans and their families and his speech aboard the uss *Arizona* Memorial at Pearl Harbor, which Mary Kate Grant and I, respectively, would write. Each would mark the fiftieth anniversary of the Japanese surprise attack at Pearl Harbor, which cost 2,403 American lives, drew the United States into World War II, and forever freeze-framed the day. Bush said that he would not apologize for America dropping the atomic bomb at Hiroshima and Nagasaki in 1945 to end the war. Negating an invasion, President Truman had been right to save the lives of U.S. and Japanese soldiers and civilians. Americans of Japanese descent were not to be called Japanese-Americans—no hyphenated identity—but "Americans with a Japanese background." Amen.

Next week I met with Bush in the Oval Office. Friends of his had died in the Japanese attack. As the reader has seen, a day later Bush, seventeen, had tried to enlist. Too young, he was told to return at age eighteen. Bush did, becoming the Navy's youngest bomber pilot. "Look, I have to be careful," he said of the half-century-later uss *Arizona* Memorial speech. "I don't want to break down." Writing, I didn't say that I hoped Bush would—not for effect alone, or even mostly, but so others would see the honor and emotion—the character—that his staff saw each day.

For several weeks I worked on the speech, gleaning letter, anecdote, and history from the day that still "live[d] in infamy." Tony Snow was helpful editing: hard, but not harsh, grading every word. "This is a very good speech," went a November 29 memo, "but it can be a great speech, and it must be." Next week a final draft was approved by Snow, David Demarest, then the president. Only later did I learn that in Hawaii Bush was still so afraid the speech would make him break down that he almost didn't give it. Demarest asked Brent Scowcroft, Bush's friend and national security adviser, for support. Liking the speech, to be nationally telecast, Scowcroft reassured the president. In his book *White House Ghosts*, Robert Schlesinger wrote, "Bush spoke at 8:10 A.M. on a morning much like the infamous one a half-century earlier: bright sun in a mostly clear sky, a slight breeze. The water gleamed. And he spoke with unusual eloquence."

December 7, 1941, "was a bright Sunday morning," Bush began. "Thousands of troops slept soundly in their bunks. Some who were awake looked out and savored the still and tranquil harbor.

"On the stern of the USS *Nevada*, a brass band prepared to play 'The Star-Spangled Banner.' On other ships, sailors readied for the 8 a.m. flag raising. Ray Emory, who was on the *Honolulu*, read the morning newspaper. Aboard *California*, yeoman Durell Connor wrapped Christmas presents. On the *West Virginia*, a machinist's mate looked at the photos just received from his wife. They were of his eight-month-old son, whom he had never seen," Bush said, voice cracking.

"Think of how it was for these heroes of the Harbor—men who were also husbands, fathers, brothers, sons. Imagine the chaos of guns and smoke, flaming water, and ghastly carnage. Two thousand four hundred and three Americans gave their lives. But in this haunting place, they live forever in our memory—reminding us gently, selflessly, like chimes in the distant night."

Aboard the memorial, you could see how "every fifteen seconds a drop of oil still rises from the *Arizona* and drifts to the surface. As it spreads across the water, we recall the ancient poet: 'In our sleep, pain that cannot forget falls drop by drop upon the heart, and in our own despair against our will comes wisdom through the awful grace of God.' With each drop, it is as though God Himself were crying," Bush said, voice again breaking. "He cries, as we do, for the living and the dead."

The president had no teleprompter, only note cards, which he held. It was as if they grounded him, providing reference. "The men of Pearl Harbor . . . knew the things worth living for were also worth dying for: principle, decency, fidelity, honor.

"So look behind me at Battleship Row—the gun turret still visible and flag flying proudly from a truly blessed shrine," Bush began his peroration.

"Look into your hearts and minds: You will see boys who this day became men and men who became heroes.

"Look at the water here, clear and quiet, bidding us to sum up and remember. One day, in what now seems another lifetime, it wrapped its arms around the finest sons any nation could ever have—and carried them to a better world.

"May God bless them," Bush's voice almost whispered. "And may God bless America, the most wondrous land on Earth."

Tom Brokaw saw Bush, tearing, and said, "Obviously a difficult speech by President Bush, who gets emotional at events that involve veterans, especially from World War II." It showed Bush's fear of private turning public—also mercy, resolve, sincerity, kindness, and fellow feeling for veterans, alive and dead.

If America had seen this Bush more often, 1992 might have ended quite differently.

ELEVEN

Into the Abyss

Bush returned to an administration lessened by the December 4 resignation of Chief of Staff Sununu, who had been accused of using government jets for personal trips, such as skiing excursions, and classifying the trips as official, for purposes such as promoting conservation or Bush's "Thousand Points of Light." Once he took a government limousine from Washington to a rare stamp auction at Christie's auction house in New York. Sununu spent $5,000 on rare stamps, sent the car back unoccupied, and returned to DC on a government jet.

During one week forty-five newspapers printed editorials damning Sununu, some urging his exit. White House counsel C. Boyden Gray ordered him to repay the government more than $47,000 for the flights, which he did, not stilling critics, who acidly assaulted Sununu's alleged sense of entitlement. Today many of those same people ignore Barack and Michelle Obama's use of Air Force One and the White House itself as a piggybank, Sununu's misconduct akin to throwing a spitball in Sunday school.

Bush's decision to dispatch Sununu briefly reduced criticism of the administration, which revived after the president went to Japan, came home to stump New Hampshire, and began a campaign that even to a GOP Cassandra seemed impossible in 1991 to lose. Sununu's exit deprived Bush of the person who, though born well-off, had the most sensitive blue-collar intuition of any high Bush aide. Atwater was recently dead. Ailes had left to create Fox News. I thought of

Sununu as, first, Pat Buchanan, then Ross Perot, snatched political bodies that had backed Bush in 1988.

As it happened, Sununu proved inextinguishable, remerging in 2012 as an aide to Republican presidential nominee Mitt Romney, a man not unlike Bush in policy and person. At seventy-three Sununu became what the GOP lacked in 1992—a take-no-prisoners surrogate. One day Sununu told MSNBC's Andrea Mitchell that President Obama was "lazy and disengaged." Most journalists, including Mitchell, thought the criticism shocking. Others, looking at Obama's vacuous record, felt that Sununu was being kind.

My last December 1991 memo to him mimed others that he received and what nascent talk radio urged daily—the Bush campaign's need to *attack*. That year's March Gallup Poll had given the president a 91 percent approval rating. In November 1992 he got 37.5 percent of the total in the general election—a historic plunge. Like most me-tooers, the GOP's free fall was largely caused by playing on the other team's turf.

The Clintons' mantra was, "It's the economy, stupid." Since their media chorus and the GOP campaign agreed, that maxim became the slogan of the election. Bypassed was Bush's magnificence in Desert Storm—how he literally reshaped the globe. Obscured was Gorbachev dissolving the Soviet Union on Christmas Day 1991—a land until very recently consigned to oblivion. Ignored was Bush's integrity—and how lower interest and inflation rates made it much easier to buy a home and afford a family. Forgotten—as if they never happened.

Instead, by Election Day "It's the economy, stupid" meant two things: (1) the worst unemployment since 1984 and (2) the president's breaking his "No New Taxes" pledge. Each kept Bush from connecting to the economically restless middle class. Given that, my December 1991 memo proposed how we could use our agenda to polarize the electorate—recognizing that to Democrats bipartisanship meant a Republican white flag.

First, the Bush White House needed to treat its friends better than its enemies. By late 1991 Bush's problems lay with Reagan-Nixon conservatives, who felt estranged over taxes and social issues. Movement rightists like Buchanan, Ed Rollins, even Newt Gingrich were a symptom, not cause, of GOP disarray. In their view, correct or not, we had needlessly destroyed bridges to Reagan's legacy.

Second, a key was to discuss Republican issues—drug use, the death penalty, a strong defense, cultural decline, permissiveness, and equal opportunity, not preferential treatment. A decisive polling majority backed us on every issue. Instead, Democrats controlled the playbill—education, the environment, child care, and other issues where they held an edge. Discussing them did little to convince Dems or independents to vote Republican.

Better late than never—albeit terribly late—the GOP needed to define differences between the parties, recalling that "us vs. them" had won every time it had been tried since Nixon's 1968 election—and could again by preempting Buchanan, sidelining Perot, and setting the agenda. Instead, too many Republicans acted like Nelson Rockefeller had never died—and Reagan had never lived. Me-too could lose in 1992. One reason was a culture it had allowed, like a fungus, to infect.

As noted in chapter 9, Bush grew to adulthood liking the American Western—with jazz and the Broadway musical, among other things, uniquely American. As 1960s through '90s "edge" coarsened an increasingly sick culture, the Western became preciously anachronistic—a life preserver in a cesspool age. The white hats won. Honesty trumped irony, even if now seen more on late-night TV than in the wide-screen theater. Either place a favorite Everyman, like Bush, was steady and underestimated, trim, old-shoe, and solid, projecting depth, stoicism, and the guy next door.

Unlike Henry Fonda, Glenn Ford was not a laconic icon in the saddle. Unlike John Wayne, he never pined to become Paul Bunyan via Pecos Bill. Unlike Jimmy Stewart, he became neither institution nor caricature: the shy fox taken as a naïf who ends up taking the taker.

By the time Ford was a teenager, the son of a Canadian railroad executive wanted to act. "It's all right for you to try," said his father, "if you learn something else first. Be able to take a car apart and put it together. Be able to build a house, every bit of it. Then you'll always have something." Learning, the tyro went off on his own, as Bush did in Texas oil.

At Ford's late 1940s to '60s acting peak, he worked on wiring, plumbing, and air conditioning at home. At one time or another, he was a roofer, plate-glass window installer, and five-dollar-a-week Santa Monica bartender. Years later, famous, Ford drove regularly by the bar. "There are too many places here that won't let me forget how I started."

Imagine Madonna aping such a modest blue-collar pulse. You can't; the dots don't connect. In one five-year period, Ford took off an average twenty-one days between movies, in 1960–61, filming four simultaneously. "I like to work," he said, making eighty-five films. In *Blackboard Jungle* the native Quebecer was a valiant teacher. *Pocketful of Miracles* bared a bootlegger of bonhomie. *Dear Heart* cast a lonely businessman. *The Big Heat* vaunted a vengeful cop.

Always, Ford's genre was the big-skied/hearted Western— *Cimarron, The Man from Colorado, 3:10 to Yuma, Cowboy,* TV's *The Hacketts*—ideal for his dry, born-for-the-heartland voice. Like Jim Davis, Morgan Woodward, the grand Ben Johnson, the great Ward Bond, he embodied the frontier's dirt and sagebrush vantage of Old World nobility and New World meritocracy.

Diane Holloway said of 1950s TV and cinema: "[They] and we were kinder than today. Life in general was more polite." I once asked Bob Costas why Maureen Dowd wrote, "We're cruder, more self-involved, and more over-the-top than ever." He said, "Television and film have a lot to do with it." We would have been better people with more Westerns as our guide.

Ford, who died in 2006 at ninety, never confused himself off screen with anyone, including Bush. He was an entrepreneur, brooked multiple marriages, and was a World War II marine. He was a Democrat till campaigning for Reagan for the job Poppy later had. Yet he played many Western characters suggestive of Bush, luring overwhelmingly the same constituency. Ford mourned how to some decency had become for squares. In a cycle of irony, squareness made him special.

It let him refuse to throw good taste after bad, even as culture became our lounge lizard and America the lounge. If character was Bush's core, it also helped make Ford a great character actor. Watching Ford on film, you grasp why Bush, to the surprise of many, ultimately thrived in politics too.

In 1946, the same year Glenn Ford starred in three films, including the film noir classic *Gilda* with Rita Hayworth, director William Wyler released the Oscar-winning film *The Best Years of Our Lives*, about soldiers returning from World War II and their families greeting them and homecoming's joys, worries, and confessions of the heart. If virtually anyone in the Bush administration took a polygraph test, they would likely say that 1992 was among the worst years of their life. Why? "Because in four years we went from maybe the best campaign in modern history [1988] to maybe the worst," said a friend. Because George Bush was a president who should have been reelected: a superb diplomat, great role model, proud of his country's past, buoyant about her future, untouched by scandal, putting strict constructionist Clarence Thomas on the Supreme Court, and keeping government growth smaller than it had been or would be again. *Time*'s Hugh Sidey, covering ten presidents from Ike through Bush 43, said 41 "ran the government better than any other modern President"—a grand president at war and peace.

The year 1992 was awful because of misjudgment—ours. As Bill Clinton increasingly seemed the probable Democratic nominee, we thought that America would never choose a man like him. He wrote that he "loathed the military," was said to be a serial adulterer, and had admitted to using drugs. Aides spoke of thwarting "bimbo eruptions," women with whom Clinton even recently had an affair and who might come forward to testify. At the 1992 GOP Convention in Houston, Buchanan defined Clinton's concept of service: "When Bill Clinton's time came in Vietnam, he sat up in a dormitory room in

Oxford, England, and figured out how to dodge the draft." I recall a March train ride from New York to DC, concocting an attack line similar to the GOP's that fall: "Bill Clinton cheated on his wife, the law, and the country. What makes you think he won't cheat on you?" *Despite* the Bush campaign, it was all going to be so *easy*. We were wrong because the country's culture—therefore, much of America— had changed.

The year 1992 was ugly because Bush deemed campaigning separate from governing, unlike Clinton, who thought each a natural extension of the other. Because few in the Bush campaign grasped Poppy's 1988 lunch-bucket coalition. Because the national media, for reasons of culture and ideology, became Clinton's shameless amen corner. "You and I know that the media was blatantly biased against Bush," Nixon wrote me a few days before Christmas 1992. "This can't be blamed on his personal press relations. No President in my lifetime has been more considerate of the press than he was. Yet, when the chips were down they showed their liberal bias and then compounded the injury by sanctimoniously claiming they were always fair and objective."

The year 1992 was errant because Bush could articulate "the vision thing" he gently mocked for the world but not for America. He lost because he let the election become a referendum on the mild 1990– 91 recession. "When things turned around I'd say, 'Good news, the fourth-straight quarter of growth,'" the president said of 1992. "By then people weren't listening. I couldn't break through." Bush lost because he didn't insist that a presidency must involve foreign policy and moral leadership, at which he excelled. He liked the culture of the Western but was not comfortable defending it. Bush lost because he noted his feats too seldom—say, the Soviet Union's dissolution or how, as Buchanan said, "under Bush more human beings escaped from the prison house of tyranny to freedom than in any other four-year period in history." On one hand, this kept the media from accusing Bush of ignoring the economy. On the other, he let people who opposed him dictate what he said.

Go figure: as Communism dissolved in late 1991, the campaign of the U.S. president who helped dissolve it began to sink. On December

16 Transportation Secretary Samuel Skinner disastrously succeeded Sununu. As new chief of staff, the ex–Eagle Scout remained a fine transportation secretary. Skinner hired a management consultant, Eugene Croisant—to many known as "French Breakfast Roll Man"—who, looking for a fall guy, unfairly found one in communications director David Demarest, vainly suggesting he be fired. In December Bush told a press conference that "given the way the economy failed to recover as was widely predicted three months ago, this science of economics is inexact at best," adding that his early January 1992 trip to Asia would accent exports—"jobs." On January 8 Bush, run ragged, vomited at an official dinner into the lap of the Japanese prime minister, the photo making page 1 from Terre Haute to Tokyo. The new year had begun as badly as the old year closed. It would make you laugh if it hadn't already made you cry.

On the same day Bush grew ill, Skinner told the *Washington Post* that the campaign's "obvious" problem was a failure to convey "a significant number of things the President has done" domestically. "Indeed, after three years of neglect," wrote Schlesinger, incredulous, "the speechwriters suddenly were being told that they were the key to the presidential reelection." The January 28 State of the Union address, said pollster and campaign chairman Bob Teeter—a technician, not strategist—would launch, in effect U-turn, the campaign. If it didn't, the next major address would—ad infinitum. "Nineteen ninety-two," said humor writer Doug Gamble, "was not a very funny year."

A mid-January Gallup poll for the first time showed more thumbs down than up for the president. The eighteen-month recession, costing 1.2 million jobs, was wide but shallow. Reagan's 1981–83 black dog and Obama's 2009–12 black hole were far more severe. Unlike Poppy, both presidents won a second term—but why? Each was a better politician. Reagan's "Stay the Course" and Obama's "Whatever's Wrong, Blame W." topped Bush 41's changing message. The latter left office before recovery became clear—1992's third and fourth quarters growing at 3.5 and 5.8 percent, respectively. After a while—say, early 1992—41 spoke to an outcome-based jury.

First, Bush traveled to New Hampshire, where Buchanan, on the primary ballot, was already auguring much of the GOP 1988 convention platform: fair trade, faith in the public square, American unity vs. identity-group politics. The Granite State had saved the then veep in 1988. Sununu's fresh firing didn't help now. "For six decades, I've been your neighbor," read Bush's text, "playing here as a kid, speaking at your Rotary, attending the local school board. Our dreams spring from a common source: Family, school, church, community." Horace Greeley, born not far from Amherst, said, "Go west . . . and grow up in the country." Bush had come north again, he said, "to return to *home* country."

Each writer had prepared text tailored for a city on Bush's January 15 schedule. When voters say they like unscripted candidates, they often commit what Churchill called a "terminological inexactitude"—an untruth. Rarely deviating from text, Reagan was among the great rhetoricians of our time. Disliking text, Bush would ad-lib whenever possible, as he did going "north." In Portsmouth he told civic leaders that he didn't want to sound like "Mrs. Rose Scenario" but thought the economy would soon revive. In Dover Bush told voters that his concern was for them—"Don't cry for me, Argentina." In Exeter a town-hall meeting heard him say what he had told aides for months: "Message: I care"—true but also sure to fuel cynicism.

I found it endearing. Most had no idea what Bush meant or why he said what he did.

For weeks the January 28, 1992, State of the Union address had been held aloft as the key to the Magic Kingdom, the event that would propel Poppy from the darkness of the recent past back to the sunlight of Desert Storm. All now depended upon the speech—a short, thematic address that would stir Bush emotionally, the economy psychologically, and the nation inspirationally.

Such cosmic expectations were, of course, a mistake. So was limiting the text to Sam Skinner, Richard Darman, Bob Teeter, the president, and its author, Tony Snow—exclusivity narrows outlook. I found

Tony kind and generous, loving to debate politics and college basketball, and an artist of the editorial page. Weaned on print, Tony found it hard to write for the ear, not eye, the former more rhythmic and lilting. Bush got his draft January 24 and rejected it. Called to Washington, Peggy Noonan registered at a DC hotel under the name of "Garbo," craving anonymity, like the actress. All weekend she toiled on the address. Straightaway the folly bloomed of waiting ten weeks for a speech to substitute for a vision.

About this time Reagan released a video in New Hampshire about his old running mate: "To those who question whether George Bush should be reelected, here is my two-word answer: Saddam Hussein." Bush's election-year disapproval rating soon approached another two-word answer: Jimmy Carter's. Likeable and effective Press Secretary Marlin Fitzwater became new communications director, succeeding Demarest, who became lead speechwriter, succeeding Snow, the new head of media affairs. Buchanan had intensity, a fervid style, and the middle-class belief that Bush had sold out jobs. The president had global insight, international cachet, Barbara, and the familiarity of a friend.

Bob Hope introduced him at a rally. Bush said, "He was telling me one result of Columbus's voyage was trade that first introduced broccoli to the Europeans." Drum beat. "They've been our friends all these years anyway." Another stop evoked the Cold War. "The Evil Empire is not merely E-V-I-L. It's D-E-A-D." Everywhere Bush bashed Congress. "Last year we liberated a country in the desert sand. This year we must liberate our economic proposals from congressional quicksand." And anti–free traders like Buchanan. "Protectionists believe in *isolationism*—in an America *running scared*. We believe in *ourselves*—in an America *standing tall*."

It sounded right but felt all wrong. How could a foreign policy wizard be in trouble, polls conveyed, against a mere protest candidate, said the White House, even a speaker as riveting as Buchanan? Moreover, what was there to protest, aside from an economy that, like a rubber band, contracted and expanded? Somehow a lot, the new year was about to say.

In February I gave a number of speeches in several moderate Upstate New York districts, then summarized my thoughts for Demarest:

There is little passion—little belief that he's *our* guy—little desire to walk on glass for George Bush. R. W. Apple's recent *New York Times* piece speaks eloquently to this point: "Pragmatists [i.e. Bush] have trouble building constituencies. Mr. Reagan had a band of die-hard supporters who could be counted upon no matter what. Mr. Bush's fans come and go with the rapidly changing political weather. And he has never convinced conservatives that he is one of them."

This explains why Buchanan's savaging of NEA [National Endowment for the Arts] pornography and racial quotas is scoring points among GOP loyalists otherwise disposed to back Bush. Our response, I believe, must not be intellectual but *cultural*. Buchanan is using Andover, Skull & Bones, and what he dubs "pampered preppies" as a metaphor for GB. *We* must react by focusing on Bush's persona—e.g. his courage in trekking to west Texas. Although Bush's background differs from most Republicans, we can say, he believes in their values and will act on their behalf.

In Upstate speeches I said that when you elect a President you choose not just policies but a person. Look at George Bush: Which among his qualities would you not want your kids to emulate? I spoke of the President as a war hero—a moral person—"like Mrs. Bush, he knows all the hymns"—a family man with a loving wife. With the nuclear family under attack, what a remarkable defense—a man of honesty and modesty.

I noted how as a child, GB's moniker was "Have Half"—he gave half his lunch to other classmates—and how he refuses to brag about himself. I referred to his bravery and responsibility—what we call *character*. At the end of each speech, people approached me, saying, "I didn't know he was *like* that." More than capital gains, tax credits, or Democrat liabilities, it is Bush the person we must make the lynchpin of the 1992 campaign.

We seldom did.

One day I was at the computer when a White House colleague flew through my door. "You know Buchanan, right?" he said.

"A little bit," I said. I knew Nixon fairly well, Buchanan only faintly.

"Well, tell him to get out," he said. "This is all *his* fault."

"No," I said. "This is *our* fault." I am not sure he heard me, leaving as quickly as he came.

On February 19 New Hampshire primary exit polls predicted a Buchanan upset. After CPR revived the West Wing, final results showed Bush winning, 53–38 percent. For once the conventional view was right: the scoreboard showed the president's weakness more than the challenger's strength.

On February 8 Andrew Rosenthal of the *New York Times* previewed Bush's chief obstacle, aside perhaps from his campaign—media bias. He wrote of how Bush, attending the National Grocers Association convention in Orlando, Florida, lingered at the mockup of a check-out lane. According to Rosenthal, who was not even at the convention, Bush signed his name on an electronic pad used to detect check forgeries, then said, "If some guy came in and spelled George Bush differently, could you catch it?"

"Yes," Bush was told, Rosenthal wrote, and the president shook his head in wonder.

Rosenthal used the incident to make it seem that Bush had never encountered a supermarket barcode reader—ludicrous, we know now; preposterous even then to anyone who knew of Bush's past shopping in Houston (and at Sam's Club after leaving the presidency). Bush was merely being shown a new type of scanner that could weigh groceries and read mangled and torn bar codes. Rosenthal didn't care about that; he wanted to make Bush seem "out of touch."

Ultimately, Bush trudged slowly through the primaries, winning 73 percent of the vote to Buchanan's 25, balance divided. At this point, he easily beat Clinton in a two-way Market Opinion Research matchup, 50–38 percent. The same poll cautioned that Clinton had a 43–25 favorable/unfavorable rating. The Arkansas governor, a self-styled centrist, or New Democrat, lost the Iowa caucus but finished a surprising second in New Hampshire, terming himself "the Comeback Kid"—a pliant press promptly slobbering over his candidacy. On one hand, he became the first baby boomer presidential nominee, embodying its toxic mid-to-late 1960s culture. On the other, his first national exposure was a woman, Gennifer Flowers, revealing reports of an affair.

Clinton denied it, appearing on television's *60 Minutes* with his wife, Hillary Rodham Clinton, who said that she was not like singer Tammy Wynette, twanging "Stand by Your Man," even as she did. The joker was a man appearing previously in this narrative: wealthy Texas businessman Ross Perot, who had ears like *Mad* magazine's Alfred E. Neuman, a visceral dislike of Bush, and twitting Clinton, said, "I'm a Rhodes scholar, too. R-O-A-D-S." His theme song was "Crazy," by country music's Patsy Cline—art as life. Even many Republicans liked him—until grasping that Clinton could not have asked for greater providence than Perot.

Bush and Clinton both endorsed the North American Free Trade Agreement (NAFTA), but the president had signed it—thus, got the blame or credit. Perot called NAFTA "a giant sucking sound," killing American jobs or outsourcing them abroad. In addition, he sensed voters' fear that internal and external debt was eroding the maxim of "pay as you go," embodied best and most recently among all presidents by Ike. Our children would unfairly get the bill, said Perot, vowing a plague on both political parties, and each's voters complied. In 1992 his name appeared on all fifty state ballots, Perot winning 19,741,065 votes and 18.9 percent of the electorate—most successful third-party presidential nominee since TR in 1912.

Ironic were the deserter's principles—sane tax, spend, and size of government. The Perotistas were overwhelmingly white, traditional, and moderate to conservative, their DNA Republican. By 1992 three in four Americans felt the economy was fairly or very bad (distant). Six in ten said their own finances were better or unchanged since 1988 (up close). They were buying a blame-Bush narrative a year and a half after economists had told him the economy would boom. Worse, after a 1988 campaign in which Willie Horton had been named so often you might think he was Bush's running mate, the cultural affronts to decent people galvanizing the GOP since 1968 as an issue had been cavalierly thrown away. In June 1992 Perot's 39 percent led Gallup's trial vs. Bush's 31 and Clinton's 25 percent. Another colleague of mine said, "*This* is Perot's fault." "No, it's not," I said—first Buchanan, now Perot—"It's *ours*." Shakespeare said, "The fault lies not in our stars but in ourselves."

In *Time*'s 1988 election issue, historian Garry Wills noted protest candidates Pat Robertson and Jesse Jackson, whose "power populism" Bush enlarged to become that year's "candidate of grievance." After their withdrawal, the president "tapped a yearning for moral rebirth that Ronald Reagan was supposed to have brought to America already. Yet Reagan's rhetoric, unable to re-create the America he invoked, made that and America's absence more haunting for those who saw a Sodom around them instead of the Eden they had been promised." In 1988 Bush upheld "Robertson's agenda of prayer in school, harsh penalties for drug dealers, a return to patriotism, opposition to abortion, and a full frontal attack on liberalism." As president, though, Wills said, Bush did little to assist that agenda. Indeed, "the loss of family values, the irresponsible sexuality of the young—what Jackson called 'babies making babies,'" was more pronounced by 1992. Poppy had not kept Sodom from the gates.

Needing a new script, Bush looked for one with a fervent fraction of the old. In Cleveland he announced health-care legislation, saying, "As long as I am President, we will not go down the road of national health care." In Miami he backed legal tort reform: "I don't want to get into trouble with the Bar Association, but I once quoted to someone that line, 'An apple a day keeps the doctor away.' He said, 'What works for lawyers?'" In Wisconsin Bush noted how "America has helped win the peace abroad. The Cold War is over—and America won." Bush wanted now "to discuss winning the peace at home by changing the child support system." None packed the punch of pulverizing the ACLU.

In March 1991 black motorist Rodney King was beaten by four white Los Angeles police officers. On April 29, 1992, an all-white jury returned a verdict of not guilty in the case. Almost immediately, riots began that lasted nearly a week. Bush asked David Demarest to draft a strong law-and-order speech. On his own Tony Snow wrote "a deep-think piece on racial relations in the United States," as it was described to the *New York Times*, conceding racism and the need to end it and, some thought, using it as an excuse to break the law. Bush chose Demarest's no-nonsense draft, addressing the nation next night from the Oval Office. "What we saw last night and the night before in Los Angeles is not about civil rights," Bush said. "It is not about the great cause of equality that all Americans must uphold. It's not a message of protest. It's been the brutality of a mob, pure and simple. And let me assure you: I will use whatever force is necessary to restore order. What is going on in LA *must* and *will* stop. As your president I guarantee you this violence will end."

Such martial rhetoric was sadly unusual for post-1988 Bush at home—no give, gloves off. More sternness might have reminded many why once they supported him. That week I wrote a speech for a format Bush used too rarely: the radio address. The president said that he was troubled by the court decision—but that rioting rose from "a simple lack of respect for human life. The first civil right of all Americans is the right to be free of violence." Bush traveled five times in the next month to California. Few thought he could win the state—Clinton routed him by 1.5 million votes—but his job description included being the nation's captain/chaplain.

On May 8, saying, "Blessed are the peacemakers," Bush hailed LA police and fire fighters who had fought six thousand fires and made twelve thousand arrests. He was governing like a president, strong and fair. Such conduct might eventually have marginalized Perot. Instead, political antennae weak, the new Bush White House campaign team borrowed its leitmotif from the 1960s television show *Get Smart*—KAOS, not CONTROL.

In 1988 CBS debuted the television show *Murphy Brown*, starring actress Candice Bergen as an investigative journalist and news anchor for *FYI*, a fictional CBS TV newsmagazine. In 1992 Brown, an unmarried character, became pregnant, decided to have the child alone, and joined the pendulum toward illegitimacy that abetted post-1960s poverty, dysfunction, crime, inferior education, and lack of parental authority, among other defects. Vice President Dan Quayle was appalled by the show's approval of having children sans wedlock, which not long ago would have earned opprobrium. In a May 19, 1992, speech at the Commonwealth Club in San Francisco, he was courageous enough to say so in a seminal speech citing the collapse of family values as a leading cause of that month's LA violence.

"It doesn't help matters," Quayle said, "when prime-time TV has Murphy Brown . . . mocking the importance of fathers by bearing a child alone and calling it just another lifestyle choice." A day later Marlin Fitzwater was asked—assaulted—by the media whether his boss agreed. The right response loyally (Quayle *was* veep) and politically (let the Dems own illegitimacy) would have been to defend the vice president and attack TV as uncivilizing—what polls showed America thought then, and now. Instead, to quote Thatcher, precincts of the White House went "wobbly." Unaware of Quayle's speech, it was caught between two "family values"—opposing abortion but wanting two parents for a child. Fitzwater told the press, "Murphy's demonstrating pro-life values, which we think is good. She is having the baby, so we're not very comfortable getting involved in criticism of the show." Marlin had unintentionally deserted Quayle by not saying marriage should precede a child—KAOS.

In 2002 Bergen said in an interview that she *supported* much of Quayle's speech, saying, "Nobody agreed with what he said more than I did." A decade earlier the White House too late got its act together. In a May 17, 1992, speech at Notre Dame, Bush said the Census Bureau showed that relative to other countries the United States had the "highest divorce rate, the highest number of children involved in divorce, the highest teenage pregnancy rates, the highest abortion rates, the highest percentage of children living in a single-parent household, and the highest percentage of violent deaths among the young." Broken families—Quayle's point—were breaking America. In May a fifth grader in Marietta, Georgia, asked what he as a student could do. "I'm an old-fashioned kind of guy," Bush said. "I think it's good when the people are patriotic and salute the flag and stand for the Pledge of Allegiance and say we are One Nation under God." It was an answer impossible to conceive of Clinton giving—an answer out of 1988—if only Bush had given it more often.

Ross Perot was many things—but stupid he was not. "The American people don't care about position papers," he said. "They care about *principles*." Ironically, Bush could have used this to his advantage because it played to his, not Clinton's, strength. "Slick Willie upholding 'traditional values' is akin to Hollywood hailing chastity," I wrote domestic policy aide Jim Pinkerton. "In one speech, Dan Quayle has succeeded where often we have not: raising family values—right vs. wrong; responsibility vs. irresponsibility—to a primary place in the campaign. This dovetails with Bush's persona—a President who believes, as he says, that 'life means nothing without fidelity to principle.'"

We shouldn't shrink from Quayle's message, I wrote. "Instead, we should *use* it to flog the Left because the V.P. has struck a nerve." As it was, trying to repackage old lamps as new, Bush outlined a six-point plan to "revive America": an anti-drug initiative, expanded urban community services, welfare reform, an inner-city jobs program, the revolutionizing of American education, and home ownership. "We know critics will say, 'You've proposed these before.' That's true," Bush said, fingering Congress, "but they have not been tried." Many still haven't.

Previously, before a major speech or course correction, the writers met with the president, Sununu, and Demarest. In June 1992 we held the most bizarre meeting of any in my time in the White House. Standing at the end of a large table in the Roosevelt Room, pollster-turned–campaign chairman Bob Teeter passed around, as Schlesinger writes in *White House Ghosts*, "an elaborate chart he had produced on his computer, laying out a structure that he wanted the speechwriters to follow in drafting speeches on such topics as education, values, jobs, and crime." Each topic had a box in the chart, but one was empty. It read, "Theme/Slogan/Name." Teeter told us, "What I want from you is to help fill this empty box." Overnight, writers were to mine themes that should have been concocted months before. Mentally, each writer's jaw must have dropped a foot. *Get Smart* was one thing. Getting this was quite another.

I don't know if World War II made Teeter's box, but its theme filled the Rose Garden June 4 as Bush spoke on the fiftieth anniversary of the Battle of Midway, the Pacific theater's turning point, to heroes no longer young but in memory never old. The Men of Midway "knew that no one ever *walks* away from appeasing an aggressor. He only *crawls*," said Bush. They did neither, waging "war to win the peace." Two days later Thatcher's successor as British prime minister, John Major, helped commemorate D-day at the White House. Bush recalled what Dwight Eisenhower said when honored by the city of London in 1945: "To preserve freedom, a Londoner will fight. So will a citizen of Abilene." Bush was playing to another strength—national defense.

In mid-June the president pounded the Democrats on health care, eerily presaging Obamacare: "The last thing we need is the government playing doctor." At another stop he portrayed Clinton as far left on abortion, preferential treatment, spending, and government: "If they had their way, Mother's Day and Father's Day would be replaced by Big Brother's Day."

On July 4 the Bushes, trying to solidify the rural America that had convincingly backed him, Ike and Reagan twice, and Nixon thrice, traveled to the aptly named Faith, North Carolina, "a town an hour or so from Siler City, where [*The Andy Griffith Show*'s] television's Aunt Bee is buried," Bush said. Then, inevitably: "If she were with us, I wonder if she'd be serving broccoli." The president ad-libbed, to laughter, "I hope not."

Bush loved the "picture-postcard holiday," especially that morning's Main Street parade. He was thinking of trying bungee jumping, but "Barbara didn't go for it. She said it's okay for a candidate to throw his hat into the ring—but not his whole body." The president said, "We meet in small-town America—in many ways, the spiritual heart of *all* America."

Bush observed that when someone in Faith was sick, "neighbors bake casseroles; and if needed, help pay medical expenses. When someone in Faith loses his job, neighbors provide support and love. You show why America would be better off if we spent more time *caring* about each other and less time *suing* each other."

Four values, he thought, sustained rural America: faith in immediate and extended family; in self-reliance; in God; and in America's divine blessing. Faith had 553 inhabitants, but each Sunday more than eight hundred congregants attended church. Listening, I likened it to voting in Chicago: more would cast a ballot than lived in a ward. "Your mayor tells me this way he keeps track of who's coming and going."

Bush told how a small boy's prayer expressed such faith: "God bless mother and daddy, my brother and sister," it began, continuing, "and, oh God, do take care of yourself, because if anything happens to you, we're all sunk."

A president could express faith too. "I'm appalled by a recent Supreme Court ruling outlawing voluntary prayer at graduation ceremonies—and I throw down the gauntlet," he said. "If the Supreme Court won't act, I hope the Congress will. I call on Congress to pass a constitutional amendment. We need the faith of our fathers back in our schools."

Bush concluded with Eisenhower's quote about the "priceless privilege" of being raised in an American small town. Twenty years later almost to the day, a man died who proved Ike right.

Like politicians, athletes, and columnists, most actors die, are briefly mourned, and recede into memory. An exception was Andy Griffith, dead, July 3, 2012, at eighty-six, in his beloved North Carolina. Since then television marathons have hailed 1960–68's *The Andy Griffith Show*. Watching, we still treasure it in a quiet way too deep for applause.

By 1960 the University of North Carolina graduate, then thirty-four, had buoyed film, record comedy, and Broadway. A quarter century later, Griffith began TV's long-running *Matlock*, won a Grammy for *25 Timeless Hymns*, and made the Gospel Hall of Fame. Any or all would have forged a remarkable career. In between, *Griffith* made it legend.

The Andy Griffith Show debuted number four in 1960–61 Nielsen ratings, never missing the top ten. It left the air—Griffith wanted to try film—number one in 1967–68. *Return to Mayberry* became 1986's highest-rated TV movie. Another *Mayberry* special was a huge hit in 1995. Why do reruns today seem original, their wearability almost magical?

First, the cast still scintillates. Ironically, Griffith hated that first series year. "I played a hick," he said, stuck in his 1950s stage role in *No Time for Sergeants*. Thereafter, he played a Will Rogers Sheriff Andy, wry and calm and wise. When Don Knotts as manic deputy Barney Fife left in 1965—also for film—the show lost some of its magic. From 1961 to 1965, though—the Xanadu we recall—the series was, to quote *Mary Poppins*, "practically perfect in every way."

Knotts won five Emmys. Griffith's and Ron Howard as son Opie's tie formed the program's core. Frances Bavier as Aunt Bee so loved North Carolina that, as Bush said, she is buried in Siler City. We also embraced cousins Gomer and Goober Pyle and prim Helen Crump, Griffith's steady, and primitive Ernest T. Bass, trolling from the hills, and the Darling family, playing bluegrass heaven. Said the *New York Times*, "The characters have remained tantalizingly real."

Next, episodes mime dowries from the past: Barney's sidecar; "Opie the Birdman," adopting three baby songbirds after accidentally killing their mother with a slingshot; the Fun Girls, as alien to Aunt Bee as propriety to Cannes. Bass can't get a girl without a uniform. "Man in a Hurry" sees the light as Andy and Barney sing "Church in the Wildwood." Opie asks, "But what about the little one—the trembler?" before a pack of dogs is rescued. "You beat everything, you know that?" Andy would say to Barney. Weekly, brilliant writing, acting, and editing did.

Finally, the place remains Griffith's utterly incalculable gift, making Mayberry perhaps the world's most famous small town, more renowned than Cooperstown or Bedford Falls. Mayberry was fictional—based on Andy's Mount Airy, North Carolina, boyhood home—except that it was so exquisitely unerring that it could have been constructed only by someone who grew up, said a critic, "with such deep respect for the people and places of his childhood"—indeed, who never left, not even when Griffith worked on Broadway or in Hollywood.

Historically, many have deemed the small town—insipidly, some still do—backward, even biased. This series showed it less narrow and narcissistic than the big city. Said the *New York Times* upon Andy's death, it created "the notion that the moral center of the country lies somewhere in a small town"—more self-contained than self-obsessed.

A friend suggests that given Mayberry, *Matlock*, film, and other shows, TV could start a Griffith channel. Each Monday night Andy would tell his *Griffith* audience, "I appreciate it, and good night." Recalling, you appreciate how "our series was about love," he said, and a culture kind and courteous and sensitive and sentimental, mastering what a writer called "the kingdom of art."

Sheriff Andy, Barn, Opie, Aunt Bee, Goob, Gomer, and above all, Mayberry still inhabit our psychic home, as lyric as a songbird and sturdy as their town. No wonder we fell in love.

On July 8, 1992, Sam Skinner spoke to the White House staff not of a rural or suburbia or working-class stratagem. Instead, he said he had finally found a new communications director. Steve Provost, thirty-two, a spokesman for Kentucky Fried Chicken, had previously been a speechwriter for former New Jersey governor Thomas Kean (a bad sign: Kean was a decided liberal) and had never worked in the White House or for a presidential campaign (worse, according to political Washington). I shared Provost's affection for political sloganeering and cheer lines. He understood that a presidential campaign, with its slam bang and smash mouth and do unto others before they do unto you, was a God-awful arena in which to educate the public. Steve realized that selling chicken and a candidate are more alike than not: be catchy, creative, cut through the clutter. What he didn't grasp was political history and a fractured electorate and voters whom Bush had owned and then had lost and might—had to—retrieve.

On July 9 Bill Clinton chose Tennessee senator and 1988 presidential candidate Al Gore as his running mate. Improbably, that week Ross Perot, leading the Gallup three-way trial, withdrew, saying that staying in the race with a "revitalized Democratic Party" would cause it to be decided by the House of Representatives. Eight days after picking Gore, Clinton gave his acceptance speech, vowing a "New Covenant" for America and the closing of the economic gap under Reagan and Bush between the rich and the poor. Politically, the talk was brilliant. "Covenant" had a biblical lilt familiar to millions of evangelicals—an anchor of the post-1968 Republican majority. The income gap addressed the growing disparity of another GOP anchor—blue-collar Reagan Democrats. The effect was a historic-high thirty-point convention "bounce." Clinton had got 25 percent of Gallup vs. Bush and Perot. With Perot gone, the GOP comatose, and Gore spawning boomer synergy, he now swamped Bush, 55–31 percent.

The White House reaction was denial and incomprehension. How could Bush's 91 percent approval become 31 percent vs. Clinton? Had the president changed? Had America? Skinner decided it must be the speech staff Bob Teeter had summoned weeks earlier to save them. In early 1992 Snow hired Scripps-Howard reporter Andrew Ferguson. Grant, Davis, McNally, and Lange had voluntarily left months before. In July Provost hired several part-time writers to swell the staff. A month later he fired half the staff. Even survivors found it wrenching. I recall coming upon a friend sobbing in his office. In the *Washington Post*, a Herblock cartoon showed Bush campaigning: "I'm concerned about jobs, jobs, jobs!—My job, Dan Quayle's job, my speechwriters' jobs—." Those axed were talented, what happened not their fault. The shake-up three months before Election Day was puzzling (so late, for what?) and telling (like trying to dump Quayle as number two, missing the point). The problem remained the message: What was Bush's for a second term?

After their convention Clinton and Gore began a bus tour around the country, their sound system blaring Fleetwood Mac's "Don't Stop Thinking about Tomorrow." Earlier the Arkansas governor had attacked Sister Souljah, a rap musician, for her sewer lyrics. The bus tour gave Clinton another chance to flaunt a spurious centrist pose: he backed the death penalty, supported uniforms in public schools, and seemed oxymoronic—a moderate national Democrat. Officially, the Bush campaign said that every major-party nominee gets a "bounce" from his convention. Unofficially, Bush began to personally zing his opponent, referencing Clinton's bus tour and the Democrat's admission that he had smoked marijuana—but not inhaled. "People ask me why my opponent keeps saying the things he does," Bush said. "Maybe he's been inhaling too many bus fumes."

One afternoon in Wisconsin, Bush visited one of the country's largest newspaper-producing areas. "The paper produced here makes some of America's finest newspapers." Pause. "It also helps make the *Washington Post*." Moreover, the president witnessed Wisconsin governor Tommy Thompson sign landmark welfare-reform legislation. Thompson said it passed the two criteria of another great governor whenever a program was proposed. "Is it right?" New York's late Thomas Dewey said. "Will it work?" Bush told how a writer was asked what he would take if his house were on fire and he could remove only one thing. The writer replied, "I would take the fire." Bush, too, liked what worked.

At Barcelona's 1992 Summer Olympic Games, what worked was the U.S. team. On August 11 it arrived at the White House for a South Lawn ceremony. Usually braving politicians, Poppy relished this chance to mingle. "It's an honor to see you," he said, "though I almost didn't recognize you without [NBC broadcaster] Bob Costas as a voice-over." The president noted that America had caught Olympic fever. That week "Barbara asked me to help her re-arrange a couple of chairs. I said, 'What's the degree of difficulty?'"

One by one, Bush unfurled tales of American Olympians. Shannon Miller overcame a bone chip in her elbow. Gail Devers beat Graves' disease, which the First Couple tried to keep at bay. Ron Karnaugh

Into the Abyss

wore his deceased father's hat, making every father proud. Bush was especially wowed by the synchronized swimmers, explaining, "Maybe it's because I live in a city where it's tough to get any two people to agree on anything."

I never got the feeling that the presidency burdened Bush, or that 41 regretted for a second his decision to seek it. That was especially true when the host and guests were athletes and young at heart, like Bush telling wrestler Bruce Baumgartner, "Any time you feel your heavy weightlifting isn't enough of a challenge, you're welcome to drop by and bench-press the federal budget."

The 1992 American team had KO'd the opposition: 108 medals—the most since 1904 for a non-boycotted Olympics. The people's choice was Pablo Morales, a swimmer who medaled in 1984, missed the team in 1988, but came back in 1992 to earn a gold medal at the ripe age of twenty-seven. "Let that be a lesson," Bush said. "Youth and inexperience are no match for maturity and determination!"—an analogy, he hoped, for Bush vs. Clinton.

"Now let's have a picture, then I want to meet each of you," Poppy told the team. "After that, it's off to a barbecue for your Olympic-sized appetites." My guess is that aides had to drag the president away.

Ross Perot had, if anything, a worse late summer than Bush—first announcing he would not run for president, then charging, sans evidence, GOP-inspired disruption of his daughter's wedding as the cause. "They have photos that they're threatening to use, and I want to spare embarrassment," he said. Immediately, most of Perot's support fled to Clinton—one outsider to another. "Think of him as a halfway house," said Tony Snow, astutely. "With the affairs and the draft-dodging, a lot of people weren't comfortable with backing Clinton right off the bat. So what you had was people leaving Bush for Perot, then Clinton when Ross withdrew. Perot was sort of a bridge. Without him, you never know, but my guess is they'd have stayed with Bush."

Instead, Bush trailed in a CBS / *New York Times* poll, 52–35, when the GOP Convention opened Monday, August 17, in Houston. With the economy seen as stalled, Bush chose to let the social Right write the platform, largely dictate the speaking schedule, and pick the keynoter. Buchanan would tie his ardor, poetry, and empathy for the unsung and dispossessed into a salute to the Forgotten Man, saying, "This election is about more than who gets what. It is about who we are. It is about what we believe and what we stand for as Americans."

Every religion survey shows the national media as secular—indeed, intensely hostile to faith. It abhorred what Buchanan said next: "There is a religious war going on in this country. It is a cultural war, as critical to the kind of nation we shall be as the Cold War itself. For this war is for the soul of America." Liberal RINOS disdained Pat too, since they would rather surrender than fight and are good at it, having surrendered for the last half century. Buchanan proceeded, "And in that struggle for the soul of America, Clinton and Clinton are on the other side, and George Bush is on our side." Later, the media maintained that Buchanan's "culture war" speech limited the Bush campaign to extremists. Predictably, its bias made a farce of fact.

For one thing, the last five decades suggest that Buchanan was correct. As Quayle's wife, Marilyn, a lawyer, told the convention a night later: "Not everyone demonstrated, dropped out, took drugs, joined in the sexual revolution, or dodged the draft"—'60s America more divided than at any time since the Civil War. For another, most convention speakers, including AIDS activist Mary Fisher, were softer—and the speaker list far more varied than that of the Democratic Convention in New York, which barred any utterance remotely sympathetic to causes backed by a majority of Americans in poll after poll: prayer in school, a strict drug policy, pro-life in the final term of conception, and opposition to racial or sexual quotas.

According to A. C. Nielsen Co., Buchanan's August 17 speech reached nearly 20 million viewers. Ronald Reagan followed. "Whatever else history may say of me when I'm gone," he said, "I hope it will record that I appealed to your best hopes, not your worst fears, to your confidence rather than your doubts." It has. Twenty-two million viewers saw the last major address of the Gipper's incomparable career: How many would watch Bush's Thursday, August 20, acceptance—and how would the speech affect his campaign?

I penned that morning's prayer breakfast text at the University of Houston. The pre-acceptance speech reviewed America's religious history, how Communism's fall in Eastern Europe "had at last let people wish Merry Christmas to each other without fear of being labeled religious" and how "one of God's great soldiers, Billy Graham, had returned from there six years earlier predicting that freedom would outlast tyranny."

At the time many shook their heads—but Graham knew "something they didn't. He knew the chains of oppression forged by men were no match for the keys to salvation forged by God," said Bush, adding that he asked Billy and wife Ruth to stay at the White House the night before the troops started Desert Storm. "I thought a lot that night. About the thousands of people praying in churches," Bush said. "About my home church—St. Martin's—its prayer book, crosses, and handmade Christmas cards made in Sunday school for our troops in the Gulf."

Bush thought about the troops themselves—"the finest sons and daughters any nation could ever have"—and how blessed he and Mrs. Bush were to have the Grahams as longtime friends. In 1992 he counted how between them the families had ten children and thirty-two grandchildren. "Now, that's the kind of expansion that would make even the federal bureaucracy jealous!" he told the crowd.

Bush's acceptance speech, a pastiche of cheer line, foreign policy review, second-term domestic preview, and attack on Clinton, was, like the State of the Union, a committee job. About 34 million people watched—most of the convention. Bush, however, got only a two-point bounce, Clinton leading, 51–36 percent, with time running out. The GOP was more in need of prayer than ever.

Churchill said of a prosaic desert, "This pudding has no theme!" Republicans left the convention still looking for theirs. Trouble was fourfold. According to CBS / *New York Times*, a 53–38 percent majority disapproved of Bush's job performance. Worse, said Bob Teeter, the electorate had changed since 1988 to the Democrats' advantage, composed of 27 percent Bush Republican, 17 percent swing GOP, 15 percent anti-GOP, and 37 percent anti-Bush Democrat. Third, the GOP National Committee regularly asked people if America was on the right or wrong track. When Bush took office, respondents said right track, 53–37 percent. Wrong now romped, 80–16. Fourth, in 1989–90 most defined Bush as "takes firm stands . . . caring very well . . . likeable . . . competent . . . strong." A majority now said "changes his mind too much . . . uncaring . . . not likeable . . . not competent . . . weak." They could have been—were—describing two different people.

Desperate, most Republicans favored one of two schools for the campaign's last ten weeks. One was to make Clinton the issue, like McGovern in 1972 and Carter, Mondale, and Dukakis in 1980, 1984, and 1988, respectively. It was possible, despite the polls. The second strategy was for Republicans to show they were as tolerant as Democrats—an approach 180 degrees different from that of the prior quarter century. The two strategies were, if not exclusive, extremely hard to mesh. In the end, exhausted, you gravitated one way or the other.

The first strategy portrayed the Clintons as the embodiment of DC consultants, lawyers, lobbyists, and what USA Today termed "ex-'60s, longhaired, anti-war McGovern-Democrat liberal types." They were "educated at some of the world's most elite universities," wrote the Post, correctly and parochially. According to the GOP, they fancied themselves as tastemakers, a moral dilemma whether to eat at Dominique's or The Palm. By contrast, Reagan aide Lynn Nofziger, surveying a Republican crowd, once heard a capital reporter say that it seemed rather dowdy. "Yep, that's us," Nofziger chortled. "The dowdy middle class." Its view toward elitism would embronze us vs. them, a strategy which had prevailed over Democrats since Spiro Agnew coined an "effete corps of impudent snobs."

The second strategy was newer—thus, less secure. Buchanan's Monday speech had torn up the GOP elite's pea patch—too divisive. The media went ballistic—though polling put Bush closer to Clinton on that night than on any other day of convention week. The result was a

Republican emphasis on tolerance that lasted through October. Some found it a Caspar Milquetoast effort worthy of the party's insipid mid-1970s slogan, "Republicans Are People, Too." Bush disagreed, deciding to talk about tolerance, since he found inclusion right and smart. On September 11 he spoke in Virginia Beach, Virginia—home of the Revered Pat Robertson, a key member of the religious Right:

> Intolerance is not a word stamped "Liberals only." Too often we conservatives have not been vigilant—but overzealous—forgetting why America was founded—to bring *in*, not drive *away*. Too often our politics have been of the closed door. So sometimes we forget how God asks us to hate the sin—but, yes, to love the sinner.
>
> As conservatives we should ask ourselves: How can we condone homosexual- and lesbian-bashing, the burning of abortion clinics, the smearing of *non*-Americans as *un*-American? Have we not endorsed the view—even accidentally—that since only *our* way is *good*—others must be *bad*?
>
> When God looks down from Heaven, He does not divide black from white, rural from urban, stay-at-home mothers from single mothers. He says—as we must: "All are welcome at my table."
>
> When we sing the song "Jesus Loves the Little Children," we don't mean just those who are affluent or who have two parents, we mean *all* the children in the world. Each *is* precious in His sight.
>
> Barbara and I had six kids—one died, five are living. I believe all are precious—just as all Americans will be welcome at the table as long as I am president. I believe too, that different means neither *better* nor *worse*.
>
> In the only election that really counts, God won't ask, "Were you English-speaking? Were you 'foreign'?"—whatever that means. He won't ask, "Were you—quote, unquote—'successful'?"
>
> Instead, God will ask, "Were we kind? Were we selfless? Did we lend a hand—believe in prayer, and keep God's faith? Did we *truly* live—did we *try* to live—a good and honest life?"

The president closed with a story about a man who had tried—"a man of God," he said. Like his father and grandfather, he was a Baptist preacher and "had dedicated his life to the church." Then, in 1982 his wife became infected with HIV, the virus that causes AIDS, from a blood transfusion during pregnancy. She died in 1991, at thirty-eight, at their home in Dallas. Their youngest child died too. Their first son, ten, also with HIV, had survived. "But, you know," said Bush, "*I wonder if decency has.*"

The president told how when some found that the minister's wife had HIV, they began avoiding him. Five times he and his family were discouraged from attending Baptist churches. In the end he was asked—told—to leave the ministry. Today, Bush continued, "He works on the National Commission on AIDS. Recalls his wife. Tries to sort out his life. Thinks about what he was taught in Divinity School: 'God will bless your life if you believe in him.'" The truth, said Bush, "is that God didn't decide to shun this man. *We* did—*you* and *me*. Too often we have forgot that our fate is indivisible."

Bush might have had a powerful argument—"Be a light unto the world"—notably with born-again blacks, Hispanics, and evangelicals. However, little time remained, the economy was still seen as sick, messages were still muddled, and Bush was still deemed "out of touch" as he tried to solidify his base—too many "stills" seven weeks before the election.

In Texas the president told a conservative briefing: "I am pleased to be at this Woodstock for conservatives. I don't think there's been so much conservative passion in one room since the last time Pat Buchanan played solitaire." In California Bush noted why Calvin Coolidge was Ronald Reagan's favorite president: "'The American people aren't overtaxed,' he said. 'The government in Washington is overfed.'" In DC the Bush speech staff endured a final makeover. Desperate, the president got Secretary of State James Baker to return as White House chief of staff. In turn, Baker brought aides Margaret Tutwiler and Robert Zoellick to head communications, demoting Provost to chief speechwriter.

On October 1 Perot, seeming as confused as Bush staff personnel, reannounced as a candidate six weeks after having withdrawn. In Gallup's last poll before Perot's reentry, Clinton had led Bush, 50–40 percent. Clinton now had 49 percent, Bush 34 percent, Perot 7 percent. Two facts helped the on-and-off-again Texan rise. One was the Bush campaign's leisurely DC rhythm. Writers often had little weekend company in the White House as the calendar turned to fall. On Fifteenth Street Bush campaign offices evoked March 15, 1991, as much as October 15, 1992; little sense of crisis loomed. Moreover, Perot had a fortune to spend on media and was quite glad to spend it—$12.3 million on infomercials, including an ad with 10.5 million viewers. Buying his way back into the race ultimately gave Perot the highest percent of the vote ever for a candidate sans any electoral votes. It also made him the only third-party candidate ever allowed to debate both major party nominees.

Bush pollster Fred Steeper curiously welcomed Perot's reentry: "He'll be important if we accomplish our goal, which is to draw even with Clinton." That meant that Bush must clear the last preelection hurdle—three ninety-minute debates vs. Clinton and Perot: October 11 in St. Louis; 15, Richmond; and 19, East Lansing, Michigan. They were the first debates in which three presidential nominees shared a single stage and to include one "town-hall meeting," letting voters ask questions.

An October 13 vice presidential debate also matched Quayle, Gore, and Perot's running mate, former admiral James Stockdale, the highest-ranking naval officer held as a prisoner of war in Vietnam. We recall chiefly Stockdale's opening: "Who am I? Why am I here?" Tuning out, many viewers' first impression of the admiral was also their last.

Behind by double digits, the president hoped at the first debate to knock the Democrat out. Instead, he left barely standing—and his strategy aground. In the late 1960s, Clinton had been a Rhodes Scholar at Oxford University. Early in the debate Bush assailed him for organizing Vietnam War demonstrations "against" his "own country on foreign land [London] . . . when young men are held prisoner in Hanoi or kids out of the ghetto were drafted. . . . It's not a question of patriotism, it's a question of character and judgment."

Expecting the assault, Clinton gave a rehearsed response—to me, reckless and rock-bottom: "When Joe McCarthy went around this country attacking people's patriotism, he was wrong . . . and a senator from Connecticut stood up to him, named Prescott Bush. . . . Your father was right to stand up to Joe McCarthy. You were wrong to attack my patriotism. I was opposed to the war, but I love my country."

Superficially glib, Clinton's technique of using a rival's family member was inexcusable. Bush should have said, "What kind of man are you to invoke my father's name? My father knew men like you who talk a good game but can't do the job—and he had contempt for every one. All you do is use people as props: my father, the country, our citizens. Governor, they are not *props*—they are *Americans*. You say I attack your patriotism. A transcript of what I've just said will show that's untrue. I question your character and judgment," the president might have said. "Anyone who attacks America abroad isn't fit to lead America at home. Anyone who 'loathes' America's military isn't fit to be its commander in chief."

Instead, Bush's rebuttal began: "I have to correct one thing. I didn't question the man's patriotism," only character. "What he did in Moscow [Clinton visited there as a student], that's fine. Let him explain it. He did it. I accept that. What I don't accept is demonstrating and organizing demonstrations in a foreign country when your country's at war. I'm sorry. I cannot accept that." Would America? A CNN / USA Today poll found 47 percent of those watching named Perot the victor; 30, Clinton; and 16, Poppy. A harsher Bush counterattack might have changed those numbers, "soft on defense" having clubbed the Dems at least since 1968.

Four days later the candidates spurned the traditional lectern format for an October 15 "town hall"—the first presidential debate with stools and an open stage, surrounded on three sides by the audience, the crowd and moderator asking questions. This debate came closest to being stacked. First, the issues were domestic only—Clinton's sweet spot. Second, the debate moderator, ABC News's Carole Simpson, took the subject of "character" off the table—no questions on it would be allowed. Like CNN's Candy Crowley in a similar 2012 tussle, she seemed to be auditioning for a future role as a Democratic Heidi Fleiss.

In one memorable vignette, Bush was seen checking his watch, as if like Nixon in 1960, he couldn't wait for the debate to end. In another, the candidates were asked about the national debt's effect on them personally. Bush replied haltingly, saying, "I'm not sure I get it. Help me with the question, and I'll try and answer it." Perot asked anecdotally how many Americans would be able, as he had, "to live the American Dream." Clinton replied effectively, saying that as governor of Arkansas in 1979–81 and 1983–92, "I have seen what's happened in this last four years when—in my state, when people lose their jobs there's a good chance I'll know them by their names." America, he rued, had not reinvested in its people.

Politically, Clinton could not advertise America's longest peacetime prosperity under Presidents Reagan and Bush; as Lyndon Johnson said, "If you have a one-eyed grandmother, you don't put her in the living room." So he mourned, "We've gone from first to twelfth in the world in wages. Most people are working harder for less money than they were making ten years ago." Clinton said he would use government to do only what *it* could do—stimulate the economy while cutting the deficit by 50 percent by 1996. (In 2000 George W. Bush called such facts and figures Al Gore's "fuzzy math.")

The CNN / USA Today poll showed a Clinton second-presidential-debate rout: 58 percent chose him vs. Bush's 16 and Perot's 15 percent. Time slip-sliding away, Election Day stalked the White House. It was a place especially precious on the weekend, when I could walk through the Rose Garden, by the Oval Office, or through the East Wing and other sites where the official portraits of each president and First Lady hung. The White House is luminous, lovely, and elegant. At this point Bush's campaign seemed solitary, inchoate, and sad.

The last debate, on October 19 at Michigan State University in East Lansing, seemed like bumper cars crashing into one another along the boards. Using psychological projection, Perot charged the GOP with raising "dirty tricks" to a "sick art form." Evoking malaise, Bush said that Clinton's economic program would repeat "what it was like when we had a spending President and a spending Congress and interest rates . . . at 21.5 percent under Carter." Clinton artfully one-upped the incumbent: "I will not raise taxes on the middle class to pay for these [his] programs . . . furthermore, I am not going to tell you to 'read my lips.'"

Moderator Jim Lehrer of PBS asked Bush why he seemed less buccaneering in domestic policy. "We have had major accomplishments in the first term," the president said, blaming Congress for the rest. Perot was asked if his being MIA from the race in July-August foretold a president ducking SOS decisions. "I'm here tonight, folks," jabbed Perot, telling the public that he was not a quitter. "I've never quit supporting you." Bush harpooned Clinton's record as governor; his "being on one side of the issue one day and another on the next"; and his deception about his draft record and military service. Would anything stick?

In the end Clinton reverted to "It's the economy, stupid" and Bush's "No New Taxes" vow and saying that he would not be diverted by foreign policy. "In that first debate, Mr. Bush made some news," Clinton recalled, by announcing that Jim Baker would oversee domestic policy. "Well, I'll tell you," the Democrat said. ". . . The person responsible for domestic policy in my administration will be Bill Clinton." Bush replied smartly, "That's what worries me."

Like the first debate, CNN / USA Today gave the verdict to Perot: 37 percent vs. Bush's and Clinton's 28 apiece. Election Day lay fifteen days away. Bush could no more reverse the calendar than King Canute reverse the tide.

Through his life, when Bush has been a distinct underdog, challenged, even threatened, he has replied competitively, almost maniacally. It saved his life in 1944. In 1964 and 1970, he campaigned as a Republican when Texas Republicanism wasn't cool. In 1970 he concocted

Into the Abyss

a plan to become President Nixon's spokesman in the Big Apple as UN ambassador. After 1980, aware that most of the Reagan inner circle mistrusted him, he made it hard for any future vice president to exceed his loyalty to the president. In 1988, behind by seventeen points, ridiculed like few presidential nominees, he ran a stinging, withering campaign. Bush was at his best when Bush was at his lowest—in that sense, he, not Clinton, was the *real* Comeback Kid.

Now, in the 1992 campaign's last two weeks, he seemed everywhere, leaving it to others to abandon hope. The Republican electoral lock seemed as ancient as a daguerreotype. Clinton had New England, the industrial Northeast, the formerly GOP West Coast, and much of the Midwest in the bag. Bush had to draw Atwater's "inside straight" but in late October was still speaking in states usually colored red. In Gainesville, Georgia, Bush said, "The scariest moment of [last night's] debate was when Governor Clinton said he wanted to do for the United States what he's done to Arkansas." Spartansburg, South Carolina: "Governor Clinton says it's not the character of the president but the character of the presidency. They're one and the same." Gastonia, North Carolina: "Remember the misery index invented by the liberal Democrats, unemployment and inflation added together? It was 21 percent [under Carter]. Now it's 10." In every speech he called Al Gore "the Ozone Man" for his fixation with global warming. "I've never seen a guy with such crazy ideas."

Bush went to New Jersey, a swing state he had won in 1988, and Kentucky, where Clinton's southern lilt was beguiling, if not convincing. He signed the Poultry Act of 1992 in Louisiana, with its history of liking such rogues as Clinton, but which shared Bush's "favorite bumper sticker: 'Annoy the media: Re-elect Bush.'" In Michigan, another 1988 swing win, the president addressed the International Association of Chiefs of Police, saying, "People who act like animals have no place in decent society." The Gipper could not have said it better. On October 27, 1992, in Ohio, Bush tried to say that the recession had been over since 1991. He announced that growth had risen for the fifth-straight quarter, at 2.7 percent, later revised to 3.5, and unemployment had fallen for the third-straight month.

It is hard to define the clang of noise and chant and caffeine and game plan and faded dream and changing hope that is an American presidential campaign. Celebrities are drawn for reasons noble, ignoble, or somewhere in between. On October 28 Bruce Willis and the Oak Ridge Boys joined Bush in Strongsville, Ohio. On election eve Poppy said, "These Oak Ridge Boys are really great. I wish you could have been with us on the plane—every single one of you. . . . I wish you could have heard these guys singing those beautiful gospel songs. It made us—not a dry eye in the house." In Columbus Arnold Schwarzenegger joined Bush about the same time that "they [Clinton and Gore] say we are less than Germany and slightly better than Sri Lanka." Said Bush, "My dog, Millie, knows more about foreign affairs than these two bozos."

By then incessant thirty- and sixty-minute infomercials had boosted Perot's polling support near 20 percent. Bush's manic campaigning—in one day, five states; saying of Clinton's promised hundred-day economic plan, "You're more apt to see a UFO than you are his plan"; relentlessly quoting Horace Greeley's "Fame is a vapor, popularity an accident, riches take wing: only character endures"—had brought him within single digits. "We had the momentum," said Bush. "The crowds, the polls, character as the issue" until an October surprise halted his last-week surge and, as he said, "put the last nail in our campaign."

Lawrence Walsh was a Columbia Law School graduate, Thomas Dewey protégé, deputy attorney general, and American Bar Association president who was named in December 1986 as independent counsel in charge of the Iran-Contra investigation. On Friday, October 30, 1992, Walsh, by now the prototypal RINO, re-indicted former Defense Secretary Caspar Weinberger on one count of "false statements." The indictment mocked long-standing Justice Department policy of not indicting a political figure out of a grand jury after August of an election year. Indeed, Walsh went further, implicating Bush in the scandal, though the accusation was irrelevant to the indictment. Clinton administration attorney Lanny Davis later called the decision to indict before, not after, the election "bizarre."

Into the Abyss

That day, however, Clinton echoed Walsh's take. A day later Bush replied with little of the politesse of his Greenwich breeding. "Over the past twenty-four hours, Governor Clinton has become panicked. He uses the word 'pathetic.' Well, he ought to know a performance like that when he sees one," Bush said. "He's afraid for the power that he's lusted for, the political viability that he wrote about when he was demonstrating against this country over in England, is going to slip away from him. [So] he's begun a series of personal attacks on my character, and he has basically called me a liar." Such charges, Bush said, weren't new. "I have responded to them repeatedly and under oath . . . in numerous investigations in a six-year, Democrat-run political fiasco that has cost the taxpayers $40 million."

Next day Bush canvassed Michigan and Connecticut, then New Jersey, Pennsylvania, Kentucky, and Louisiana on election eve, ending in Texas, at Houston's Sports Arena, introduced by Bob Hope, where nostalgia was in vogue. "What an awesome array. What a great homecoming and a great welcome back," Bush began. "Texas, that's where it all started for Barbara and me: forty-four years ago, when we moved out to Texas, West Texas, we voted in our first presidential election out there; here in Houston, thirty years ago, when I gave my very first speech on my own behalf. And tonight, in Texas, I will give my last speech ever on my own behalf as a candidate for reelection as president of the United States."

Bush's talk was home talk. Among friends and family, he could confide—and did. "Pundits" said he was behind. "So what? I have a feeling the gods are smiling on us, and I know we're going to win this campaign." Even in a time "of uncertainty and transition, the American people share our values. And that's one of the reasons we'll do it, some simple, commonsense beliefs that Barbara and I learned right here in the great state of Texas"—belief in faith, family, and friends; that America always will be "one Nation under God"; in "the word of honor." Texas is where "I learned about character. Character is what you are when no one's looking and what you say when no one is listening."

Bush readily conceded that "I've never been too hot with words.

In fact, some of the more elite pundits say I can't finish a sentence," on occasion "being right." The people knew, however, that "I care very deeply about our nation. And I believe that we must treat this precious resource with great care," helping and being kind to people. It was our dowry, passed on "to our kids and to our grandkids." Voting was a ritual too; Bush requested theirs. Then it was over—the campaigning, the soliciting, the trying to talk in voters' language, which so entranced John F. Kennedy—"The damnedest thing is I love it," JFK had said. So did Bush, who, unlike JFK, saw electioneering as a prelude to, not part of, governance.

On Election Day 1992, scuttlebutt passed less on the Internet—it barely existed—than by word of mouth. Even in the East, citizens had barely begun to vote as I arrived at the White House, hoping for the best but expecting the worst—my presidential two-step in every election save 1972 and 1984, when even yard signers, precinct captains, and the corner drunk could presage a Nixon and Reagan sweep.

In the 1981 film *Body Heat*, William Hurt said of the Kathleen Turner character, "She would do what was necessary." What was necessary for Bush was to win Ohio and New Jersey; any path to 270 electoral votes led through them.

Numbers are statistics, but not always static. In 1992 Michigan and Pennsylvania headed ten states that haven't voted Republican since. In 2000 and 2004 the Democrats didn't win a single southern electoral vote. By contrast, Bill Clinton won four states of the Confederacy in 1992—and became the first Democrat to win every northeastern electoral vote since Lyndon Johnson in 1964. Clinton also won many states that Republicans had regularly won after LBJ's tsunami: California, Colorado, Illinois, Montana, Nevada, New Mexico, Vermont, even New Hampshire, Bush's 1988 savior—and New Jersey, by 79,341 votes. In 1988 Bush followed Nixon's advice to "carpet bomb" Ohio, treating it as intensely as a governor would. Four years later Clinton edged him there by 90,632 votes. Perot's 1,036,426 Ohio total was mostly white, moderate, and middle/working class—Bush's base. Poppy had not done "what was necessary."

Early Election Day, talking with Nixon's office, I found that New Jersey and Ohio, achingly close, were gone—thus the election. In eleven northeastern, midwestern, and mostly southern states, Perot's candidacy topped Clinton's victory margin over Bush. As it was, despite Perot, an unpopulist Bush high command, a tenacious Democratic economic game plan, and 1992 recession less reality than myth, Clinton got only 43.5 percent of the electorate, or 44,909,906 votes. Put another way, Bush's 37.5 percent, or 39,104,550 votes, was the lowest incumbent's total seeking reelection since William Howard Taft's 23.2 percent in 1912 vs. Theodore Roosevelt and Woodrow Wilson.

According to CNN / USA *Today* polling, 34 percent of the electorate was conservative, 19 liberal, and 38 moderate. Perot drew more support from Bush conservatives than Clinton liberals. Clinton trailed narrowly among married men and women, leading widely among unmarried. Two in ten whites favored Perot; the rest tied between Bush and Clinton. Minorities broke heavily Democratic. White Protestants, nearly half the vote, preferred Bush, 47–33. Catholics and especially Jews supported Clinton, whose backing was also strong among voters ages seventeen to twenty-nine and sixty and older. Bush tied in between. He also had an edge among college graduates. Clinton led at the poles: no graduation or a postgraduate education.

Family finance fractured, as it has since Hoover: those who made under $50,000, particularly under $15,000, backed Clinton; over $50,000, Bush. Clinton won the East; as Bush said in his "last speech" in Houston, "I got the book-learning back East, but I learned about life right here in Texas." The Midwest backed Clinton, 42–37 percent, Perot interceding. The South repaid Bush's love, 43–41. The West was on the cusp of turning almost as solidly Democrat as the South once had been: Clinton, 43–34.

In the 1980s Lee Greenwood made "God Bless the USA" the GOP's unofficial anthem, akin to the Democrats' "Happy Days Are Here Again." The Republicans' song should really be "Don't Fence Me In." In cities with over 500,000 people, Clinton detonated Bush,

58–23, Perot invisible. Among cities with 50,000–499,999, Clinton decisively led, 56–33. In suburbia, once as reliable as Ward and June Cleaver, the president lost, 40–39. In rural America, they were tied. One in five backed Perot, who talked their own language down to the cornpone and the twang.

Perot lacked, of course, what Bush possessed—the depth that the small town and suburbia once had recognized and would again. At 10:20 p.m. election night, the president spoke at Houston's Westin Galleria Hotel to concede. "Well, here's the way I see it. Here's the way we see it and the country should see it, that the people have spoken. And we respect the majesty of the democratic system." Bush had just called Clinton in Little Rock "and offered my congratulations. I want the country to know that our entire administration will work closely with his team to ensure the smooth transition of power."

To the nation, 41 observed, "We have fought the good fight, and we've kept the faith. And I believe I have upheld the honor of the presidency of the United Sates. Now I ask that we stand behind our new president." It was not a night for speeches, he said, but Bush wanted to share a special message "with the young people of America. Do not be deterred, kept away from public service, by the smoke and fire of a campaign year or the ugliness of politics."

As for the president, he planned to get "very active in the grandchild business" and to find ways to serve. "The definition of a successful life," he said, "must include serving others." How one might do that, hearing Bush conclude, and what form it might take, was a question not without its mystery.

TWELVE

A Morning After

The shock of losing the presidency, expected or not, yielded to simple sorrow by the time Bush returned to the White House the afternoon after Tuesday's election. "Maybe you didn't read the election returns," he greeted cheering staff near the Rose Garden. "It didn't go out the way we wanted. Now we will go inside, readjusting. But you have given us a marvelous life." Bush praised Dan Quayle—"The guy almost killed himself out there, hard work day in and out, and what he wasn't doing Marilyn was"—concluding, "It's been a wonderful four years . . . and I think we've contributed something to the country. Maybe history will record it that way." On Saturday Bush began his weekly radio address by saying, "Way back in 1945, Winston Churchill was defeated at the polls. He said, 'I have been given the Order of the Boot.' That is the exact same position in which I find myself today"—not a position he "would have preferred, but it is a judgment I honor." Bush hoped there would be "no finger pointing, no playing the blame game," but inevitably there was.

Depending on the source, he should never have vowed not to raise new taxes. Others thought the vow no crime but breaking it a blunder. His domestic agenda was overly me-too—or was it so robust that Bush had to raise revenue to afford it? He should have dumped Quayle. He should have used the vice president more effectively. Bush should have gone to Baghdad. W.'s later misadventure proved he was right not to. He should never have let Buchanan keynote the GOP Convention. Bush wouldn't have had to if he had grasped

Pat's and later H. Ross Perot's core. The president should have emulated Buchanan's populism—thus blocking Perot. He should have remade the GOP in the image of his dad—corporate, socially liberal, and prone to compromise. He should not have hyped Desert Storm, as if running for reelection in a rear-view mirror. He should not have pledged a "kinder, gentler" nation; if America wanted that, Alan Alda, not Reagan, would have been the first actor-president. In 1995 Bush, looking back, told me, "I should have spent more time on speeches, on the importance of words generally. That's the one thing I'd do differently." Your choice. Take your pick.

Any one of or a combination of these ideas might have brought victory, which seemed so sure for most of 1991. Later, leaving the presidency, Bush quoted Theodore Roosevelt, who thought that credit or blame belonged to those "who actually strive to do the deeds." You caught a whiff of that the day after Election Day. "I can only say it was my administration, my campaign," Bush told the staff. "I captained the team, and I take full responsibility for the loss. No one else was responsible. I am responsible." A week later he asked a poignant farewell dinner with the Senate leadership at Union Station if writer Steve Provost's comparison of him to Churchill's "Order of the Boot" had been "overly harsh." Probably not, he concluded. "Listen, being in the company of Churchill ain't that bad. I gave him [Provost] a little raise and sent him back to Kentucky Fried Chicken."

Thus began an interregnum of sad songs and long farewells—as Maurice Chevalier sang indelibly in *Gigi*, "I remember it well." First, Bush told "private life" what it would soon be up against. "You've created a bit of a monster," he told Senate wives about Mrs. Bush. "You've given her a whole new self-confidence which is"—he paused amid laughter, self-confidence being her excessive, not recessive, gene. The president concluded, "Give her a wide berth because she's a bundle of energy, shifting gears from the present." That day, a week after the election, author Timothy Naftali relates, the Bushes made an impromptu late-night visit to the Vietnam Veterans Memorial. Designer and architect Maya Lin's huge *V* slices into the Mall in front of the Lincoln Memorial. Veterans were marking the tenth

A Morning After

anniversary of the memorial's birth with a daylong reading of the 58,137 names carved into its black-granite face of those who died in the one major war America lost.

Just before midnight the president was taking a solitary walk on the South Lawn when the notion came to him. He woke Barbara up and asked the Secret Service if a last-minute visit to the Mall could be arranged. Bush didn't want attention—as always, he remembered his mother: be a sportsman; accept the verdict. What he wanted was to find the reason, thus dim the hurt, of his rebuff. He had thought he would win. His life had been based on service. Now the country he loved had for the moment turned its back. Why? For a long time he did not understand. That month Bush wrote brother Jonathan a letter. "I will always regret not finishing the course," he said, recalling a Kenyan runner in the Summer Olympics who had limped across the finish line forty-five minutes behind the leaders. "He was hurting bad. 'My country didn't send me all the way to start the race. They sent me here to *finish* it.' I didn't finish the course, and I will always regret that." Both knew that a greater regret lay ahead.

Bush's trek to the sacrosanct *V* recalled the two achievements he deemed the proudest of his life: Poppy's pre-voting-age service in World War II and conducting two wars as what Gen. Wesley Clark called "a brilliant commander in chief" that buried the curse of Vietnam. Asked as president what he wanted on his gravestone, Bush drew a simple marker with a cross and his serviceman's identification number on one side and "He loved Barbara very much" on the other. Many Vietnam veterans had been greeted shamefully on their return from service. As much as any American, Bush restored the military to its rightful niche, the Gulf War turning veterans into heroes. It was natural for him to tear that night at the Vietnam Memorial—also, less than two weeks later, at losing the person who had loved him most since birth.

"It was the idea of obligation to others, as preached by Dorothy Bush, that drove the President into a life of service, now winding down in bittersweet days," wrote *Time*'s Hugh Sidey as Bush and his daughter Dorothy (Doro) flew to Greenwich, Connecticut, to be by his mother's side in her final hours. Bush was losing the job he had wanted his adult life. His "Mum," he called her, had most forged his *entire* life. Sidey wrote, "George Bush was shaped and tempered by his mother's nature. His was a soul finally formed by strata of love and discipline relentlessly laid down. Bush was lucky, so very lucky, to be rooted in a woman like [her]."

Bush and his daughter "sat next to her bed sobbing," the president confided that night. "Her little frayed Bible, her old one was there, and I looked in it and there were some notes that I had written her from Andover." Dorothy Walker Bush, ninety-one, died later that day. "Her death," wrote Sidey, was "added anguish in the President's season of political rejection, a burden few men have known." Yet—this is the thing—leaving the office he had worked a lifetime to attain, hosting one holiday function after another, smiling, guesting, retrieving names, telling stories—I recall this from a Christmas party—or meeting Clinton in the Oval Office November 18, Bush never revealed to the outside world the inner turmoil of a broken heart. You went on, never complained, took refuge in what lay ahead.

Even in transition, events intruded. In 1992 Bush had declined to involve America in possibly keeping Yugoslavia from breaking up: too regional, not vital to self-interest. By contrast, he ordered an airlift to get needed supplies to the interior of the East African nation of Somalia after its government fell in 1991 and rival warlords prevented their delivery by truck. When airfields were attacked, U.S. forces withdrew. The UN sent Pakistanis to move the supplies, but they soon retreated. On November 24, 1992, UN Secretary General Boutros Boutros-Ghali asked Bush for military aid to open the truck routes. The president and Colin Powell thought the job could be done quickly, with few casualties, then given to the UN.

By December "over a quarter million people, as many people as live in Buffalo, New York, have died in the Somali famine," Bush said in a nationwide TV address, announcing a substantial American force to move into Somalia. Our objective would be limited: "To

　　　　　　　　　　　　　　　　　　　　A Morning After

open the supply routes, to get the food moving, and to prepare the way for a UN peacekeeping force to keep it moving." As in Desert Storm, America would "not stay one day longer than is absolutely necessary." Instead, Clinton inherited the deployment.

One year earlier, on December 7, Bush's voice had caught aboard the USS *Arizona* Memorial at Pearl Harbor. Now Bush lay a wreath at the U.S. Navy Memorial and hailed two new ships in the U.S. naval fleet: USS *Ross*, lauding Medal of Honor recipient Donald Ross, whom Bush met a year before and who died the following May, and USS *Pearl Harbor*, its name evoking the mountaintop conflict of our time.

Trying to lighten the leaden mood of loss, Bush also asked his favorite impersonator, Dana Carvey, to help launch Christmas at the White House by importing his "Wouldn't be prudent" shtick. "He said to me on the phone, 'Are you sure you really want me to come there?'" said Bush of Carvey. "And I said, yes. And he said, 'I hope I've never crossed the line.' As far as I'm concerned, he never has." For the final time, the Bushes proceeded to guide staff and guests through their favorite season—the People's House at Yuletide—more magical than songs crooned by Bing Crosby via Karen Carpenter to Perry Como.

On December 8 Bush released his annual Christmas message. Two days later he presented congressional medals to Powell and Norman Schwarzkopf, lauding arguably the greatest U.S. military victory since Inchon in 1950. Next day Medals of Freedom were awarded to, among others, David Brinkley, Richard Petty, Elie Wiesel, Isaac Stern, Ella Fitzgerald, Audrey Hepburn, and TV's Johnny Carson. "Johnny," said Bush, "I don't care what you say, I still think Dana Carvey does a better impersonation of you than he does of me." Carson and his family stayed overnight, among 120,000 visitors to see the 1992 Christmas decorations: thirty trees placed around the White House, each decorated with icicles, tinsel, and white lights, needlepoint, toy trains, eleven-foot-tall toy nutcracker soldiers, the gingerbread house transformed into Santa's Village, and the massive eighteen-foot-high Blue Room tree, with eighty-eight ornaments representing eighty-eight different gift givers.

Mrs. Bush began planning Christmas at the White House in February each year. Her first theme as First Lady was 1989's "A Storybook Christmas." Next year's was "Nutcracker," in honor of Jacqueline Kennedy's first motif. Like the holiday, the White House fused past and present. The East Room boasted a baroque crèche originally given to Lady Bird Johnson. In the East Colonnade, Mrs. Bush re-created Pat Nixon's red poinsettia tree. She also used a collection of official presidential Christmas cards, starting with President Eisenhower's. One year Mrs. Bush read that most DC shopping stores had inexplicably begun prohibiting Salvation Army ringers. You didn't need proximity to hear her hit the roof.

"Who can think of Christmas *without* Salvation Army bell ringers?" she huffed, heading in a White House car for the only mall allowing bell ringers on their property. That night TV viewers saw a very public First Lady donate, effectively saving Christmas for the army. Donations soared when the ringers were reinstated. Mrs. Bush so loved the group that it joined White House entertainment for public tours, choirs, and individual singers. Andrew Jackson said, "One man with courage makes a majority." Barbara Bush showed that one woman with courage can right a wrong. Years later she affectionately recalled her grandchildren quietly leaving family functions to hear the bell ringers in the Grand Foyer, making beloved carols even better. As First Couple, the Bushes "had enjoyed four fabulous White House Christmas seasons and had awakened to four Christmas mornings at Camp David," read the book *Christmas with the First Ladies*, published in 2011. "They had entered the White House with two grandchildren to spoil with Christmas cheer and left with twelve."

In 1991 the man often termed the "Education President" chose Texas A&M University at College Station, Texas, as the site for his presidential library over Yale, his alma mater; Rice University, in Houston, his home; and the University of Texas, in Austin, the state capital. In mid-December 1992 Bush gave a speech on foreign policy at A&M, observing that "in thirty-six days we will have a new president." Like Mrs. Bush, he was shifting gears.

A Morning After

Back at the White House, the president said, "This is about as much fun as I've had since the election," welcoming the first non-U.S. World Series titlist, the 1992 Toronto Blue Jays. Bush, however, said he wished U.S. trade representative Carla Hills was there to explain herself: "I thought she understood that our free-trade agreement with Canada didn't mean that the United States would trade away the world's championship." He continued, "I was playing baseball some forty years ago, hitting [a lowly] eighth, 'second cleanup,' we called it." The audience laughed. Bush smiled, wryly, perhaps recalling his .224 overall college batting average. He then asked Jays manager Cito Gaston to "come over here. This is a rookie ball player who needs a job," 41 confessed, showing Cito his special Topps Co. Bush baseball card. "And I'm going to give you this baseball card. Take a look at him. You need a good-fielding first baseman? I'm your man."

Humor eased the transition, as did weightier material, like NAFTA, among Canada, Mexico, and the United States, which Bush signed December 17. "Today, for the first time in years," he said, "more capital is flowing into the Americas for new investment than is flowing out. Every major debtor nation, from Mexico to Argentina, has negotiated a successful agreement to reduce and restructure its commercial bank debt under the Brady plan." Nick Brady was secretary of the treasury. Bush told him, "Okay, we'll call it the Brady plan, but if it's successful we're going to call it the Bush plan." Tongue in cheek, both agreed.

Bush signed NAFTA at the Organization of American States, which he often visited as vice president and president. He was "thrilled" that his final visit would build what he called "a better future for our children and for generations yet unborn." The agreement spurned tariffs on products traded among the countries; restricted patents, copyrights, and trademarks; and hailed "the combined energies of our 360 million citizens trading freely across our borders." He thought that NAFTA would link America "in a permanent partnership of growth with our first- and third-largest trading partners"—and that new President Clinton would build on its beginnings.

Bush couldn't know that support for free trade would be hurt by twenty-first-century illegal immigration—or that millions of Americans would temporarily regard NAFTA less as a tool of national sovereignty than of pluralism gone mad. A banner "Reconquista"—California-plus is Mexico's—flew under Mexico's flag in a citizenship-for-illegal-aliens parade in California. "Open the borders!" read another. Marchers shouted, "Our land! Not yours!," trashed compromise, and called law abiders "nativist," "racist," and "xenophobic." The American flag was inverted, taken down, even burned.

Bush 41 hadn't intended such narcissism; instead, hoped to save what works. What worked were relationships in which allies helped each other. John Major paid a December 1992 visit, the Bushes "inundat[ing]" the British prime minister and his wife at Camp David with Christmas carols, said Poppy. Major, closer in temperament to Bush than the theatric Margaret Thatcher, said, "The last two years have been remarkably good not just for the United Kingdom but for Europe to know we've had such a good friend here in the White House."

Bush referenced UN aid from the Persian Gulf to the former Yugoslavia: "When it comes to taking decisions that affect the lives of troops, I would view a British [or any allied] soldier the same as I would if these were United States soldiers there. We owe them prudence in making these decisions." Dana Carvey—not to mention the troops' parents—would agree.

Bush had said on November 2, 1992, "I love it when that national talking-head media take me on. I love it, because I like a good fight. There's no reason my holding back anymore." The campaign crowd in Akron roared. "Every time somebody holds up one of those bumper stickers, it says, 'Annoy the Media. Re-elect Bush,' and everybody in this country knows what it means. You know what it means. Everybody knows what it means." That day he gave mock amnesty to campaign photographers—to Bush, "photo dogs"—against any charge of bias. On December 23, leaving for Christmas at Camp David, Bush did the same for "Helen Thomas [United Press International] and

A Morning After

all the rest of you guys. So have a wonderful Christmas and a very happy new one." Two days later, six years after the arms-for-hostages scandal that threatened his candidacy for president had begun, Bush gave a real pardon to six officials from the Reagan administration: former defense secretary Caspar Weinberger; former national security adviser Robert McFarlane; Elliott Abrams, former assistant secretary of state for inter-American affairs; and former CIA officers Duane Clarridge, Alan Fiers Jr., and Clair George.

Weinberger was to stand trial on January 6, 1993, on charges that he had lied to Congress about his knowledge of the arms sales to Iran and attempt by other countries to subsidize the Nicaraguan rebels. Iran-Contra independent prosecutor Lawrence Walsh's October 30, 1992, re-indictment of him was an election eve ploy widely viewed as meant to hurt Bush, especially since Walsh did not learn of the Bush diary till December 11. Had Weinberger gone to trial, the diary's Iran-Contra contents, if any, would have been public. Bush, however, obsessed not over that but Reagan aides' "patriotism"—a word he used in the pardon statement; to him, the incident was a policy error, not crime. The president returned from Camp David with other things on his mind: a January 1 recognition of the Czech and Slovak Republics; a next-day state dinner hosted by Russian president Boris Yeltsin in Moscow; and a news conference with Yeltsin, signing the treaty on further major cuts in strategic offensive arms of Russia and the United States—START II.

"Today, the Cold War is over, and for the first time in history an American president has set foot in a democratic Russia," Bush said on January 3. "This historic opportunity would simply not have been possible without our combined common effort." He recalled how in August 1991, defying a coup against the government, Yeltsin climbed atop a turret of a tank to speak to the crowd, defending "Russia's democratic destiny." Bush also wanted "to salute the heroism of the Russian people themselves, for it is they who will determine that Russia's democratic course is irreversible."

Bush flew home to give a January 5, 1993, speech at a place of victory and memory. As a boy, I loved Douglas MacArthur's elegiac 1962 farewell at the U.S. Military Academy: "Today marks my final roll call with you, but I want you to know that when I cross the river my last conscious thoughts will be of The Corps, and The Corps, and The Corps." I first visited West Point in 1991, writing President Bush's commencement speech. The World War II Navy hero and Yale '48 had often been there, most recently a month after Army edged the football Middies, 25–24, in December 1992. "Let me begin with the hard part," Bush now said. "It is difficult for a Navy person to come up to West Point after that game." Laughter. "Go ahead, rub it in." Laughter. "But I watched it." The moral, he said, is that "losing is never easy. Trust me, I know something about that."

It seems improbable now, but for a long time, Sunday was not America's football day. "When we grew up, pro football players were . . . a bunch of pot-bellied longshoremen," broadcaster Vin Scully has recalled of the 1930s and '40s. By contrast, Auburn played Alabama, Penn State met Syracuse, and Ohio State confronted Michigan. Saturday was our day, bub, and don't you forget it. Few forgot in 2012, as Bush and millions of others watched an Army-Navy spectacular worthy of the term. No Bowl Championship Series berths were decided. No Heisman Trophy candidates prowled the late-autumn turf. No future NFL star paraded his résumé. It didn't matter. It never does.

Navy's Midshipmen entered the game 7-4-1. Army's Black Knights of the Hudson—perhaps sport's greatest moniker—were 2-9. Worse, they had lost to Navy ten-straight times. Each team's corps marched into the pregame stadium at Philadelphia, a sight NBC voice Dick Enberg, now seventy-nine, still calls "chilling." The game then began: a brio of West Point rushing (370 yards) and Navy leading (17–13) and din rising above the field, crashing against the seats, and ricocheting off the tiers.

With a minute left, Army, still behind, reached Navy's 14-yard line, first down and surging. Senior quarterback Trent Steelman, already thrice losing to the Middies, gave the ball to his fullback, who mishandled it, causing Army's third fumble, Navy recovering. Steelman, the only Knight to ever run and pass for 2,000 yards, his record 44 rushing scores topping even Glenn Davis's 43, went to the bench, sat by himself, and began to cry.

Teammates left the son of Bowling Green, Kentucky, whose grandfather served in World War II and uncle in the Persian Gulf, alone. Disconsolate, he put his jersey over his face. Traditionally, the losing Army-Navy team sings its alma mater first. For four years Steelman, Army's captain, had vowed to "sing second." Now he sat, sobbing, as Army's alma mater began. Hundreds of practice hours and thousands of dreams and one battle plan—"Beat Navy!" shared by plebes and cadets and millions who relished MacArthur's "friendly fields of strife"—had crashed around him. It broke your heart to watch.

In the postgame melee his mates, 2012 Army coach Rich Ellerson and Army's chief of staff hugged him. Somehow Navy coach Ken Niumatalolo found Steelman, put an arm around his shoulder, and whispered that this too shall pass—a less random than common act of kindness showing why the military is Gallup's most admired institution. In World War II, Gen. George C. Marshall was asked if he had a secret weapon to win the war. "We do indeed," he said. "The best damn kids in the world." As Army-Navy shows, they still are.

Those kind of kids heard Bush discuss the presidency at West Point in January 1993. "Any president has several functions," he told them. "He speaks for and to the nation. He must faithfully execute the law. And he must lead. Leadership, well, it takes many forms. It can be political or diplomatic. It can be economic or military. It can be moral or spiritual leadership. Leadership can take any one of these forms, or it can be a combination of them." It was essential to his most important role—commander in chief—and to anyone who might join the military. "There is no higher calling, no more honorable choice, than the one that you here today have made. To join the armed forces is to be prepared to make the ultimate sacrifice for your country and for your fellow man."

Bush recalled how Secretary of War Stimson had urged his class at Andover to complete its college education before entering the service. "A half century has passed since that day when Stimson spoke of the challenge of creating a better world. You will also be entering a new world, one far better than the one I came to know, a world with the potential to be far better yet. This is the opportunity of your lifetimes. I envy you for it, and I wish you Godspeed. And while I'm at it, as your commander in chief, I hereby grant amnesty to the Corps of Cadets."

If you were a cadet, a Navy man had saved the best for last.

Leaving the presidency, Bush seemed to want to meet the turning points of his past. On January 8 he visited the CIA at Langley, Virginia, which had swelled his foreign policy curriculum vitae in the mid-1970s and, as we have seen, whose headquarters now bear his name. Bush's remarks to CIA employees began at 1:15 p.m.: "Anything to keep from having to go back to work," he said to laughter. "I know how it is." The president vowed "to be a voice after I leave for keeping this intelligence community the strongest, the best in the entire world, which it is now." He then gave CIA Director Bob Gates, "my right-hand person and trusted adviser when at the White House," the National Security Medal, the highest medal a president can give for the nation's defense. (Adm. Jonathan T. Howe also received it on January 13.)

Five days later the East Room of the White House bulged with fellow feeling, time passing, and the memory of the man who helped George Bush become president, learn about leadership, and remake the world. This morning Bush welcomed the fortieth president back to "give him the Presidential Medal of Freedom, with distinction." It reminded the forty-first president of another morning—Inauguration Day of 1981—"and how the clouds . . . gave way as he began his speech." Ronald Reagan turned America's winter of discontent, said Bush, "into a springtime of possibility."

It was common to say that Reagan championed liberty. As Bush observed, Reagan also saw its triumph coming. "We recall your stirring words to the British parliament [in 1982]. Here were the words: 'The march of freedom and democracy . . . will leave Marxism-Leninism on the ash heap of history.'"

Bush mentioned Reagan's restoring American military strength and morale: "When I became president, [he] passed on to me the most dedicated and best-equipped fighting force that the world has ever seen." Reagan also signed the INF Treaty, "the first agreement to eliminate a whole category of nuclear weapons." This, in turn, led to START I and then START II, which Bush and Boris Yeltsin had signed ten days earlier.

"When Ronald Reagan's favorite president died in 1945, the *New York Times* wrote, 'Men will thank God on their knees a hundred years from now that Franklin D. Roosevelt was in the White House,'" said Bush. "Well, Mr. President, it will not take a hundred years; millions thank God today that you were in the White House. You loved America, blessed America, and with your leadership helped make America that shining city on a hill."

Listening, I was struck not for the first time but more forcibly than ever by Bush's attitude toward Reagan. It cannot have been easy to succeed the Gipper—following a John Wayne or Louis Armstrong, an American Original. Yet Bush never showed anything but generosity—a true tenderness of tone. Reagan was, as Bush said, "only the third president to receive the Medal of Freedom—the first to receive it in his own lifetime."

Reagan's Alzheimer's disease was not diagnosed for another year. Thus, it is likely that the Gipper grasped Bush saying, "And I consider him my friend and mentor, and so he is. And he's also a true American hero"—which more than ever he remains.

The term "Points of Light" originated in Bush's 1988 acceptance speech—Reagan's grand last full year as president. It became synonymous with Poppy's presidency, but what did it mean? Some "say it's religion," said Bush. "Others say, well, it's a patriotic theme, like the flag, and others think it's an image of hope."

To Bush, Points of Light were all of the above, and more—"what happened when ordinary people claimed the problems of their community as their own—the inspiration and awakening to the God-given light from within, lit from within, and it's the promise of America."

In January 1993 Points of Light assembled from all fifty states at the White House, "each of you finding within yourselves your own special genius for helping others," said Bush. "Each discovered the imagination to see things that others could not; the human dignity in the eyes of a homeless man; the musicians and business leaders in an inner-city gang; the light and laughter in the shadows of a shattered life."

That day Bush recognized the 1,014th Daily Point of Light, the Lakeland Middle School eighth-grade volunteers from Baltimore, showing that "somewhere in America, every serious social problem is being solved through voluntary service, for therein lies the greatest national resource of all." It didn't matter who you were. "Everybody's got something to give: a job skill, a free hour, a pair of strong arms." This is what Bush meant by saying that any definition of a successful life must include serving others.

He and Mrs. Bush would soon leave Washington, but the president, still honorary chairman of today's Points of Light Foundation, an international nonprofit, had a final thought. "If I could leave but one legacy to this country, it would not be found in policy papers or even treaties signed or even wars won; it would be return to the moral compass that must guide America through the next century, the changeless values that can and must guide change." He meant "a rekindling of that light lit from within to reveal America as it truly is, a country with strong families, a country of millions of Points of Light."

That compass had lost direction, Bush knew, families ravaged, Americans' collective fire dimmed. In 1835 Alexis de Tocqueville is alleged to have said, "America is great because she is good." If Bush could wave a wand or strike his brightest Point of Light, he has said, it would be to make America *good* so that America could remain *great*.

"Perspective is all," a teacher told me. Bush revealed his perspective about leaving the presidency his last weekend at Camp David, which he loved, as all presidents do. Reagan's closest personal ally was, without question, Thatcher. Bush's was his last guest that last weekend, Canadian prime minister Brian Mulroney, with whom he had developed an almost brotherly rapport.

"For me and for Barbara, this is a fond farewell as we leave this

A Morning After

job," Bush said at a press conference with his neighbor up north four days before leaving office. "And it's most fitting, in our way of looking at things"—which was inevitably personal, for him and Barbara, both as the First Couple and as individuals—"that Prime Minister Mulroney and his wonderful family are with us here today."

Mulroney hailed his host's stance on free trade; the Clean Air Act, which enabled the Canadian-American treaty on acid rain; and Bush's "remarkable assembling of the coalition in terms of the Gulf War probably without precedence, certainly in recent decades."

Bush then talked about turning out the lights. "It's going to be low-key. There's no point in trying to continue something that isn't"—the presidency. "And I'm trying to conduct myself with dignity and hopefully in a spirit of total cooperation with Governor Clinton." He continued, "No bitterness in my heart. January 20th when I walk out of that capitol, I'm a private citizen. And I hope I'll be treated as a private citizen by my neighbors in Houston."

A friend of mine shook his head. "Too mentally healthy to be a politician," he observed of the president. Leaving office, Bush had a Gallup approval rating of 56 percent, up 19 percent from Election Day 1992. "Where were they when we needed 'em?" another friend said. Probably out voting for Perot.

As we have seen, Bush's emotions generally were kept in check, as a successful politician learns—see Reagan. They rose to the surface, however, for anything that involved the military, his love life-long and deep down. It evoked Bush's youth, friendship and loyalty, embrace of country, the heroic and awful grandeur of World War II, perhaps guilt for having lived, surely joy for life itself.

On January 14, 1993, Defense Secretary Dick Cheney and Gen. Colin Powell hosted an Armed Forces Salute to the President. Bush's ad-lib open and close etched his quintessence, in a way matched by no writer's text.

"I am honored by this salute," Bush began. "But you guys have got it backward. I came over here to thank all of *you*, past and present of our armed forces. There is no doubt that the all-volunteer force is one of the true successful stories of modern-day America."

He ended, "Let me speak not as president and not as commander in chief, but as a citizen, as an American. I look back on my service to this great nation with pride. I think my three years in the Navy did more to shape my life than anything that's followed on. And I'm very honored to stand with you all here, today, honored that we share this sacred bond of duty, honor, country."

Ironically, the all-volunteer force, replacing the draft, had made that service less common to the country, less unifying as a force. Not to the bomber pilot–turned–president, though. Like his generation, George Bush will always feel that sacred bond. "Duty, honor, country" is what he was—and will forever be.

THIRTEEN

America's "Vision Thing"

An old adage says, "When God closes one door, He opens another." I am not sure whether this is so, though I think it more often true than not. I am sure that you haven't lived until you've been fired by the American people. This happened to President Bush and hundreds of his friends—White House appointees, including me—on Election Day 1992. Overnight, we had to decide what to do, if not for the rest of our lives, at least for the next chapter.

For the president, as we shall see, it meant a personal rejection, a painful adjustment, and the knowledge—to the last, Bush had expected to win—that he would leave the presidency in two months, not four years. Like other aides, my timetable was upset too. I had hoped to leave the White House midway through a second term, forgetting the ancient Czech proverb "Plan for next year and make the devil laugh." Now, I would be, if not thrown in the street, at least forced to show Hemingway's "grace under pressure"—fast.

The first imperative was to grasp, as Bush did instantly, that the White House was over—done that, look ahead. It is true that, at any age, working for the president—in his case, *being* president—is the greatest honor you could have, or would. It is also true that life involves different chapters—and you don't read a book by starting at the end.

I knew that I would not miss argument for argument's sake—the ego and gossip that fuel White House politics. I knew I would miss almost everything else, and have: the building's history, grounds, architecture, and wonder; tourists who rightly expected us to act mannerly; colleagues who shared a devotion to Middle America; the library that held or could find any book relative to the presidency; ghosts whose footprints still patrol the halls. I miss what Nixon writer Bill Gavin called "Bush's talented speechwriting team" and our researchers. I loved Air Force One, the West Wing bustle, the Oval Office quiet as a church mouse on a weekend, past White House writers most gracious with their time, the knowledge that no matter what you later did—books, academe, political office—to a speechwriter, this was the summit. Virtually every once presidential writer that I know concurs.

As is often true, the answer of how to follow this involved, as Bing Crosby sang, "eliminat[ing] the negative." I knew I would largely spurn, say, corporate speechwriting. "There is nothing smaller," Richard Nixon said, "than a big businessman." This did not mean that I wouldn't occasionally write for a good company. (They do pay well.) It did mean that 1992 had so seared my consciousness that I would—could—not work only for one employer. Many colleagues—Sununu, Demarest, Snow, other writers—had been treated shabbily by the crass profession of inside politics. The lesson stung.

At least for a time, no one person would control my—what?—fate, future, bank account. I would sell the only asset I had: me. In spring 1993 I began writing stories for *Reader's Digest*. Its managing editor, Bill Schulz, was one reason for the magazine's then-nonpareil 17.5 million circulation. I also hosted a series at the Smithsonian Institution's National Museum of American History in Washington, did talk radio for Baltimore CBS Radio affiliate WBAL, wrote speeches for Anheuser-Busch Brewery's legendary public relations guru Mike Roarke, and signed a contract with Macmillan to write *The Storytellers: From Mel Allen to Bob Costas, Sixty Years of Baseball Tales from the Broadcast Booth*.

About this time I heard that George Bush, though not despondent, was adrift about the loss to Clinton. Tales about former aides blaming the president for losing the election likely reached and hurt him too. I have never grasped how hirelings can turn on politicians who stoked their career. Schulz, a friend, told me that spring that he admired my loyalty. Taken aback, I said that Bush made it easy. What wasn't easy was to raise $43 million to pay for the 69,050-square-foot George H. W. Bush Library and Museum, with 44 million pages in such traditional papers as memos, letters, and reports, flanked by an academic curricula at the George Bush School of Government and Public Service. Each would open in 1997 on ninety acres of Texas A&M University.

My interest in the library may have stemmed from my grandmother, who earned her college degree in the 1920s, an act then deemed Bolshevik. It reflected my parents, both teachers, especially my mother, a high school librarian for a quarter century. I also wanted to help someone I admired, knowing that Bush's library funds would largely accrue from speeches—and keeping overhead down would keep their remainder up. On behalf of ex–White House writers Mary Kate Cary (née Grant), Beth Hinchliffe, Mark Lange, and Ed McNally, I wrote Bush on June 3, 1993, "to say that if you need speeches, opinion/editorials, or other commentary in the years ahead, we would like to freely volunteer our time to help you in any way we can."

Poppy replied next week comically, and typically. "The answer, before you change your minds: I accept your offer!!!!" He invited those of us on the East Coast to Maine "to get things moving. Inasmuch as Ed and Mark are out west maybe you and Les Girls, make that politically correct—'Les Women,' can come up here first. If that makes sense let me know and the plane tickets will be in the mail."

Seals and Crofts sang, "We may never pass this way again." I already had.

My mother was born two hours southwest of Kennebunkport. Decades later, our family tried to vacation each year in Blue Hill, Maine, three hours northeast of Bush's home. The tiny shops and fishing community had it all: the *Boston Globe*, the Red Sox on the radio, nautical art, model ships, coffee brewing in every diner, and the Atlantic close by.

In June 1993 Mary Kate, Beth, and I met in Boston, drove to Kennebunkport, and traveled up the strip of land called Walker's Point jutting into the ocean onto the estate used for family holidays, weddings, and receptions—also to host leaders from Margaret Thatcher to Mikhail Gorbachev. We then passed through the checkpoint on Walker's Point Road, gated and guarded by Secret Service officers, near the driveway leading to the main house and a circular driveway. In the middle of that driveway was a huge flagpole flying the American flag.

"When either President Bush was present while in office, the Presidential flag was hoisted just below the U.S. flag," said then–*Newsweek* White House correspondent Tom DeFrank, the longtime 41 friend who covered both presidencies. During *père*'s term TV journalists used the flagpole as a backdrop. "It was beautiful, evocative of New England, so different than [Bush] 43, vacationing at the [Crawford, Texas] ranch," laughed DeFrank—as different as the presidents. "Bush 41 was more cerebral, comfortable with the issues, and experienced. Forty-three was more instinctive, decisive, acted from the gut, didn't lose much sleep when he'd made a decision."

Covering Bush in Kennebunkport meant "lobster every day, balmy weather, civilized and sophisticated, old-line money; Bush's Brahmin and patrician, which is not to say elitist, side," said DeFrank. "After all, he'd get up there and first thing he's playing golf on a public course." DeFrank had covered Jimmy Carter in Plains, Georgia, whose nearest hotel, Best Western, the press dubbed Worst Western. Tom was from small-town Texas, yet felt Crawford had "such an utter lack of civilization, looked like a grasshopper plague, that it made Plains look like Kennebunkport."

In late 1991, a time of political turmoil for Bush 41, Kennebunkport's large central home built in 1903 was severely damaged by a series of nor'easters. Bush had it totally rebuilt, in a clean New England shingles mode: nine bedrooms, four sitting rooms, an office, a den, a library, a dining room, a kitchen, and various patios and decks. Next door were a four-car garage, a pool, tennis court, dock, boathouse, and guesthouse, with spacious lawns on either side of the house ready for baseball, horseshoes, and other sports of the day.

America's "Vision Thing"

Today President Bush and the three writers sat on the deck overlooking the Atlantic, talking shop and watching grandchildren toddle by. Mary Kate, Beth, and I wore hats in the sun because Mrs. Bush told us to. The Harry Walker Agency in New York handled Bush's speaking schedule with him and Chief of Staff Jean Becker. We decided that memoranda, letters, and assignments would go from Kennebunkport and Houston through me to the writer—say, Beth Hinchliffe or Mark Lange. The writer would research, write a draft, and fax it—e-mail began about 1993—to Bush, who edited a finished product. The schedule remained intense into 1996, after library construction had begun and an official dedication set. Bush was unfailingly gracious, quick to edit and revise, and glad to have one postpresidential job resolved.

Looking back, Becker artfully balanced each volunteer writer's schedule. I was writing three books and an ESPN TV series based on another, *Voices of The Game*. Leaving DC, I returned to Upstate to do National Public Radio affiliate analysis, receiving an Associated Press award for "best commentary" in New York State—"Great going on the big award," Bush wrote in the kind of personalized note he loved. "Well deserved, say I!"—and teach English, specifically, Presidential Rhetoric and Public Speaking at the University of Rochester. "Dear Professor—Rochester is the winner here—so are the students, who will learn how to speak English," said Bush, who reinvented it regularly. My last Bush speech was his 2004 eulogy to President Reagan, though if he needed a quote or phrase I would drop everything today.

Anticipating a reader's question, it inevitably was a jolt to hear the president by phone, no matter how often. That was also true of getting a handwritten note, often signed "George Bush, Older #41." An early letter to the speech team read, "Yeah team!!! Thanks for all the work so far. You said 'No pay', but that cannot be." In reply, I thanked Bush for the chance to get to know him better than I had as a White House writer while he busily managed the Free World—his obsession with outdoor sports of every shape and kind; a reluctance to criticize Clinton even privately; how each family home in

Maine and Texas was put together but not put on, in the old-money New England Protestant way; and 41's easy and loving repartee with Barbara, born of a marriage most would kill for—sixty-nine years in 2014, the longest-ever-wed presidential couple.

Working, it also struck me that not only but especially in America could people so different in status, family, and background develop a close working relationship—this was true too of Bush with many others—based not on class but strains of an individual. In my case that meant work and lifelong love of politics and literature; faith; interest in animals and baseball; love of New England, Bush's and my mother's home; and Texas, his, my wife's, and a sister's adopted home. Up close, I saw, as much of the nation hadn't, Bush's amalgam of gentleness and steel. Once he spent forty-five minutes looking for a grandchild's stuffed animal. Bush would end a phone call by making you feel as if he didn't want to waste more of your time, not his. He refused, whatever the cost, to curry favor with what he felt the more demagogic elements of his party. All this—and to get paid. I told him it would go toward our "house fund."

It is a fact that many—especially but not exclusively Democrats—thought that upon leaving the presidency Bush would never return to build or buy his house in Texas. He had used the Lone Star State simply as a backdrop for his career, they sneered, noting that his voting residence in 1988 and 1992 had been the Houstonian Hotel. Born in the foreign East, educated in the alien Ivy League, Bush seemed to them a pseudo-Texan—not coarse enough for Longhorn politics. In spring 1980, when his candidacy for president collapsed, Bush put his Tanglewood house on sale and bought his family's manse at Walker's Point. If he were going home, cynics carped as 1993 approached, it would be there—except it wasn't. Texas had long ago become home.

"I'm sure some people didn't think we were going back to Houston till the house was built, the curtains hung, and George and I were in the kitchen, cooking tacos," barbed Mrs. Bush, who like her husband, simply loved the place. First, the presidential library would be

America's "Vision Thing"

in Texas. Second, Bush had moved into a roomy presidential office within the Park Laureate Building on Houston's Memorial Drive. Third, like the parents, their children largely lived in the South. Last, as anyone who has spent time in Texas knows, it is unpretentious, patriotic, religious, and hooked on family, work, and friends—a good definition of the former First Couple. By 1993 it fit like a glove.

The site of Bush's new Houston home stemmed from his 1981 sale of the Tanglewood property, which made a profit and began a dispute with the Internal Revenue Service (IRS). To resolve the scuffle, Bush signed an affidavit in 1985 in which he agreed to build his retirement home on the lot at 9 West Oak Lane South, within the West Oaks Addition subdivision—but within the Tanglewood area. A 1992 *Houston Chronicle* review called the area "charming" and redolent of Connecticut—Bush's childhood home. That year a *New York Times* story called Bush's 5,280-square-foot lot "a postage stamp of a vacant lot, and most associates doubt that Mr. Bush intends to build a home there."

The *Times* was as wrong about Bush's intent as it had been earlier that year about his supposed ignorance of a checkout counter. Once again the record gave Bush the last laugh. As part of the sale, completed around 1989, the family had an option to buy an extra 4,320 square feet of land, which the *Times* should have checked and which the Bushes exercised in 1992. Annoying the media, the family moved from a friend's temporarily rented Tanglewood home into their new residence in late 1993.

That year the Bushes invited my future wife, Sarah, and me to their new house shortly before Christmas. Enough decorations populated the residence to conjure past holidays at the White House. Mrs. Bush again reminded me of Angela Lansbury. The former president justified his marquee as America's oldest teenager by offering a glass of wine and then guiding us to the kitchen.

"You guys like pretzels?" he said, yanking a huge plastic barrel from a cabinet. "Ever see anything like this? This is a great deal, just got it at Sam's Club. I love these things." We returned to the den, where we drank and munched. Bush and a group of friends then went to a

Rockets pro basketball game, where we watched the crowd proudly welcome its friend and ex-president home.

Next morning I perused the *Times*, as I did daily for the heck of it. Typically, the newspaper never printed a retraction about the Bushes having built their lovely home in Texas after all.

Each president must choose a postpresidential model. Jimmy Carter became a humanitarian; Richard Nixon, best-selling author; Bill Clinton, globe-trotting sage. Bush 41 intended for his life to help others. That would only peripherally include, he thought, leaving office, a *public* life. "Bill, I want to tell you something. When I leave here, you're going to have no trouble from me," Bush told Clinton in November 1992. "The campaign is over, it was tough, and I'm out of here. I will do nothing to complicate your work, and I just want you to know that." Bush was through with politics. The 1992 campaign had been rough, even vicious. His family would take longer than Poppy to forgive. If you had said that real friendship would bloom between Bush and Clinton, most would reply that Jupiter had just aligned with Mars.

Postpresidential speeches that Bush gave to build his library inevitably critiqued 1989–93. "Think about the kaleidoscope of social and political change during our four years," he began. "The fall of the Berlin Wall, and the reunification of Germany; the dismantling of the Soviet state; the historic coalition that ejected Saddam Hussein from Kuwait; the good-faith dialogue of a lasting peace between age-old enemies in the Middle East. We faced a new world every day, it seemed, and the archives will help show how we answered the call to lead as no other nation could." Inevitably, the litany impressed the audience. As Henry Kissinger said, it had the ancillary advantage of being true.

Bush's speeches almost always discussed the decision not to go to Baghdad in 1991. About ninety-two hours after the ground war began, the president ordered his leadership team to the Oval Office: Colin Powell, Dick Cheney, Brent Scowcroft, Bob Gates, Dan Quayle, and Jim Baker. "Colin said the time had come to end the fighting—

the U.S. does not slaughter people along a highway of death for the sake of killing people," Bush stated, asking if Norman Schwarzkopf agreed. Powell said yes, "but walked over to the Oval Office desk and pulled the secure phone out of the drawer—you remember that classic photo," 41 recalled. Powell said, "Get me Schwarzkopf." Thirty seconds later, he was on the phone. "The question put to him was direct," said Bush. "So was his answer. He said, 'Our mission is complete.'"

Thus, Desert Storm ended after a hundred hours, Bush said. "And because of it, ancient enemies of the Middle East sat across the table from one another to talk peace for the first time in centuries." In 1992 Secretary of State Baker oversaw a regional peace conference in Madrid that Bush had promised Mikhail Gorbachev in 1990 between Israel and Arab entities, including the Palestine Liberation Organization (PLO). "History will recall Madrid as a major turning point toward peace," Bush continued. "The historic peace meeting held in Washington in September 1993 would not have occurred without the Madrid meeting, which stemmed from Desert Storm, which stemmed, in turn, from U.S. leadership."

Clinton invited the Bushes to spend the night in the White House, then attend the signing of the peace accord between Israel and the PLO. Mrs. Bush, believing that her husband had lost to a lesser man, refused. Bush, feeling that the accord was largely his, went. Still sorting out as an ex-president what next to do, he accepted straightaway an April 1993 offer to return with Mrs. Bush to the scene of his greatest triumph, receiving a royal tour of Kuwait at the invitation of its people. The Kuwaitis gave the library a generous gift—and Bush the chance to forget Election Day. "To see the nation we liberated from the terror of occupation, there's no way to express the power of those feelings," said Bush, truly moved.

Mrs. Bush's diary recounted the response: "We drove to Bayan Palace and all along the way were people cheering and waving George Bush posters and American flags and Kuwaiti flags." Over and over, Kuwaitis thanked the president. "One little kid touched my heart when he told me: 'If it weren't for Desert Storm, I would have no country.' What a moment." Looking back, Bush would tell an audience in 1993 that the perception of "being a 'foreign policy' president wasn't too helpful last November. But you know something? I have no regrets. I did what was right—for your [the audience's] kids and my grandkids."

The Kuwaiti trip was a family affair: in addition to Barbara, sons Jeb and Marvin and George W.'s wife, future first lady Laura. Also along: Baker and former treasury secretary Brady. Later, 41 found what a price they almost paid. Profoundly grateful to Bush, the Kuwaitis wanted nothing to spoil his visit—especially an Iraqi plot to kill the ex-president that they found days before the U.S. delegation's April arrival. Locating a Toyota Land Cruiser with almost ninety kilograms of plastic explosives, the Kuwaitis arrested seventeen people, some of whom admitted to coming from Baghdad, but didn't tell their guests or the U.S. Secret Service, which might have canceled the trip. When the party left, U.S. authorities were told, experts examining the device and interviewing captives. Ultimately, the Clinton administration found that Saddam Hussein had approved Bush's murder. Its retort: a June 26 cruise missile strike at the Iraqi Intelligence Service. Next day America's ambassador to the UN, Madeleine Albright, gave proof of the Iraqi plot to the Security Council. Hussein may not have got the message, but it is assumed that a grateful Bush did.

Back home, Poppy spurned advice that he embrace this or that cause. Too soon. Not his style. Don't be a braggadocio, he could hear mother Dorothy saying. "I need more time, more quiet time, more grandchild time, more time to forget and to *remember* [his emphasis]," Bush is quoted in Timothy Naftali's *George H. W. Bush*: "I don't have myself cast as a big and important person. I want to be a tiny point of light, hopefully, a bright point of light, but I don't crave sitting at the head table; nor do I burn with desire to see that history is kind to us."

This is where and how I hope Bush's circa 1993–96 speeches helped. They helped build—if not his *legacy*, a word he loathed—the bricks and mortar of nearly forty-five thousand feet of archival and office space and almost twenty-five thousand feet of public exhibition space, created by the architectural firm of Hellmuth, Obata and Kassabaum (now HOK), enhanced by the George Bush School's curricula, offering four, including two master's degree, programs. The speeches also let Bush, eschewing *I*, detail what his *team* had achieved.

By and large, Bush enjoyed speaking three or four times a week to political, economic, and civic groups. They helped him to remember what went right—what he had done that would last. He grew more relaxed and funny, increasingly, the private man on display. Like any effective speaker, Bush referenced subjects both in the news and in the audience's specific field. He also loved to quote household names from his (here, World War II) generation—Bing Crosby saying of Bob Hope, "There is nothing I wouldn't do for Hope, and there is nothing he wouldn't do for me. We spend our lives doing nothing for each other."

As president the time-challenged Bush played robo golf, somehow squeezing a full round into half an afternoon. Involuntarily retired, he poked fun at himself: "I'm adjusting just fine. Now I can really lay back and enjoy a relaxing hour playing eighteen holes of golf."

By now two members of the Bush family had written *New York Times* best-selling nonfiction books. "I'm glad to be here," 41 told one group, "though I admit I'm still recovering from the call to our office inviting the two most popular and eloquent Bushes to conclude this conference. I told my assistant to say, 'I'd be delighted.' She said, 'They want Barbara and Millie.'"

Both Bush adults often spoke to the same group. "I understand Barbara told you she's up each morning at 5:30 to work on her latest book," he said. "She didn't tell you that when she takes a break, she terrorizes our neighbors—because after all those years of backseat driving in government cars, she's now the proud owner of a Mercury Sable and a driver's license. If you visit Maine in the summer, or Houston the rest of the year, here's a warning: give that blue Merc station wagon plenty of room to roam."

Many speeches involved an award. In October 1993 Bush returned to Washington to receive the Association of the United States Army (AUSA) George Marshall Award. "I loved it when I was here, but I do not miss Washington," he told the AUSA. "I don't miss the press.

I am enjoying trying to stay out of their first strike zone. But what I *do* miss is dealing with our great military." The Marshall Award was both a tribute and metaphor, named "for a man who made a difference—not wishing it, but willing it."

As democracy triumphed in the 1980s, some called it "accidental." It wasn't, Bush said. "It's just that men like George Marshall made its victory seem providential." First, he believed in peace through strength. In 1918, as operations officer responsible for World War I tactical plans, Marshall helped Gen. John "Black Jack" Pershing acquire artillery, flamethrowers, and something called "tanks," then emerging. The material let the "famed First Division prepare for a local offensive at Cantigny in France, where our troops won the first battle ever won by Americans fighting in Europe."

In World War II, as Army chief of staff, Marshall taught a second lesson: "America thrives when, in Arthur Vandenberg's words, 'Politics stop at the water's edge.' To this day, I don't know whether he was a Democrat or Republican. I do know that he helped us win World War II [ending in 1945]." Finally, Marshall taught that America must be engaged, not merely strong. In 1947 the then secretary of state announced his plan to help Greece and Turkey: "Our policy is directed not against any country but against hunger, poverty, desperation, and chaos." Bush said, "Think of 1918, 1945, or foreign aid in General Marshall's plan. Each showed a strong, bipartisan, and fully-engaged America"—Bush's what-if goal in a second presidential term.

Instead, Bush increasingly was frustrated by Clinton's seesaw on Somalia. On October 20, 1993, the *Washington Post* editorialized as Army Rangers were withdrawn, "In all since the Oct. 3–4 firefight in which 18 U.S. soldiers were killed and scores were wounded, the Clinton Administration has [now] added troops to or withdrawn them from Somalia at least five times. 'This whipsawing of the force package and the description of what we think we're doing is fairly typical of this administration so far,' said one senior officer. 'The MTV generation doesn't seem to have much of an attention span.'" Bush was honored at a CARE dinner in New York for his humanitarian work in Somalia. A day later Edward Ney, chairman of Burson-Marsteller and Bush's former ambassador to Canada wrote, "Having a standing, clapping, cheering crowd for five to ten minutes at the end of your speech must have made you feel great."

Bush did when in 1994 he received the Sylvanus Thayer Award at the U.S. Military Academy. Surveying the soldierly audience, he said, "Now I know how Bob Hope feels." He then thanked the group for inviting a Navy man to speak at West Point. "I didn't want to press my luck, so I left the goat outside." Bush said that he knew the meaning of Douglas MacArthur's "'In the evening of my memory, always I come back to West Point.' For Barbara and me, call this the twilight of our memory. We are proud to be honorary members of the Long Gray Line."

That year the British media focused on a passage in Margaret Thatcher's new book, *The Downing Street Years*, in which Thatcher cited a need to "stroke" Bush's ego. At a London dinner, the former president jibed, "Barbara can't understand why. She said that yesterday while telling me how great I am." Bush then picked out four passages to defuse tension and lightly show, as Paul Harvey would say, "the *rest* of the story."

On page 768 Thatcher wrote, "I had breathed a sigh of relief when George Bush defeated his Democrat opponent in the U.S. Presidential election." Bush read this, then told the dinner, "Margaret, so did I."

Bush read how on page 763 Thatcher wrote of the G-7 summit, "It was chaired by President Bush, who was now imposing . . . his own style on the U.S. Administration." To this he added, "Margaret, my style being praised by you is like being called Man of War by Secretariat."

On page 820 Thatcher described their meeting at Aspen in the first days of the Gulf War: "He was firm, cool, showing the decisive qualities which the Commander in Chief of the greatest world power must possess." Bush, too, would never forget that week, being told by Thatcher never "to go wobbly."

Finally, Thatcher wrote of "the President and [her husband] Denis playing 18 holes of golf in the pouring rain—a very British occasion." Bush eyed Mr. Thatcher, saying, "Only one thing has changed on the course. Now that I'm no longer President, it's amazing how many people *beat* me."

In Manchester, England, Bush recalled George Bernard Shaw terming Britain and the United States two countries separated by a common language. "That's funny," Bush added. "Some say English is my only *foreign* language." Speaking to the Joint Israel Appeal, he said that the tiny nation, at forty-six younger than the Bushes' marriage, recalled a verse he once read on a little stone church in Sussex: "A vision without a task is but a dream, a task without a vision is drudgery, a vision *with* a task is the hope of the world."

Bush referenced criteria for U.S. involvement abroad that we used in dozens of speeches during his presidency and beyond. "When I committed forces to the Persian Gulf in late 1990 and early 1991—as I had in Panama earlier and would later in Somalia—I needed answers to three questions. One, What is the mission? Two, How to reach it—how do we win? Three, How and when do we get out once the mission's achieved? If I could satisfy those criteria, I acted. If not, we did not—*must* not."

As we have previously seen, when the United States overran Iraq in 2003, Colin Powell summarized the reality of not having an exit strategy: "You break it, you own it." By contrast, Bush 41 told me that all three of his criteria, especially the third, kept him from seizing Baghdad in 1991. It is safe to say that his "vision with a task," to quote the little stone church in Sussex, was and remains clear.

It would be incorrect to say that 41's postpresidential speech parade passed without incident. In 1997 Bush was to appear at the University of Toronto to receive a doctor of laws degree, where, we learned, several dozen professors, flaunting liberal tolerance, were prepared to walk out during the first few minutes of his speech. Their "beef," to use a favorite Reagan word: Bush's CIA stint, Iran-Contra role, and invasion of Panama had flaunted, as Toronto English professor David Galbraith said, "a contempt for legality and democracy." Another university professor, political science's John Kirton, thought that a

America's "Vision Thing"

bit unhinged. "Bush's contribution was truly historic," he said. "He presided over the end of the Cold War, and accomplished it peacefully, which is quite a feat."

As Bush's appearance neared, I did what I always did when Bush needed to be funny: called Doug Gamble, who has graced this narrative for his humor in the 1988 acceptance speech. Born in Montreal, Doug moved to Hamilton, Ontario, at age eight and Toronto at eighteen; became a *Toronto Star* humor columnist; and crossed the border to LA in 1980 to soon write one-line phrases for Joan Rivers, Bob Hope, Phyllis Diller, Rodney Dangerfield—and Ronald Reagan. After Walter Mondale had accused Reagan of government by amnesia, the president replied, "I thought that remark accusing me of having amnesia was uncalled for. I just wish I could remember who said it." Another: "For the last four years, I've been urging the press to be more positive. Today I picked up the *Washington Post* and saw a story that said, 'We're positive the president will lose the election.'" Another: "The other side's promises are like Minnie Pearl's hat. Both have big price tags hanging from them." (TV writer Ray Siller was Reagan's other brilliant humorist.)

In 1987 Bush inherited Gamble, soon happy that he did. "Despite my critics, I have good reason to be confident," the vice president would say. "Shirley MacLaine told me recently that I was Martin Van Buren in another life." After Bush's election, speechwriter Joshua Gilder gave Gamble credit second only to Bush. Gamble wrote many of 41's best one-line jokes for use by his writers. A decade later, with teachers from other colleges joining Toronto's faculty in demanding that Bush's honorary degree be revoked, Gamble scored again in his "home and native land." Poppy spoke before an imminent Canadian postal strike, which coincided with the possible teacher walkout. One Gamble line explored a reason for the professors' conduct: "I can only assume they're walking out in sympathy with the postal workers." Another line referenced the Toronto hockey team's hated 1970s and '80s owner: "I haven't seen such a mass exodus from an arena since Harold Ballard bought the Maple Leafs." As usual, Bush chose the Gambleism with which he felt most comfortable: "Sometimes I'm too optimistic. When they first got to their feet I thought I was getting a standing ovation."

In fact, only a few teachers walked out during Bush's talk. Sadly, 41 never had to use a zinger. Afterward, though, students devoted to free speech and higher learning turned over what they believed was the former president's official car. It wasn't. Bush's real auto left, undisturbed, by another route. Hating student violence, Gamble had seen it in Canada before moving south. Living in Carmel, California, he now continues to dispense good humor to Republicans across the land.

Bush's 1990s return to public life was as unexpected as Gamble's 1980s entrance. In late summer 1993, we devised a running joke to lace 41's speeches. Bush said that he had vowed not to criticize Clinton for a full year after the November 1992 election. He then said, "And I've kept my promise." Chuckles. "But, you know, I checked the calendar this morning." More laughter. "Only __ days to go." Applause. The criticism was gentle. Bush backed democracy in Haiti but called U.S. ground forces there "a tremendous mistake." Unlike Clinton, he did not support the overthrown president, Jean-Bertrand Aristide. At home, Bush attacked Clinton's bid for health-care reform. Poppy's interest was becoming less his party than his sons. In 1994 George W. and Jeb ran as Republican candidates for governor of Texas and Florida, respectively. Suddenly, Poppy was back in politics, agreeing to campaign for both.

W. was said to be his mother's son: direct and acerbic. "I have my father's eyes and my mother's mouth," he often said, to laughter. Jeb was closer to dad, soft-spoken and sensitive. Bush found it harder to be a member of the candidate's family than the candidate: "As the front guy you slug back. The family has to take it, be resigned. It's the worst thing in the world." Worse is to lose, which Barbara, urging W. not to run, thought he would do against Ann Richards, loathed by the clan since her acidic 1988 convention speech: "Poor George, he can't help it. He was born with a silver foot in his mouth." Early polls in Florida showed Jeb ahead of Lawton Chiles, Election Day proving the saw that "a week in politics is like a year anywhere else."

Jeb lost to Chiles amid charges of vote fraud similar to 1960 Chicago. W. showed discipline veiled for most of his forty-eight years, Bush's on-message campaign burying Richards by 334,066 votes. The family victory was almost as fulfilling as 1988's.

In April 1995 an incident widened the gulf among how Bush *père* was viewed by wings of the Republican Party. White supremacists exploded the Alfred P. Murrah Federal Building in Oklahoma City, killing 168, among them former Secret Service agent Al Whicher, on Bush's protective detail when Poppy was vice president and president. When a GOP angel, the National Rifle Association (NRA), refused to repudiate attacks on federal law enforcement after the bombing, Bush resigned his NRA life membership, saying, "Al Whicher was no Nazi. He was a kind man, a loving parent, a man dedicated to serving his country—and serve it well he did." Bush would not abide this diatribe against a friend. "Your broadside against federal agents deeply offends my own sense of decency and honor," he wrote NRA executive vice president Wayne LaPierre. Some NRAers responded, heatedly: 41 raised our taxes, gave us Clinton, and now this—what was next?

One was Grover Norquist, an NRA director, who founded the influential advocacy group Americans for Tax Reform in 1985—Darth Vader and Banquo's ghost to the Left and Right, respectively. Since the 1990s each Republican presidential nominee, most governors, and almost every congressional candidate had signed Norquist's "no new taxes" pledge—the tie that bound the scattered GOP. Its genesis was Bush breaking his 1988 convention pledge: "Bush managed the collapse of the Soviet Union, kicked Iraq out of Kuwait, had a 90 percent approval rating. However, he agreed to a tax-increase deal [consisting of] two dollars of spending cuts for every one dollar of taxes. And he lost the Presidency." To the Right's elite, Bush raising taxes made all that he did suspect. That was not the view of his Secret Service detail, which idolized him—nor most conservatives, furious here at the NRA—nor those helping to dedicate the Bush Presidential Library and Museum at Texas A&M in College Station, the eleventh presidential library to open to the public.

To reach it, a visitor travels Highway 290 north from Houston to

Hempstead, keeps north on Highway 6 to Bryan, takes Business 6 at College Station to the second light and turns left on FM 2919, then sees George Bush Drive at A&M. You turn right and proceed to the Bush library, which links a museum, archives, Centers for Presidential, Leadership, and International Studies, and classroom space for the Departments of Economics, Sociology, and Political Science. Also visible at the November 6, 1997, opening were a Gulf War exhibit, replicas of Air Force and Camp David offices, Bush exhibits, and a display of family books, videos, and computer goings-on, as well as five presidents—the current (Clinton), three past (Bush, Carter, and Ford), and a future (George W.)—and their wives, plus Lady Bird Johnson and Nancy Reagan.

The guests of honor arrived by train the day before. Huge flags bannered "Welcome to College Station," "Aggies 4 Bush," and "Gig 'em George." A bronze statue put every visitor in freedom's saddle: *The Day the Wall Came Down*, by Veryl Goodnight, showing horses jumping over pieces of the Berlin Wall. An estimated fifty thousand people heard Governor Bush proclaim, "Here, objective historians will look at his record and conclude President Bush was a man who knew his priorities and never wavered from them. President Bush was a man who entered the political arena and left with his integrity intact. President Bush was a leader who stared tyranny in the face and never blinked. George Bush was a great president of the United States because he is first and foremost a great man."

Increasingly, tentatively, W.'s "great man" began to leave his cocoon. In 1997 the International Parachute Association invited Bush to be guest of honor at an annual meeting, during which he recalled bailing out of the Navy Avenger in 1944 as his two crewmates stayed behind. "As I recounted these errors, something happened," Bush next day wrote his children. "For some reason, I went back to a thought I had way in the back of my mind. It has been there, sleeping like Rip Van Winkle, alive but not alive. Now it was quite clear. I want to make one more parachute jump!" He expected Barbara to object, but as he continued, "in the final analysis I will convince her (1) that it is safe and (2) that this is something I have to do, must do." Colin Powell was incredulous. "Are you planning to jump from a *plane*?" he asked. "It's the talk of the Pentagon. I know you look forty-five, but you're seventy-two. How are your ankles, knees, etc.?" Bush went ahead anyway. Eleven days before the jump—J-day—he called each of his children. All gave consent, though not carefree advice.

Finally, on March 25, 1997, "caught up in the spirit of it all, totally hyped"—wearing his Desert Storm boots, white helmet, and white gloves—Bush termed it his "White Elvis suit"—and having learned the jumpers' secret handshake, ending with index fingers pointed at each other, a signal to pull the rip cord, Bush jumped with the U.S. Army's famed Golden Knights—successfully. To 41, it was almost surrealistic. "The floating to death took longer than I thought, but I wish it could have gone on twice as long," he said. "I didn't hit hard, but a gust of wind seemed to pull me back . . . I was down. It had gone well. I had lived a dream."

Mrs. Bush hugged him. To millions of Americans, this was the most appealing Bush since the Persian Gulf. The media covered it around the world. That year, discussing a speech, he suddenly told me, "You know, it's the damnedest thing. I was worried people would laugh at me. I did it to honor my mates, and to prove that old guys can still do things." Bush started laughing. "I go abroad, and even foreign leaders ask, 'Tell me about the jump!'" They were still asking in 2009 and 2014 when incredibly he jumped to celebrate turning eighty-five and ninety, respectively.

Acting against type, Bush jump-started his popularity with the jump—but what about his legacy? Refusing to write a memoir—too many *I*s—he finally agreed to collaborate with National Security Adviser Brent Scowcroft, whom Bush trusted implicitly, and James McCall, a young staffer and historian, on a book about his administration's record, the Gulf War, and the Soviet Union. In 1998's *A World Transformed*, Bush and Scowcroft wrote first-person passages, including excerpts from Bush's diaries, which relatively few then knew existed. A year later other diary entries and letters from childhood to the present were published in *All the Best, George Bush: My Life in Letters and Other Writings.* The entries and letters largely affirmed the Bush I thought I knew and had written for on that assumption for a decade—kind, sentimental, stoic. They form a revealing window on Bush's mental and emotional world.

Another window was even clearer: a father's regard for his sons, and nation's regard for him. The current Gallup Poll says that most Americans view Bush *père* favorably, many very, giving him a 60 percent approval rating. The *Wall Street Journal*'s Peggy Noonan writes, "He is increasingly acknowledged as a great diplomat, a patriot, a steady and sophisticated president, an exemplar of the greatest generation." Many in Bush's own party, especially conservatives, however, still bay for the Gipper.

In 2008 such GOP presidential candidates as Mike Huckabee, John McCain, and Mitt Romney spoke at a regional convention in Tennessee. Its largest-selling button read, "I Miss Ronald Reagan." Bush told W., "The Far Right will continue to accuse me of 'Betraying the Reagan Revolution'—something Ronald Reagan would never do." Bush did not betray the Reagan Revolution as much as politically he failed to strengthen it. In 1998 W. and Jeb again ran for governor. This time both won, partly because of a remarkably selfless dad.

Pop wrote each that August:

So read my lips—no more worrying. At some point both of you may want to say, "Well, I don't agree with Dad on that point," or "Frankly I think Dad was wrong on that." *Do it* [author's emphasis]. Chart your own course, not just on the issues but on defining yourselves. No one will ever question your love of family—your devotion to your parents. We have all lived long enough and lived in a way that demonstrates our closeness, so do not worry when the comparisons might be hurtful to your Dad for nothing can ever be written that will drive a wedge between us—nothing at all.

In effect, George Bush was freeing each son to further his career by using him as a foil.

The amazing fact, thought Tom DeFrank, is that George W. Bush's triumph, which his dad helped make possible—a two-term presidency, something that escaped the father—ultimately helped resurrect Bush Sr. in America's and the world's sight. "One of the great ironies of their relationship is that the performance of the son helped remake the father's image," DeFrank believed. "Bush 43 talks compellingly about his father's 'unconditional love', and that must be true since he opposed much of what 41 did. His stewardship helped rehabilitate the father's relationship with the American people and with history."

To Noonan, Bush was a foreign-policy "realist." He was "prudent after the end of the Soviet Union, he was tactful, and when he said he had to go to war in Kuwait he built a world-wide coalition, did the job he said he would do, and stopped when that job was done." Increasingly, she felt Bush deserved a Nobel Peace Prize for "his work in the days after the [fall of the] Soviet Union" and his help making Germany whole and free. In response, friends were "no longer startled and usually nod in agreement."

DeFrank understood, thinking Poppy the "last great Republican moderate" and the "best human being in the White House since Gerald Ford." The result: George H. W. Bush was much more "respected, and in many cases, truly revered" than on leaving office in 1993.

An example of 41's "unconditional love" was religion. George H. W. Bush was intensely, but privately, religious. Antipodally, as Timothy Naftali wrote, "following a hard-drinking, hard-partying adolescence that stretched until age 40, George W. Bush embraced evangelical Christianity" in a most sincere but public way.

On December 13, 1999, the Iowa Caucus only six weeks away, each GOP candidate in a presidential debate in Des Moines was asked by moderator John Bachman to name his favorite political philosopher or thinker. Bush answered, "Christ, because he changed my heart," later saying he thought the question to mean, "Who's had the most influence on your life?" To many, it was a thoughtful, even inspired, choice. It won Iowa, helped W. survive later primary defeat, and almost surely made his presidency possible. Elites went hysterical. Chris Matthews, host of MSNBC's *Hardball*, foamed about W.'s coalition living "under a tent." Reverend C. Christopher Epting, bishop, Episcopal Diocese of Iowa, hissed in a nasty December 15 *New York Times* article that a profession of faith by candidates "could be a turn off for those who fear a heavy-handed Christianity in the White House." Apparently, it was worse for the more than 80 percent of Americans who call themselves Christian—*his own flock*—to profess their religion too openly than not to profess it at all.

Bush the Elder was sufficiently moved by this to write Epting, starting, "This is not a political letter. It is simply a letter from a father about one of his sons. It is written from the heart. Certainly it is not intended to be offensive in any way." He noted that he had felt uncomfortable as president wearing "my religion on my sleeve" but that "what he [George] said was true. Jesus Christ did turn our son's life into something virtuous. Christ as revealed in the Bible has taught him to love God and love people and that's what he is doing." Bush observed that *fils* had read the Bible twice, from cover to cover, "respected all faiths, and never tried to impose his views on others." Moreover, Bachman had asked Bush to "expand on his views only after George made a simple statement about Jesus Christ." The camera switched to the next candidate, missing what "those in attendance tell me . . . was a tear in our son's eyes."

Epting wrote back, substituting "Mr. Bush" for the more polite "Mr. President," saying the "awkwardness" he had cited in the *Times* dealt with Jesus being called "a political philosopher or thinker." This seems extremely curious, since even those sans a Christian or any faith concede philosophy pervades the Sermon on the Mount, the Last Supper, and other teachings. More curiously, Epting ended with a nauseous assault against "a narrow fundamentalism . . . far from . . . Christ." I myself feel awkward around fundamentalism's public profession of faith. However, there is little narrow about its huge appeal, as even a cursory glance at membership shows. Instead, narrow better describes the appeal of liberal Protestant sects like the reverend's Episcopalianism or my boyhood Presbyterianism. Bush wrote as a loving father seeking understanding for his son. Perhaps Epting, now assisting bishop, Episcopal Diocese of Chicago, might try to understand why so many people are no longer buying what denominations like ours are trying to sell.

A month later Bush addressed the Nixon library, saying, "My time for contributing to this work in the public arena is now past. I had my chance, and did my best, and hopefully got a few things right," he said, modestly. "Of course, 1992 did not work out the way we hoped, but I have tried not to criticize my successor—understanding that he has a hard job to do, and that there are plenty of good people in the loyal opposition out there fighting for many of the beliefs that I share." Bush's belief in bipartisanship was as rare as his humility in the 2000 public square. "They don't need one more back-bencher in Houston, Texas, saying, 'Hey, wait a minute. I used to do it this way.' My sons don't need me doing that, either." What they, especially W., needed was less for Dad to speak on their behalf than to raise money: first in the older son's primaries vs. John McCain; then the general election vs. Al Gore—to Bush Sr., still "the Ozone Man."

After W.'s victory in Iowa, Bush introduced him in New Hampshire by saying, "This boy of ours will not let you down." McCain made sport of the fact that it took a man to be president, whereupon W. lost the primary by nineteen points, after which Dad seldom introduced him again. Instead, he utilized his network for money and personnel; appeared, like Barbara, wherever the campaign thought useful; and after eight years of Bill Clinton, including an affair in the Oval Office with an intern only seven years older than his daughter, reminded Republicans, then the general electorate, what it had *liked* about Bush—someone worthy of the office. The South Carolina primary was *fils*'s pivot, Karl Rove his Atwater. After McCain later withdrew, Junior chose the Senior Bush's defense secretary, Dick Cheney, as vice president. At the convention, parents sat, beaming, as W. said, "Mother, everyone loves you and so do I. Growing up, she gave me love and lots of advice. I gave her white hair. And I want to thank my father—the most decent man I have ever known. All my life I have been amazed that a gentle soul could be so strong. And Dad, I want you to know how proud I am to be your son."

Bush *père* "was the last president of a great generation," W. said. "Now the question comes to [its] sons and daughters. . . . What is asked of us?" Bush Jr.'s answer was "compassionate conservatism"—to some, a Trojan horse for greater spending, ever-larger government, and social engineering in rightist garb. His philosophy didn't defeat Al Gore in November. Not being Gore and Bill Clinton was enough—barely. In September I interviewed Bush Sr. at Kennebunkport for my Rochester, New York, CBS TV affiliate series *Perfectly Clear*. He was friendly but preoccupied: the campaign was going badly. Ironically, the following debates pivoted the election, Gore losing more than Bush won—sighing and rolling eyes in one, seeming numb in another, crowding Bush physically in the last. The Old Man—W.'s affectionate moniker—viewed every minute. Mrs. Bush, the house Cassandra, would not watch.

Election Day came, stayed, and wouldn't leave. Early that night the networks gave Florida to Vice President Gore and thus, it seemed, the presidency. Jeb, the Sunshine State's governor, was aghast, having thought it solid for his brother. The Bush clan was in Austin, Bush Sr. feeling like the baseball announcer of a bad team who turned fifty in August. "I don't mind that," the broadcaster said. "It's just that when the season began I was forty-three." As Florida, mocking early projections, seesawed back toward Bush, then Gore, then Bush, then "undecided," the former president, seventy-six, told a friend, "I feel twice my age." Early in the morning, Florida was declared for Bush, giving him the 270 electoral votes needed to become president. That decision, laughed a friend, lasted "about as long as it takes to recite the oath of office."

Gore closed the gap. Florida again turned undecided, the networks throwing up their hands. Prince Al led by about 500,000 popular votes nationally—but neither candidate had a majority of the Electoral College. For thirty-six days neither would, as lawyers on behalf of each side took over, honorary family member James Baker leading Bush's. A recount began and continued until the U.S. Supreme Court *Bush v. Gore* ruling ended it. Bush the Elder no longer felt 152—seventy-six times "twice"—years old.

The night of the Supreme Court verdict, Al Gore conceded in a memorable speech. Bush 41, knowing political victory and defeat, called the White House switchboard to congratulate the vice president. He then saw the televised image of his son, about to address the nation from the Texas State Legislature. As the camera "focused on George and Laura walking into the chamber," he wrote in *All the Best, George Bush*, his body "was literally wracked with uncontrollable sobs. It just happened. No warning, no thinking that this might be emotional for a mother or dad to get through—just an eruption from deep within me where my body literally shook. Barbara cried, too. We held hands."

On January 20, 2001, the new president took the oath of office, gave his inaugural address, and went to the Oval Office, where he wanted his first visitor to be someone who had been there before. The visitor was already in the family quarters of the White House having a hot bath when he learned that "the president wants to see you." The guest rose, dried, and dressed quickly, because he knew that a president's time is precious. He made his way to the Oval Office, to be greeted by his son.

"He knew how much this would mean to his dad, and he wanted to share his first moments in this revered office with him," said Barbara Bush, later describing how George W. poignantly set the scene. He also wanted the world to know that his father had been visitor number one. For his part, to show respect for W., erase confusion with his son, and write finis to his political career, Dad said that he should now be called George H. W. Bush, restoring the patrician name he had dropped when he entered Texas politics. George W. would be known as W., Junior, or Bush 43. Dad would be dubbed Bush 41, Senior, or George H. W. The gymnastics both did to honor the other did honor to each.

The Bushes were America's first presidential father-son combination since the early nineteenth-century Adamses. A more intriguing comparison was 43 vs. 41. At first their terms differed on, among other things, the role of foreign vs. domestic policy; the urgency of tax cuts vs. need for a balanced budget; the efficacy of 43's defense secretary Donald Rumsfeld; and whether the Strategic Defense Initiative had largely won the Cold War—*fils* was more sure than *père*. These and other fissures faded in 9/11's wake.

The elder Bushes had left Houston early on September 11 to fly to St. Paul, Minnesota, to speak before returning home at night. Their private plane was diverted to Milwaukee, the Secret Service saying that their eldest son and daughter-in-law were safe in Florida and DC, respectively. That night the Bushes talked to people at a mall in Milwaukee, where they were to buy walking shoes, go for a walk, and eat at a family restaurant. Next day, terrorist strategy still murky, U.S. airspace was closed. An exception was the Bushes, flown to Kennebunkport.

Overnight 43's presidency changed from an emphasis on domestic policy—the environment, cell research, and education, working together with Democrats to pass "No Child Left Behind"—to an officially undeclared war on terrorism. "He can run, but he can't hide," Bush, quoting boxer Joe Louis, said of Osama bin Laden, leader of the terrorist group Al-Qaeda, which had planned and implemented the attack on the Pentagon and New York's Twin Towers. W. fingered the Taliban regime, Osama's sanctuary in Afghanistan, then eyed Saddam Hussein, Dad's bête noire, as a force behind Al-Qaeda. Usually Bush the Elder and Rumsfeld treated each other as the price you pay for entering politics. Independently, though, they now reached the same conclusion. In January 2002, 43 included Hussein's Iraq with North Korea and Iran in an "axis of evil." Pop would have agreed, saying, "I don't hate a lot of people. I don't hate that easy." Hussein, though, who Bush wrongly thought would be overthrown after the Gulf War, would have to involuntarily retire—or worse.

As W. debated whether to attack or not—in effect, "nation build," what he vowed *not* to do in the 2000 campaign—the media wondered if 41 was advising him on Hussein. In 2002 Scowcroft wrote a *Wall Street Journal* article suggesting Bush not invade and occupy Iraq. Would he have done so without 41's consent? Would the United States inherit a quagmire, sans exit plan, violating 41's three criteria to invade? Bush Sr. was nowhere to be heard. In an interview with journalist Bob Woodward, W. raised as many questions as he answered: "I don't remember" what, if any, advice he got from pop. "You know, he is the wrong father to appeal to in terms of strength. There is a higher Father that I appeal to." Most Americans, unlike elite journalists, grasped Bush's final sentence. What made no sense is that 43 wouldn't consult 41 about Hussein, Iraq, and the U.S. military. After 1991 who knew more about the region? Why wouldn't W. consult his dad?

Ultimately, 43 anchored a far smaller UN coalition—less than half the number of nations and 250,000 of the 300,000 troops of the initial invasion force vs. 1990–91's 800,000 troops, including half a million Americans—than his father assembled. The attack's rationale—Hussein had nuclear "weapons of mass destruction"—was never proved. Hussein *was* found, tried, and later killed. The U.S. military victory's "shock and awe" helped W. beat Massachusetts senator John Kerry in the 2004 election, stamping the Bush clan as a political "dynasty," another term Poppy hated—two presidents of three terms, two governors, one U.S. senator, and a U.S. congressman. "I want our kids to be proud, not intimidated, by what came before," said Bush Sr. "Just go where their interests are, follow where your hearts lead you, as we did when Bar and I were married."

For the former First Couple, the autumn of their lives together led to honors in full bloom. Three primary schools and two middle schools in Texas and an elementary school in Mesa, Arizona, were named for Barbara Bush, as were the Barbara Bush Library in Harris County, Texas, and the Barbara Bush Children's Hospital at Maine Medical Center in Portland, Maine. Mrs. Bush joined the Board of AmeriCare and the Mayo Clinic, though busy with the Barbara Bush Foundation for Family Literacy. This left little time for, among other things, television. With CBS's *Murder, She Wrote* series canceled in

1996 and the last *Murder* TV-movie aired in 2003, perhaps she had little to miss. In March 2003 the United States invaded Iraq—to her another reason not to watch. When ABC's *Good Morning America* asked Barbara about the tube, to quote W., "she let 'er rip":

"I watch none," she bristled. "He [Bush 41] sits and listens and I read books, because I know perfectly well that, don't take offense, that 90 percent of what I hear on television is supposition when we're talking about the news. And he's not, not as understanding of my pettiness about that." Perhaps the viewer would be. "But why should we hear about body bags and deaths, and how many this or that or what do you suppose? Or, I mean, it's not relevant. So, why should I waste my beautiful mind on something like that, and watch him suffer?"

Mrs. Bush's decision to "read books" should have brought down the house. Instead, the dissonance of a "beautiful mind" and "body bags" helped the ceiling crash. In late August and early September 2005, Hurricane Katrina devastated New Orleans and southern Mississippi, displacing thousands of vagabonds from New Orleans to Houston. Visiting a relief center, Mrs. Bush "ripped" again. "I've heard almost everyone I've talked to say, 'We're gonna move to Houston,'" she told the radio program *Marketplace*. "What I'm hearing, which is sort of scary, is they all want to stay in Texas. [Many did.] Everybody is so overwhelmed by the hospitality, and so many of the people in the arenas here, you know, were underprivileged anyway, so this"—she chuckled softly—"is working very well for them." That humor briefly worked less well for her.

A year later it was revealed that she donated an undisclosed amount of money to the Bush-Clinton Katrina Fund on the condition that the charity work with an educational software company owned by son Neil. Later, Barbara was hospitalized for abdominal pain, an ulcer, and aortic valve replacement surgery. In a 2010 interview with Larry King, she was asked about former Alaska governor Sarah Palin. "I sat next to her once, thought she was beautiful, and I think she's very happy in Alaska, and I hope she'll stay there," she said, curtly. Palin was even colder. "I don't want to, sort of, concede that we have to get used to this kind of thing [Palin felt it condescension], because I think the majority of Americans don't want to put up with the blue-bloods." It was, said a Bush family friend, less that they came from two wings of the party than from two different orbs.

Sacred Heart University and Dartmouth College gave Yale '48 honorary degrees, the latter a doctor of law. The trek to Hanover evoked a pivotal campaign of George Bush's long career, the 1988 New Hampshire primary, without which Poppy could not have become president. In 2004 and 2007, he and Mrs. Bush attended the state funeral of Presidents Reagan and Ford, respectively. A month after the Ford funeral, Bush received the Ronald Reagan Freedom Award from Nancy Reagan. Taft and Wilson, Hoover and FDR, Truman and Ike—the list swells of a president and his successor barely speaking to one another, at the inaugural or later. By contrast, Bush's growing affinity with Bill Clinton truly astonished each other's staff.

Most forget the illegitimacy many Republicans and independents attached to Clinton during and after his presidency. In late December 2004, responding to a horrific tsunami that killed nearly 300,000 in Asia, W. recruited his dad and Clinton to raise money and relief. Each traveled to the site. Both cut TV ads showing them jointly requesting help. In June 2005 Clinton vacationed in Kennebunkport, causing incredulity, double take, and murmuration. Clearly, they *liked* each other. Moreover, their budding friendship showed that two foes had turned the page—something our politics in state capitals and especially Washington DC seemed constitutionally incapable of. "This is a great example of the wonderful role former presidents and their libraries can play," said pollster John Zogby. "In a time of disunity, they remind us of unity—the many things that bring Americans together."

In 2005 both Presidents Bush, Laura Bush, foreign policy aide Condoleezza Rice, and Chief of Staff Andrew Card traveled with Clinton to attend Pope John Paul II's funeral at the Vatican. That fall local, state, and federal relief for Hurricane Katrina was slow and bungling. Stores were smashed, businesses looted; more than a thousand people died. Again W. asked 41 and Clinton to head a charitable campaign to help the victims, many homeless, their houses wrecked or gone. America reacted gallantly, sending money and supplies. The campaign further fused the two ex-presidents. In one letter Bush confessed, "I encouraged him to make [another] trip as I thought it would be fun to have him along. It was."

Once, video caught Clinton falling asleep during a Martin Luther King Day sermon. Bush wrote him, saying, "I could indeed 'feel your pain'"—Clinton's aphorism. Bush said that "I don't remember if I ever told you about the prestigious [Brent] Scowcroft Award," given in 1989–93 to the person "who fell asleep most soundly during an Administration meeting." Points were added for "recovery," waking from a sound sleep and, nodding in agreement to something just said, feigning that you had been awake all along. Joking, Clinton began calling Barbara Bush "Mom." At Bush *fils*'s 2013 library dedication at Southern Methodist University in Dallas, Clinton called himself "the black sheep of the Bush family." Even partisans laughed—because of or despite themselves.

In 2006 Bush was feted by the National Italian American Foundation for working to better the lives of all Americans. In 2008, accompanied by W., still in office, Bush met Chinese president Hu Jintao in Beijing, a final trip to the China he loved and whose bona fides had helped make him president. On January 10, 2009, each President Bush and his wife shared a special day—the commissioning of USS *George H. W. Bush* (CVN-77), the U.S. Navy's tenth and last *Nimitz*-class supercarrier, a craft that in a different form and age had helped save Poppy's life. Ironically for Bush, who didn't learn how to use a computer until he was seventy, this carrier was the first to rely primarily on a computer-based platform, automatically accounting for winds and currents, instead of the paper charts that ships traditionally had used.

The ship's historian, CMC J. D. Port, used a traditional tribute room to make sure "everyone has a sense of who our namesake was." Bush's naval career was recalled, especially his flying of torpedo bombers off the carrier *San Jacinto*. At the opening a visitor among the eighteen thousand would find a letter from Vice Adm. John S. McCain, the senator's grandfather, awarding Bush the Distinguished Flying Cross for his mission over Chichi Jima, and nearby in the hangar bay a statue of a young Bush in his flight suit. "We have a feeling that this is our grandfather," Port said. On January 9 Bush toured the ship for several hours, then next day was escorted down the pier by commanding officer of the aircraft carrier, Capt. Kevin E. O'Flaherty. "I'm feeling very excited, unbelievable, very emotional," Bush said, "very proud of the kids on this ship." The pride was reciprocal, Bush back where he belonged.

Turnabout is fair play. In 2003 Senator Edward Kennedy received the third annual Bush Library Foundation's George Bush Award for Excellence in Public Service, causing conservative jaws to drop and liberal throats to chortle. In 2014 Poppy was awarded the John F. Kennedy Library Foundation's Profile in Courage Award for "risking his reputation and ultimately his political career" by breaking his "No New Taxes" pledge to lower the deficit and fuel prosperity. On February 15, 2011, Bush, having given the Medal of Freedom to, among others, Ronald Reagan and Margaret Thatcher, received it himself, President Obama saying, "Those of you who know him, this is a gentleman, inspiring citizens to become points of light."

In July 2013 the ex-president and First Lady were invited back to the White House in recognition of the five thousandth daily Point of Light Award. Later that month, 41 asked why each member of his Secret Service detail had shaved his head. Bush learned that a member's two-year-old son, identified by his family as "Patrick," was ill with leukemia, which in 1953 killed the Bushes' daughter Robin. Bush promptly shaved his head in solidarity with the agents and Patrick, who had lost his hair. Since 1977 George and Barbara had embraced Houston's famed M. D. Anderson Cancer Center, helping to raise money for research. In 2004 the center created a clinic in Robin's name. Now a photo of Bush, smiling and holding Patrick, appeared around the world. A caption might have read, "Points of Light Are Ageless."

About three years earlier, a form of Parkinson's disease known as

Parkinsonitis, a loss of balance and mobility in the legs, had begun to affect 41. Bush increasingly relied on a cane or motorized wheelchair, "President of the United States" emblazoned on the back. Dispirited, he took heart, I hoped, from America's response to his 2012–13 stay at Methodist Hospital in Houston. Bush entered November 23, 2012, for a bronchitis-related cough. Supposed to be home by Christmas, he was moved December 23 to the intensive-care unit because of a persistent fever. Family members flew to Houston to be with Bush, the prognosis grave. In critical condition for several days around Christmas, he rallied. By December 30, several weeks before 41's January 2013 release, family spokesman Jim McGrath said that Poppy was singing with his doctors—endearing, unself-conscious, arguably more beloved than any other elder statesman of his time.

Hospital officials were stunned by the avalanche of people trying to contact the ex-president—in person and by phone, telegram, e-mail, Facebook, and Twitter—apt, since Bush, once so technically challenged that he lampooned his inability to learn Nintendo from his then-ten-year-old grandson, had improbably become e-mail and Twitter taught—his playful e-mail address ending "@flfw.com" for "former leader of the free world." What appeared so crucial in 1992—entertain, even transport, a crowd—seemed almost irrelevant a quarter-century later. What Bush did worst—glad-hand, attack—is what polling says Americans now disdain. Instead, his forte—honor and competence, a person to admire, even dub a hero—is what we say matters. America's vision of the man who coined "the vision thing" had profoundly changed in the twilight of his life.

John Zogby explains,

He was the second-oldest man to be elected president, and the second-oldest to leave the presidency. So we've come to look at him as a father figure. It's been more than twenty years since he left the office—so people have grown comfortable with him as a person. Our prism is different than when he was president. One of his sons became president, and another governor of Florida. So America thinks of him literally as a father. He built a great

America's "Vision Thing"

alliance and won a great war. That has rarely, if ever, happened since Franklin Roosevelt. So people think of him as a great commander in chief. Plus, he was a war hero as a young man and our last president from the Greatest Generation. It all fits together.

In April 2013 the George W. Bush Presidential Center opened in Dallas. President Obama and former presidents Clinton, Carter, Bush 41 and 43 gathered to hail the newest presidential library: "The headline of the . . . remarks," wrote Peggy Noonan, "is that everyone was older and nicer." Each president spoke. The oldest, George H. W. Bush, said, "God bless America, and thank you very much." He rose courageously from his wheelchair to acknowledge the crowd, whose applause was loud and lasting. "That crowd," said Noonan, "and the people watching on TV—the person they loved and honored most was him."

Time's Hugh Sidey had predicted it a generation earlier. "His presidential record was better than anybody in this dismal campaign ever admitted, and better than he could articulate. And there was something more that could never be fitted into the strictures of raucous electronic politics: the sheer decency of the son of Prescott and Dorothy Bush," he wrote in 1992's worst autumn of Bush's life. "All last week as his mother faded from this world, Bush toasted his friends and adversaries in elegant farewells. There was one night, after the ceremony ended, when there was a glimpse of the 41st President of this enduring republic standing in the corner of the mansion: he was sending Republicans and Democrats off into the night with one of his atrocious neckties flapping and his crooked grin playing across his face and his basic goodness asserting itself above all hurt and pain. History will remember."

It has.

FOURTEEN

Poetry of the Heart

W hen I was a kid," television's Roger Ailes said of growing up in Ohio, "everyone went to see Harry Truman
when he came through on the train and we thought we
knew him because Harry Truman waved to us." Depending on the
president in our modern—that is, radio and television—age, each is
reflected more or less accurately by his persona.

Herbert Hoover was a pre–White House titan in education, business, and government. Later, fortune's child became depression's
stepchild. Franklin Roosevelt flaunted self-confidence—the laugh,
flung-back head, the bonhomie. "His idea of the President," said historian Doris Kearns Goodwin, "was himself." Exhausted and inex-
haustible, FDR never let America feel pygmy or afraid.

Truman was a bespectacled machine protégé with awful sight
and superb vision: the Truman Doctrine, Marshall Plan, dropping
the atomic bomb. Dwight Eisenhower's middle-class affinity almost
became the 1950s. F. Scott Fitzgerald called style "an unbroken series
of perfect gestures." John F. Kennedy's still evokes a dreamboat home
less of Camelot than élan and grace.

Lyndon Johnson loved the raw use of power—how to inveigle,
even domineer. We like our president to get things done. Indomitable and indefatigable, Richard Nixon defeated almost everyone but
himself, needing every bit of his surpassing courage. Gerald Ford
was open, reliable, and thoroughly at ease with his assets and debits.

Jimmy Carter spurned Babylon on the Potomac for what he thought a higher calling. Ronald Reagan was "The Great Communicator" and "The Great Liberator," using language to swell liberty. Bill Clinton had all, almost lost all, and regained much of what he lost. Aside from Desert Storm, political fallibility, personal decency, and Metternich-like diplomacy, how will we recall the subject of this book?

In 1982 Bulgaria's former president, Todor Zhivkov, asked Nixon how many grandchildren he had. Nixon answered: four at the time. Zhivkov said, "Then you are a very rich man. Having grandchildren is the greatest wealth a man can have." As the "Author's Note" observes, leaving the presidency, George H. W. Bush passed a rule that any time a grandchild neared him they must "deimperialize the presidential retirement" by giving him a hug.

If grandchildren were gold—Bush today has seventeen, with three great-grandchildren—he would own part of Fort Knox. History will note his special love of children, how often he thought of them, and how that affected his desire to be a peacemaker. "My goal," he said, "is to have a world where every child has someone who knows their name."

To move the public, every president has had to conquer the yin and yang of presidential speechwriting. Regard prose as policy: a speech's main course, essential but insufficient. Deem poetry inspiration: a great dessert, an after-dinner drink. Prose details, instructs: to Barack Obama, a "teachable moment." Poetry ricochets, even chimes, playing a scale of sound, sense, and feel.

Presidential speechwriting began with George Washington's 1789 first presidential inaugural, denouncing "public prosperity and felicity" in office. Later, Thomas Jefferson said, "We are all Republicans, we are all Federalists." Like his life, Lincoln's language soared: "a house divided against itself . . . the better angels of our nature." Each was helped by friends, hangers-on, and cabinet secretaries, lending a line or phrase. Presidential speechwriting as we know it began in 1921, when Warren Harding was inaugurated. His problem wasn't a house divided—rather, corruption and backroom greed.

A critic pontificated, "Harding left the impression of a man of pompous phrases moving over the landscape in search of an idea. Sometimes these meandering words would actually capture a straggling thought and bear it triumphantly, a prisoner in their midst, until it died of servitude and overwork." Harding died after two years in office, having found at least one idea: the president needed a full-time speechwriter, creating the words that a president might speak.

Until the early twentieth century, to hear the speaking, you went where the speaking was. In 1908 William Jennings Bryan, nominated a third time for president by the Democratic Party, gave ten speeches a day, each averaging an hour, for sixty straight days—six hundred hours, to reach 5 million people. Under Harding, the office grew, more groups to be addressed, speeches given. Another factor: commercial radio, debuting in 1920 on KDKA Pittsburgh. Suddenly, a president needed writers to help this new medium help him.

Paraphrasing Lincoln at Gettysburg, the world has little noted nor long remembered the first full-time presidential speechwriter: Harding's literary clerk, Judson Welliver, may he rest in peace. In the 1980s ex-Nixon writer William Safire created a society in Welliver's name. It has about sixty members, includes writers chosen from each president since the 1930s, and fuels what the late Safire called the "strong bond among White House speechwriters." The late Clark Clifford, Truman writer and LBJ defense secretary, said, "We are rare birds and we must hang together."

Since Welliver, many increasingly grasp how presidents differ in voice, tone, rhythm, rate of cadence, and even whom they quote. As we have seen, Ronald Reagan liked to parrot the Founding Fathers, whom the Gipper used to poke fun at his seventy-something age. George Bush separated himself from his mentor in his first meeting with writers, preferring to quote Yogi Berra. As 41 said, once Yogi was talking about a batter who hit well from each side of the plate: "Wow, both ways. He's amphibious."

Harding was the first radio president. Franklin Delano Roosevelt was the first president to master radio. On March 12, 1933, FDR delivered the first of twenty-seven to twenty-nine—depending upon your definition—fireside chats over the next twelve years. Remember Bryan, speaking six hundred hours to reach 5 million people. By contrast, FDR liked return on investment, speaking for twenty minutes from the White House to 60 million or more listeners by radio.

Roosevelt had a born-for-the-wireless tenor and a born-to-perform persona. He was a natural and knew it. He also understood how vivid, simple, and personal were better: "My friends . . . you and I . . . our government." Once, lifting his hands, Roosevelt dropped them like a pianist: "Speaking, you have to strike a chord. Then you wait. Then you strike the chord again." Helping him, among others, were Raymond Moley and Harry Hopkins and Rexford Tugwell and poet Archibald MacLeish and Pulitzer Prize–winning playwright Robert Sherwood—speechwriting's Murderers' Row.

FDR's chords warned, then changed, the world: "New Deal"; "rendezvous with destiny"; "the only thing we have to fear is fear itself"; "the great arsenal of democracy"; the "Four Freedoms" of speech and religion and against want and fear. My favorite line denounced the Nazis: "You don't tame a tiger into a kitten by stroking it." Succeeding him, Harry Truman used Clifford to outline the postwar world. Truman's successor relied less on rhetoric than on reputation. Most people run for president pledging to save civilization. Eisenhower did it the other way around: defeating Hitler, then entering the Oval Office.

Ike's poetry was biographical. Kennedy's included irony, equanimity, and a fluent phrase. JFK would quote Flannery O'Connor to Robert Frost, literacy, it was said, no longer evidence of high treason. Once he called a group of Nobel Prize laureates "the most extraordinary collection of talent . . . that has ever gathered at the White House—with the possible exception of when Thomas Jefferson dined alone." It is hard to imagine that on today's iPod, iPad, or DVD.

Like FDR with radio, JFK was the first to master television. He was a voracious reader, Pulitzer Prize–winning author, and disciple of self-improvement. Before running for president, JFK put on a smoking jacket, sat in his study, and put Churchill on his record player: "This was their finest hour" and "blood, toil, tears, and sweat" and "give us the tools, and we will finish the job." Later, as president, Kennedy used Theodore Sorensen—"my intellectual blood bank"—to help draft his inaugural and Cuban Missile Crisis speech and nuclear disarmament address. He absorbed Churchill well.

Kennedy grasped the difference between writing for the eye and ear. The latter was more informal, casual, yet structured—an open, middle, and close. Before his inaugural Kennedy had Sorensen reread the Gettysburg Address, finding that 71 percent of its words were one syllable. "Let the word go forth," said JFK. It did, still should, especially about how Kennedy was not a hater, seeking to grasp other points of view.

Lyndon Johnson inherited Kennedy's writers, who penned addresses on the Great Society and voting rights: "We shall overcome." What LBJ lacked was JFK's charm. Johnson's successor lacked it too. What Nixon possessed was empathy with Middle America. In *White House Ghosts*, Robert Schlesinger suggests that Nixon had as much respect for the spoken word as any modern president. He retreated to Camp David for a major speech, did one draft after another on legal pads, and so internalized the speech he *became* the speech—in sync with, protective of, the great working middle.

Nixon warned against America "as a pitiful helpless giant"; in 1971, announced his historic trip to China; in 1974, gave his surrealistic farewell—"It [defeat] is only a beginning, always." When he wanted a quotable quote, he dialed Safire, who also wrote for vice president Spiro Agnew, he of "nattering nabobs of negativism," "vicars of vacillation," and "hopeless, hysterical hypochondriacs of history." When Nixon wanted to explain foreign policy, he used cerebral Raymond Price. When he wanted to bash liberals, he summoned Patrick J. Buchanan, who has visited this narrative. Pat saluted, sat down at his typewriter, lit the keyboard, and began.

In chapter 3 Nixon showed his grasp of politics, terming it "poetry, not prose." Successor Gerald Ford grasped little, hiring a stunning twenty-two speechwriters in his two and a half years as president.

Carter ignored how poetry relates to prose. One half of a commence-ment speech said "we have an inordinate fear of Communism"; his other half suggested that Communism was at our door. Both fell to Reagan—like FDR, singing poetry's greatest hits. This account shows him embodying America at Normandy, the Berlin Wall, after the *Challenger* exploded. The Gipper could be errant in detail, gauzy about fact. No matter. Poetry KO'd prose.

Some termed language key to Reagan's presidency. It *was* his pres-idency, Dutch's life revolving around the spoken word. Even his first job prophesied. Reagan broadcast the 1930s Chicago Cubs despite never being at a game. A wire operator at Chicago's Wrigley Field sent Morse code hundreds of miles to Reagan, sitting in the studio of WHO Des Moines. "B10" meant ball one, outside; "S2C" strike two, called. Eureka! In a "re-creation," you described a game unseen.

One day Reagan was announcing when—disaster—the wire broke. The Gipper considered having WHO play music in the lurch, then recalled three other Des Moines stations airing the same game *live*. "I thought, if we put music on," he said, "people'll turn to another station doing the game in person." What to do? Make a big *to*-do. Instantly, Reagan remembered the one thing that doesn't make the newspaper box score—foul balls. You can hit two million foul balls—and still have two strikes. Thus, in the next ten minutes, Dutch had the batter set a record for fouls.

As Reagan told it, Billy Jurges fouled to the left, right, and behind the plate, into the stands and out of the park—wherever a foul could go. Pitcher Dizzy Dean used the resin bag, mopped his brow, and tied a shoe. Rain neared. A fight began. None of this happened, but at home it seemed real. Finally, the wire revived, Reagan laughing. It read, "Jurges popped out on first ball pitched." Years later the Gip-per said, "Making things up, relating tale to fact. What better train-ing for politics?"

Bill Clinton might agree, perhaps *primus inter pares*—in Latin, "first among equals"—in presidential eye contact, gesture, and segue from teleprompter to ad lib, pleasing crowds but not necessarily his writers, who despaired of Clinton speaking not for history but for the moment. Successor George W. Bush had little poetry, timing, or grasp of the middle class. Barack Obama knew the Harvard faculty lounge and Chicago machine politics, but little of America in between.

Plato said, "Before we talk, let us define our terms." It is fair to say that to Democratic presidents, poetry means tending elements of a left-of-center coalition: New Deal, Fair Deal, New Frontier, Great Society, Obama's health care and economic stimulus. To Republicans, it means—at least it should—ideas and attitudes, a writer suggested, which should "have more to do with loyalty than with ideology"—among other things, faith, loyalty, and patriotism, an appreciation of American history, sacrifice, exceptionalism, and wonder. If, as Tip O'Neill said, all politics is local, most presidential speechwriting should be personal. That is especially true of the president I know best.

In George H. W. Bush, I found a hybrid of Andy Hardy and Walter Mitty. In one breath he could confess "I'm on a cholesterol high"; another, bravely vow "this aggression will not stand" and make it stick; another, become so choked as to be unable to speak about his then-four-year-old daughter's death sixty years earlier; another, civilly address opponents in the "just war" speech. A modest man, more complex than he or critics would admit. A heroic man, like so many of his generation. An old-fashioned man, who knew that a letter—far more than an e-mail or text message or—God forbid—Tweet—could reveal and touch the heart. A man whose poetry linked vulnerability and wearability and nobility, above all.

In 1999 Bush released *All the Best, George Bush: My Life in Letters and Other Writings*, reissued in 2013, a collection of his letters from childhood to then. One entry is especially telling: Bush's "self-typed" letter to each of his five children on December 31, 1990, as a president—and dad—sensed that the greatest decision of his presidency—the invasion of Kuwait—lay just beyond the river. "First, I can't begin to tell you how great it was to have you here at Camp David," he began.

Poetry of the Heart

"I loved the games (the Marines are still smarting over their 1 and 2 record). I loved Christmas Day . . . I loved the movies—some of 'em. I loved the laughs. Most of all, I loved seeing you together. We are a family blessed; and this Christmas simply reinforced all that."

Next came a trait I had seen in the White House and beyond—Bush's fine feeling for the person as opposed to mass. "I hope I didn't seem moody. I tried not to." He had vowed not to complain about "the loneliest job in the world." Yet "I *have* been concerned about what lies ahead. There is no 'loneliest,' though, as I am backed by a first rate team of knowledgeable and committed people." Bush had "thought long and hard about what might have to be done," having "the peace of mind that comes from knowing that we have tried hard for peace. We have gone to the U.N.; we have formed an historic coalition; there have been diplomatic initiatives from country after country." Only sixteen days remained till the UN deadline for Saddam Hussein to leave "Kuwait—totally."

As a father, what "I want you to know . . . is this: Every human life is precious. When the question is asked, 'How many lives are you willing to sacrifice?'—it tears at my heart. The answer, of course, is none—none at all. We have waited to give sanctions a chance, we have moved a tremendous force so as to reduce the risk to every American soldier if force has to be used; but the question of life still lingers and plagues the heart." Making history, Bush retrieved prior history. "How many lives might have been saved if appeasement had given way to force earlier on in the late '30s or earliest '40's? How many Jews might have been spared the gas chambers, or how many Polish patriots might be alive today? I look at today's crisis as 'good' v. 'evil' . . . yes, it is that clear."

Bush knew his stance must "cause you a little grief from time to time; and it hurts me. . . . So dear kids—batten down the hatches." Senator Daniel Inouye of Hawaii told him "to be prepared for some in Congress to file impeachment papers" if the war went badly. "That's what he said, and he's 100% correct. And so I shall say a few more prayers, mainly for our kids in the Gulf, and I shall do what must be done, and I shall be strengthened every day by our family love which lifts me up every single day of my life. I am the luckiest Dad in the whole wide world. I love you. Devotedly, Dad."

Desert Storm would proceed brilliantly, but Bush couldn't know that then. I recall his grace and poise under pressure, refusal to ignore principle, capacity for love and sympathy, and a quote he used a year later, at Pearl Harbor: "'In our sleep, pain that cannot forget falls drop by drop upon the heart,'" adding, "It is as though God Himself were crying." Bush cried that day, as does almost everyone who visits Pearl's sacred shrine.

I have often thought of that time since George Bush left the White House. He was not a nonpartisan president; no one can be, especially in this hyperpartisan era. He was, though, likely our age's least partisan president, and perhaps our most loving, as a final story shows.

In 2001 my wife and I visited Ukraine, a country that Bush, with help from others here and abroad, had helped liberate from the Soviet Union. We adopted two very young children—Travis, nine months old, and Olivia, twenty-one months old—and brought them here—brought them home. The former president found out and, unsolicited, wrote each a letter. His full text is in the photo folio.

"Dear Olivia," Bush's letter began.

"Just a few weeks ago, you arrived in your new home, Rochester, New York in the United States of America. Welcome!

"Already you are a lucky little girl—luckier than most—for you have a mother and dad who love you so much.

"And you have friends, too. I want to be your friend. I used to be President of the United States. Now, though, I am a happy, private citizen; but I know something true. Family and friends are what really count.

"All the best to you, Olivia," he concluded. "I hope your exciting life ahead in your new homeland is full of happiness, and I hope you spend all of it living in a world at peace.

"Sincerely, George Bush."

Such a letter was not—not meant to be—"Ask not what your country can do for you" or "Mr. Gorbachev, tear down this wall." That was poetry of the voice. Bush's poetry was different, which is not at all to say lesser, invoking what Faulkner called "the old verities and truths . . . [of] love and honor and pity and pride and compassion and sacrifice"—works, not words.

George Bush's was, and is, a poetry of the heart, with character at the core.

APPENDIX

Selected Speeches

The text of the first four selected speeches was released the day of each speech by the White House. The text of the final speech was released by President Bush's office in 2004.

Nixon Library Dedication Speech

Presidential Library Opening
Yorba Linda, California
Thursday, July 19, 1990

I am very proud to be introduced to this gathering by Ronald Reagan. I know how I got here. To President and Mrs. Nixon, Barbara and I are delighted to be with you on this memorable day. My special greetings to be with all my predecessors. [Many other dignitaries were cited, including cabinet members, members of the Nixon family, Reverend Billy Graham and Reverend Norman Vincent Peale, and entertainer Vicky Carr.] Our thanks for the privilege of helping to dedicate this beautiful library of the thirty-seventh president of the United States of the America.

To Lincoln, the presidency played, as he put it, America's "mystic chords of memory." To Teddy Roosevelt, it meant the "bully pulpit," reflecting American values and her ideals. It was Dwight Eisenhower—beloved Ike—who described its power "to proclaim anew our faith," and summon "lightness against the dark."

To occupy this office is to feel a kinship with these and other presidents, each of whom, in his own way, sought to do right—and thus achieve good. Each summoned the best from the idea we call America. Each wondered, I suspect, how he could be worthy of God, and man,

This year an estimated one and a half million people will visit presidential museums and libraries, exploring the lives of these presidents, passed down, like oral history, from one generation to another. They will see how each president is like a finely cut prism with many facets—their achievements and their philosophy, their family and their humanity.

For instance, not far from here, visitors will soon see the library of my distinguished predecessor, the fortieth president of the United States, and Mrs. Reagan. President Reagan, we will not soon forget how you truly blessed America.

Look next to Michigan, where a museum and library honor the thirty-eighth president of the United States, Gerald Ford, and Mrs. Ford. An entire nation is grateful for your decency, your leadership, and your love of country.

Finally, tomorrow morning the first visitors will enter our newest presidential library. They will note that only FDR ran as many times as Richard Nixon—five—for national office, each winning four elections, and that more people voted for Richard Nixon as president than any other man in history. They will hear of Horatio Alger and Alger Hiss; of the book *Six Crises* and the seventh crisis, Watergate. They will think of Checkers, Millie's role model. And, yes, Mr. President, they will hear again your answer to my "vision thing"—"Let me make this perfectly clear."

They will read of your times as president—perhaps as tumultuous as any since Lincoln's—and of your goal as president—a world where peace would link the community of nations. Yet other young visitors will not remember the years 1969 to 1974. They had not been born when Richard Nixon became president. So to help them understand our thirty-seventh president, here is what I would tell those who journey to Yorba Linda.

I would say, first, look at perhaps the truest index of any man—his family. Think of his mother—a gentle Quaker—and his father, who built their small frame house less than a hundred yards from here. Think of his daughters, Tricia and Julie. Any parent would be proud of children with the loyalty and love of these two women. Think finally of a very gracious First Lady, who ranks among the most admired women of postwar America: the woman who we know, and love, as Pat.

As First Lady, Pat Nixon championed the Right to Read program, brought the Parks to People program to the disabled and disadvantaged, and refurbished the White House and opened it to more people than ever before. She believed the White House should be alight like Washington's other monuments—and so it was. She was our most widely traveled First Lady, visiting five continents and twenty-two nations—overcoming poverty and tragedy to become a mirror of America's heart, and love.

When, in 1958, foreign mobs stoned the Nixons' car, she was, an observer said, "stronger than any man." Yet it was also Pat who moved pianist Duke Ellington, at a White House dinner, to improvise a melody. "I shall pick a name," he said, "gentle, graceful—like Patricia." Mrs. Nixon, the Secret Service called you "Starlight," and your husband has said it best: "You fit that name to a T." So once again, I won't ask you to stand up—you've already done it. But let us show our appreciation for the grace and beauty that Pat Nixon brought to the White House.

Next, I would say to visitors here: Look at Richard Nixon the man. He had an intellectual's complexity. (Knowing how you feel about some intellectuals, Mr. President, I don't mean to offend you.) He was an author of eight books, each composed on his famous yellow legal pads, who, like his favorite author, Tolstoy, admired the dignity of manual labor. He worked in the most pragmatic of arenas, yet insisted that "politics is poetry, not prose." He believed in love of country, and in God—in loyalty to friends, and protecting loved ones. He was also a soft touch when it came to kids. Believe me, I can empathize.

Let me repeat a story which President Nixon himself enjoys—I hope he enjoys it. One day, greeting an airport crowd, he heard a young girl shouting, "How is Smokey the Bear?" then living at the Washington National Zoo. The girl kept repeating the question. Not grasping her words, the president was baffled, asking an aide for translation. "Smokey the Bear," the aide mumbled, pointing to the girl. "Washington National Zoo." Triumphant, President Nixon walked over, extended his hand, and said, "How do you do, Miss Bear?"

I'd be the last to confuse verbal confusion. After all, some say English is my only foreign language. The point is, President Nixon was merely being kind, just as he mailed those handwritten letters to defeated rivals like his friend Hubert Humphrey—or saw that when the POWs returned home in early 1973 to a White House dinner each wife received a corsage. Just as Richard Nixon was extraordinarily controversial, he could also be uncommonly sensitive to the feelings of other people.

This brings me to what I would next tell those who travel to Yorba Linda. What Richard Nixon said of Dwight Eisenhower in a 1969 eulogy was true, also, of himself: "He came from the heart of America"—not geographically, perhaps, but culturally. Richard Nixon was the quintessence of Middle America, and touched deep chords of response in millions of her citizens—as president, upholding what he termed "the Silent Majority" from Dallas to Davenport, and Syracuse to Siler City.

He loved America's good, quiet, decent people; he spoke for them; he felt, deeply, on their behalf. Theodore White would say: "Middle America had been without a great leader for generations, and in Richard Nixon it . . . elevated a man of talent and ability." For millions of Americans, this president became something they had rarely known: a *voice*—speaking loudly and eloquently for their values and their dreams.

Finally, and most importantly, I would say to visitors: Richard Nixon helped change the course not only of America but of the entire world. He believed in returning power to the people—so he created revenue sharing. He believed that young people should be free to choose their future—so he ended the draft. He knew that the great outdoors is precious but fragile—so he created the Environmental Protection Agency: an historic step to help preserve, and wisely use,

Appendix

our natural resources. He helped the United States reach new horizons in space and technology—and began a pioneering cancer initiative that gave hope and life to millions.

All of this Richard Nixon did. Yet future generations will remember him most, in my view, for dedicating his life to the greatest cause offered any president: the cause of peace among nations.

Who can forget how he endured much in his quest for peace with honor in Vietnam? He knew that true peace means the triumph of freedom, not merely the absence of war. As president, he served this country's special mission to help those around the world for whom America has always been a morning star of liberty—engaging in diplomatic summitry and helping change the postwar bipolar globe.

Who can forget how in Moscow Richard Nixon signed the first agreement to limit strategic nuclear arms, giving new hope to the world for lasting peace, or how he planted the first fragile seeds of peace in the Middle East?

Who can forget how Golda Meir [former prime minister of Israel], whose statue is inside [the Nixon Library and Museum], credited him with saving Israel during the [1973] Yom Kippur War?

Even now, memories resound of President Nixon's trip to China—the week that revolutionized the world. No American president had ever stood on the soil of the People's Republic of China. As President Nixon stepped from Air Force One and extended his hand to Zhou Enlai, his vision ended more than two decades of isolation.

"Being president," he often said, "is nothing compared with what you can do as president." Mr. President, you worked with every fiber of your being to help achieve a *generation* of peace. Today, as the movement toward democracy sweeps our globe, you can take great pride that history will say of you: Here was a true *architect* of peace.

There have been literally millions of words written about Richard Nixon, but let me close with a passage from the president himself. It comes from his first inaugural address—January 20, 1969—where the new president spoke of how the "greatest honor history can bestow is the title of peacemaker."

He began by noting that within the lifetime of most present, mankind would celebrate a new year which occurs only once in a thousand years—the start of a new millennium—and that America had the "chance," he said, "to lead the world onto that high ground of peace that man has dreamed of since the dawn of civilization."

Finally, Richard Nixon concluded, "if we succeed, generations to come will say of us that we helped make the world safe for mankind. I believe the American people are ready to answer this call."

Mr. President, you helped America answer what you termed "its summons to greatness." Thank you for serving the cause of peace. God bless you and your wonderful family. Now it is my honor, as president of the United States, to introduce the thirty-seventh president of the United States, Richard M. Nixon.

Just War Speech

National Religious Broadcasters
Sheraton Hotel, Washington DC
Monday, January 28, 1991

This marks the fifth time I have addressed the annual convention of the National Religious Broadcasters. Once again, it is an honor to be back. Let me begin by congratulating you on your theme of "Declaring His Glory to All Nations." It is a theme eclipsing denominations—and reflecting many of the eternal teachings in scripture.

I speak, of course, of the teachings which uphold moral values like tolerance, compassion, faith, and courage. They remind us that while God can live without man, man cannot live with God.

His love and His justice inspire in us a yearning for faith and a compassion for the weak and oppressed as well as the courage and conviction to oppose tyranny and injustice. Matthew also reminds us that the meek shall inherit the earth.

At home, these values imbue the policies which you and I support. Like me, you endorse adoption, not abortion—and last year, you helped ensure that the option of religious-based child care will not be restricted or eliminated by the federal government.

I commend your concern on behalf of Americans with disabilities—

and your belief that students who go to school to nourish their minds should also be allowed to nourish their souls. I have not lessened my commitment to restoring voluntary prayer in school.

These actions can make America a kinder, gentler place because they reaffirm the values I spoke of earlier—values that must be central to the life of every individual and nation. The clergyman Richard Cecil once said: "There are two classes of the wise: the men who serve God because they have found Him, and the men who seek Him because they have not found Him yet." Abroad—as in America—our task is to serve and seek wisely through the policies we pursue.

Nowhere is this more true than in the Persian Gulf—where despite the protestations of Saddam Hussein, it is not Iraq against the United States, it's the regime of Saddam Hussein against the world. Fifty years ago we had the chance to stop another aggressor, and missed it. We will not make that mistake again.

Saddam has tried to cast this conflict as a religious war—but it has nothing to do with religion per se. It has, on the other hand, *everything* to do with what religion *embodies*. Good versus evil. Right versus wrong. Human dignity and freedom versus tyranny and oppression.

The war in the Gulf is not a Christian war or a Jewish war—or a Muslim war. It is a Just War—and it is a war in which good will prevail.

I am told that the principles of a "Just War" originated with classical Greek and Roman philosophers like Plato and Cicero. Later, they were expounded by such Christian theologians as Ambrose, Augustine, and Thomas Aquinas.

The first principle of a Just War is that it supports a *just cause*. Our cause could not be more noble. We seek Iraq's withdrawal from Kuwait—completely, immediately, and without condition: the restoration of Kuwait's legitimate government; and the security and stability of the Gulf. We will see that Kuwait once again is free, the nightmare of Iraq's brutal occupation is ended, and that naked aggression will not be rewarded.

We seek nothing for ourselves. As I have said, U.S. forces will leave as soon as their mission is over, when they are no longer needed or desired. And let me add, we do not seek the destruction of Iraq. We have respect for the people of Iraq—and importance of Iraq in the region. We do not want a country so destabilized that Iraq itself will be a target for aggression.

A Just War must also be declared by *legitimate authority*. Operation Desert Storm is supported by unprecedented United Nations' solidarity—the principle of collective self-defense. Twelve Security Council resolutions and, in the Gulf, twenty-eight nations from six continents united—resolute—that we will not waver and that Saddam's aggression will not stand.

I salute the aid—economic and military—from countries who have joined in this unprecedented effort—whose courage and sacrifice have inspired the world. We're not going it alone—but believe me, we *are* going to see it through.

Every war is fought for a reason. But a Just War is fought for *right* reasons—*moral*, not *selfish*. Let me tell you a story—a tragic story—about a family whose two sons, eighteen and nineteen, reportedly refused to lower the Kuwaiti flag in front of their home. For this crime, they were executed by the Iraqis. Then, unbelievably, their parents were asked to pay the price of the bullets used to kill them.

Some ask whether it is moral to use force to stop the rape, pillage, and plunder of Kuwait. My answer: Extraordinary diplomatic efforts having been used to resolve the matter peacefully, it would be immoral *not* to use force.

A Just War must be a *last resort*. As I have often said, we did not want war. But you all know the verse from Ecclesiastes: There is "a time for peace, a time for war." From August 2, 1990, to January 15, 1991—166 days—we tried to resolve this conflict.

Secretary of State Jim Baker made an extraordinary effort to achieve peace: More than two hundred meetings with foreign dignitaries; ten diplomatic missions; six congressional appearances; over 103,000 miles traveled to talk with—among others—members of the UN, the Arab League, and the European Community. Sadly, Saddam Hussein rejected out of hand every overture made by the United States and by other countries. He made this Just War an *inevitable* war.

We all know war never comes cheap or easy. War is never without the loss of innocent life—and that is war's greatest tragedy. But when a war must be fought for the greater good, it is our gravest obligation to conduct a war in *proportion* to the threat. That is why we must act reasonably, humanely, and make every effort possible to keep casualties to a minimum.

We have done so. From the first day of the war, the Allies have waged war against Saddam's military machine. We are doing everything possible to avoid hurting the innocents. Saddam's response? Wanton, barbaric bombing of civilian areas. America and her Allies value life. We pray that Saddam Hussein will see reason. To date, his indiscriminate use of Scud missiles—nothing more than weapons of terror—has outraged the world.

The price of war is always high. So it must never—ever—be undertaken without *total commitment* to a successful outcome. It is only justified when victory can be achieved. I have pledged that this will not be "another Vietnam." Let me assure you: It won't. We are fortunate to have in this crisis the finest armed forces ever assembled—an all-volunteer force joined by courageous allies. We will prevail because we have the finest soldiers, sailors, airmen, marines, and coast guardsmen any nation has ever had.

Above all, we will prevail because of the support of the American people—armed with a trust in God and in the principles that make men free—people like each of you in this room. I salute Voice of Hope's live radio programming for U.S. and Allied troops in the Gulf, your "Operation Desert Prayer," and worship services for our troops held by, among others, the man who over a week ago led a wonderful prayer service at Fort Myer, over here across the river in Virginia, the Reverend Billy Graham.

America has always been a religious nation—perhaps never more than now. Just look at the last several weeks: churches, synagogues, and mosques reporting record attendance at services; chapels packed during working hours as Americans stop in for a moment or two. Why? To pray for peace. I know that some disagree with the course that I have taken. I have no bitterness in my heart about that, no anger. I am convinced that we are doing the right thing—and tolerance is a virtue, not a vice.

With the support and prayers of so many, there can be no question in the minds of our soldiers—or in the minds of our enemy—about what Americans think.

We know that this is a Just War. We know that, God willing, this is a war we will win. But most of all, we know that ours would not be the land of the free if it were not also the home of the brave.

No one wanted war less than I did. No one is more determined to seize from battle the real peace that can offer hope—that can create a new world order. When this war is over, the United States, its credibility and its reliability restored, will have a key leadership role in helping to bring peace to the rest of the Middle East. I have been honored to serve as president of this great nation for two years now and believe more than ever that one cannot be America's president without trust in God. I cannot imagine a world, a life, without the presence of the One through whom all things are possible.

During the darkest days of the Civil War, a man we revere not merely for what he did but what he was, was asked whether he thought the Lord was on his side. Said Abraham Lincoln: "My concern is not whether God is on *our* side, but whether *we* are on *God's* side."

My fellow Americans, I believe the times will soon be on the side of peace—because the world is overwhelmingly on the side of God.

Thank you for this occasion. May God bless our country. And please remember all of our coalition's armed forces in your prayers.

Medal of Freedom Speech

Lady Margaret Thatcher
White House State Room
Thursday, March 7, 1991

Sir Denis Thatcher. Mark and Diane Thatcher. Other friends of what is indeed our Special Relationship. Above all, the greengrocer's daughter who shaped a nation to her will.

America's highest civilian award is the Medal of Freedom. We are here to present it to one of the greatest leaders of our time. For more than eleven of the most extraordinary years in British history, she helped freedom lift the peoples of Europe and the world: Former prime minister Margaret Thatcher.

She has been called the Iron Lady—irrepressible; at times, incorrigible; always indomitable. She summoned the best of the human spirit—speaking for our values and our dreams. Once she said, "Turn if *you* like, the Lady's not for turning," and she wasn't. Instead, the Free World turned to her—for counsel, for courage, for leadership that proclaimed a belief in right and wrong—not a devotion to what is popular.

It has been said that great leaders reflect their time. Margaret Thatcher did. She also transformed her time as few leaders have. Consider the 1980s and early '90s—a golden age of liberty. Remember what she meant, and how she mattered. Hers was not merely among Britain's finest hours. She helped mold perhaps democracy's finest era.

Think, first, of what she meant to the place that Shakespeare called "this blessed plot, this earth, this realm, this England." She didn't create spirit in the British people—it's been there for a millennium. But Margaret Thatcher believed in it and once again unleashed it.

She cherished human dignity and self-determination—so when an antidemocratic military moved against the Falkland Islands, Britain met the challenge. She sought to decrease what government must do and increase what the individual may do—so she put private roofs over British heads and restored economic pride to British hearts.

Like her successor, John Major, she believed passionately in free enterprise—so she used it to renew British initiative and national pride.

Margaret Thatcher didn't merely make Britain a leader in the New World Order. She defined the essence of the United Kingdom.

Think, next, of what she meant to America, knowing that although ours may be "two countries separated by the same language," Britain and America are—and always will be—joined by a common heritage and culture, civilization and soul.

Mrs. Thatcher understood the ties that bind our nations—moral and economic, political and spiritual—so she defended America and helped inspire it. No country could have had a more valiant comrade in arms. No president, as another great leader, Ronald Reagan, would attest, could ask for a better friend.

Margaret Thatcher stood with America when others stood silent. She knew that character is not what we have—but what we are. We will never forget her courage in helping forge a great coalition against the aggression which brutalized the Gulf. Nor will I forget one special phone conversation I had with the prime minister.

In the early days of the Gulf crisis, I called her to say that though we fully intended to interdict Iraqi shipping, we were going to let a single vessel headed for Oman enter port without being stopped. She listened to my explanation, agreed with the decision, but then added these words of caution—words that guided me throughout the Gulf crisis—words I will never forget.

"Remember, George," she said. "This is no time to go wobbly."

Those who work with me in the White House know we use that expression often and have used it during some troubling times. Never, ever, will be it be said that Margaret Thatcher went wobbly.

Finally, think of what Margaret Thatcher meant to the *world*. Her resolution and dedication set an example for us all. She showed that you can't lock people behind walls forever when moral conviction uplifts their souls. She knew that tyranny is powerless against the primacy of the heart.

Margaret Thatcher helped bring the Cold War to an end. She helped the human will outlast bayonets and barbed wire. She sailed freedom's ship wherever it was imperiled. Prophet and crusader—idealist and realist—this heroic woman made history move her way.

Prime Minister, there will always be an England. But there can never be another Margaret Thatcher. May God bless you and thank you for all that you have done.

Now, it is my great honor and privilege to present the Medal of Freedom. [Script:] "Three times elected Prime Minister of the United Kingdom, Margaret Thatcher led her country with fearlessness, determination, integrity, and a true vision for Britain. In over a decade of

achievement, she extended prosperity at home and made signal con-
tributions to transatlantic partnership, the unity of the West, and
overcoming the postwar division of Europe. With a strong sense of
her nation's history and of the principles which brought it to greatness, she restored confidence to the British people. The United States
honors a steadfast and true ally and a firm friend of political and
economic freedom throughout the world."

Pearl Harbor Fiftieth Anniversary Speech

Pearl Harbor, Hawaii
Aboard USS *Arizona* Memorial
Saturday, December 7, 1991

Thank you, Captain Ross. To our secretary of defense and our chairman of our Joint Chiefs; members of our cabinet; distinguished governors here and so many members of the United States Congress;
Admiral Larson; members of our armed forces, then and now; families and friends of the *Arizona* and *Utah*; fellow veterans.

It was a bright Sunday morning. Thousands of troops slept soundly
in their bunks. Some who were awake looked out and savored the
still and tranquil harbor.

On the stern of the USS *Nevada*, a brass band prepared to play
"The Star-Spangled Banner." On other ships, sailors readied for the
8 a.m. flag raising. Ray Emory, who was on the *Honolulu*, read the
morning newspaper. Aboard *California*, yeoman Durell Connor
wrapped Christmas presents. On the *West Virginia*, a machinist's
mate looked at the photos just received from his wife. They were of
his eight-month-old son, whom he had never seen.

On the mainland, people listened to football games on the radio,
turned to songs like the "Chattanooga Choo-Choo," comics like "Terry
and the Pirates," and movies like *Sergeant York*. In New York, families went window-shopping. Out West, it was late morning, many
families still at church.

At first, to the American sailors at Pearl, the hum of engines seemed
routine—and why not? To them, the idea of war seemed palpable—

but remote. Then, in one horrible instant, they froze in disbelief. Suddenly, the abstract threat was real.

These men did not panic. They raced to their stations. Some strapped pistols over pajamas, fought, and died. What lived was the shock wave that soon swept across America, forever immortalizing December 7th, 1941. Ask anyone who endured that awful Sunday. Each felt like the writer who observed: "Life is never again as it was before anyone you love has died; never so innocent, never so gentle, never so pliant to your will."

Today we honor those who gave their lives at this place, half a century ago. Their names were Bertie and Gomez and Dougherty and Granger. They came from Idaho and Mississippi and the sweeping farmland of Ohio. They were of all races and colors, native born and foreign born. Most of all, they were American.

Think of how it was for these heroes of the Harbor—men who were also husbands, fathers, brothers, sons. Imagine the chaos of guns and smoke, flaming water, and ghastly carnage. Two thousand four hundred and three Americans gave their lives. But in this haunting place, they live forever in our memory—reminding us gently, selflessly, like chimes in the distant night.

Every fifteen seconds a drop of oil still rises from the *Arizona* and drifts to the surface. As it spreads across the water, we recall the ancient poet: "In our sleep, pain that cannot forget falls drop by drop upon the heart, and in our own despair against our will comes wisdom through the awful grace of God." With each drop, it is as though God Himself were crying. He cries, as we do, for the living and the dead: men like Commander Duncan Curry, firing a .45 revolver at attacking planes as tears streamed down his face.

We remember Machinist Mate Robert Scott, who ran the air compressors powering the guns aboard *California*. When the compartment flooded, the crew evacuated. Scott refused. "This is my station," he said. "I'm going to stay as long as the guns are going." Nearby, aboard *New Orleans*, Chaplain Forgy assured his troops it was all right to miss church that day. His words became legend: "You can praise the Lord and pass the ammunition."

Captain Ross, then a warrant officer, was awarded the Congressional Medal of Honor for his heroism aboard *Nevada* that day. I salute him and the other Congressional Medal winners with us today, wherever they may be also.

For the defenders of Pearl, heroism came as naturally as breath. They reacted instinctively by rushing to their posts, knowing that our nation would be sustained by the nobility of its cause. So did Americans of Japanese ancestry who came by the hundreds to give wounded Americans blood, and the thousands of their kinsmen across America who took up arms for their country. Every American believed in the cause.

The men I speak of would be embarrassed to be called heroes. Instead, they would tell you, probably with defiance: "Foes can sink American ships, but not the American spirit. They may kill us, but never the ideals that made us proud to serve."

Talk to those who survived to fight another day. They would repeat the Navy hymn that Barbara and I sing every Sunday in the lovely little chapel up at Camp David: "Eternal Father, strong to save, Whose arm hath bound the restless wave . . . O hear us when we cry to Thee, for those in peril on the sea."

Back in June of 1942, I remember how Henry Stimson, the secretary of war, defined the American soldier and how that soldier should be, and I quote, "brave without being brutal, self-confident without boasting, being part of an irresistible might without losing faith in individual liberty."

The heroes of the Harbor engraved that passage on every heart and soul. They fought for a world of peace, not war, where children's dreams speak more loudly than the brashest tyrant's guns. Because of them, this memorial lives to pass its lessons from one generation to the next—lessons as clear as this Pacific sky.

One of Pearl Harbor's lessons is that together we could "summon lightness against the dark"—that was Dwight Eisenhower. Another: When it comes national defense, finishing second means finishing last. World War II also taught that isolationism is a bankrupt notion. The world does not stop at our water's edge. Perhaps above all, that real peace, the peace that lasts, means the triumph of freedom, not merely the absence of war.

As we look down—as Barbara and I just did—at *Arizona*'s sunken hull, tomb to more than a thousand Americans, the beguiling calm comforts us, reminds us of the might of ideals that inspire boys to die as men. Everyone who aches at their sacrifice knows America must be forever vigilant. And Americans must always remember the brave and the innocent who gave their lives to keep us free.

Each Memorial Day, not far from this spot, the heroes of Pearl Harbor are honored. Two leis are placed upon each grave by Hawaiian boy scouts and girl scouts. We must never forget that it is for them, the future, that we must apply the lessons of the past. In Pearl Harbor's wake, we won the war and, thus, the peace. In the Cold War that followed, Americans also shed their blood, but we used other means as well.

For nearly half a century, patience, foresight, and personal diplomacy helped America stand fast and firm for democracy. But we've never stood alone. Beside us stood nations committed to democracy, free markets, free expression, and freedom of worship: nations including our former enemies Germany, Italy and Japan.

This year these same nations stood with us against aggression in the Persian Gulf. You know, the war there was so different: different enemy, different circumstances, the outcome not in doubt. It was short; thank God, our casualties, mercifully few. Yet I ask you veterans of Pearl Harbor and all Americans who remember the unity of purpose that followed that momentous December day fifty years ago: Didn't we see the same national spirit when we launched Desert Storm?

The answer is a resounding *yes*. Once the war for Kuwait began, we pulled together. We were united, determined, and confident. When it was over, we rejoiced in exactly the same way we did in 1945—heads high, proud, and grateful. What a feeling. Fifty years had passed, but the American spirit was as young and fresh as ever.

This unity of purpose continues to inspire us in the cause of peace among nations. In their own way, amid the bedlam and anguish of that awful day, the men of Pearl Harbor served that noble cause, honored it. They knew the things worth living for were also worth dying for: principle, decency, fidelity, honor.

So look behind me at Battleship Row—the gun turret still visible and flag flying proudly from a truly blessed shrine.

Look into your hearts and minds: You will see boys who this day became men and men who became heroes.

Look at the water here, clear and quiet, bidding us to sum up and remember. One day, in what now seems another lifetime, it wrapped its arms around the finest sons any nation could ever have—and carried them to a better world.

May God bless them. And may God bless America, the most wondrous land on Earth.

Eulogy to Ronald Reagan

Washington National Cathedral
Washington DC
Friday, June 11, 2004

When Franklin Roosevelt died in 1945, the *New York Times* wrote, "Men will thank God a hundred years from now that Franklin D. Roosevelt was in the White House."

It will not take a hundred years to thank God for Ronald Reagan—but why? Why was he so admired? Why was he so beloved?

He was beloved, first, because of what he was. Politics can be cruel, uncivil. Our friend was strong and gentle.

Once he called America hopeful, big hearted, idealistic, daring, decent, and fair. That was America and, yes, our friend.

Next, Ronald Reagan was beloved because of what he believed. He believed in America—so he made it his shining city on a hill. He believed in freedom—so he acted on behalf of its values and ideals. He believed in tomorrow—so the Great Communicator became the Great Liberator.

He talked of winning one for the Gipper and as president, through his relationship with Mikhail Gorbachev—with us today—the Gipper and, yes, Mikhail Gorbachev won one for peace around the world.

If Ronald Reagan created a better world for many millions, it was because of the world someone else created for him.

Nancy was there for him always. Her love for him provided much of his strength, and their love together transformed all of us as we've seen again here in the last few days.

One of the many memories we all have of both of them is the comfort they provided during our national tragedies.

Whether it was the families of the crew of the *Challenger* shuttle or the uss *Stark* or the marines killed in Beirut, we will never forget those images of the president and First Lady embracing them and embracing us during times of sorrow.

So, Nancy, I want to say this to you: Today, America embraces you. We open up our arms. We seek to comfort you, to tell you of our admiration for your courage and your selfless caring.

And to the Reagan kids—it's okay for me to say that at eighty—Michael, Ron, Patti, today all of our sympathy, all of our condolences to you all, and remember, too, your sister Maureen is home safe now with your father.

As his vice president for eight years, I learned more from Ronald Reagan than from anyone I encountered in all my years of public life. I learned kindness; we all did. I also learned courage; the nation did.

Who can forget the horrible day in March 1981, [when] he looked at the doctors in the emergency room and said, "I hope you're all Republicans"?

And then I learned decency; the whole world did. Days after being shot, weak from wounds, he spilled water from a sink, and entering the hospital room aides saw him on his hands and knees wiping water from the floor. He worried that his nurse would get in trouble.

The Good Book says humility goes before honor, and our friend had both. Who could not cherish such a man?

Perhaps as important as anything, I learned a lot about humor, about laughter. And, oh, how President Reagan loved a good story.

When asked, "How did your visit go with Bishop Tutu?" he replied, "So-so."

It was typical. It was wonderful.

In leaving the White House, the very last day, he left in the yard outside the Oval Office door a little sign for the squirrels. He loved to feed those squirrels. And he left this sign that said, "Beware of the dog," to no avail, because our dog Millie came in and beat the heck out of the squirrels.

Anyway, he also left me a note, at the top of which said, "Don't let the turkeys get you down."

Well, he certainly never let them get him down. He fought hard for his beliefs. He led from conviction, but never made an adversary into an enemy. He was never mean-spirited.

Reverend Billy Graham, who I refer to as the nation's pastor, is now hospitalized and regrets that he can't be here today. I asked him for a Bible passage that might be applicable. He suggested this from Psalm 37: "The Lord delights in the way of the man whose steps He has made firm. Though he stumble, he will not fall for the Lord upholds him with His hand."

Then, this, too, from 37: "There is a future for the man of peace."

God bless you, Ronald Wilson Reagan, and the nation you loved and led so well.

BIBLIOGRAPHY

Alsop, Joseph. *FDR: A Centenary Remembrance.* New York: Viking Press, 1982.

Ambrose, Stephen E. *Eisenhower: Soldier and President.* New York: Simon & Schuster, 1990.

———. *Nixon.* 3 vols. New York: Simon & Schuster, 1987.

Baker, James. *The Politics of Diplomacy: Revolution, War, and Peace, 1989–1992.* With Thomas M. DeFrank. New York: G. P. Putman's Sons, 1995.

Busch, Andrew E. *Reagan's Victory: The Presidential Election of 1980 and the Rise of the Right.* Lawrence: University Press of Kansas, 2005.

Bush, C. Fred. *C. Fred's Story: A Dog's Life.* Edited slightly by Barbara Bush. Garden City NY: Doubleday, 1984.

Bush, George. *All the Best, George Bush: My Life in Letters and Other Writings.* New York: Scribner, 1999.

———. *Looking Forward: An Autobiography.* With Vic Gold. New York: Bantam, 1988.

———, and Brent Scowcroft. *A World Transformed.* New York: Knopf, 1998.

Cannon, Lou. *President Reagan: The Role of a Lifetime.* New York: Simon & Schuster, 1991.

Carter, Jimmy. *Why Not the Best?* Nashville TN: Broadman Press, 1975.

Connally, John. *In History's Shadow: An American Odyssey.* With Mickey Herskowitz. New York: Hyperion, 1993.

Darman, Richard. *Who's in Control? Polar Politics and the Sensible Center.* New York: Simon & Schuster, 1996.

Ford, Gerald. *A Time to Heal: The Autobiography of Gerald R. Ford.* New York: Harper & Row, 1979.

Frost, David. "The Next President." *U.S. News & World Report,* January 1988.

Gates, Robert M. *From the Shadows: The Ultimate Insider's Story of Five Presidents and How They Won the Cold War.* New York: Simon & Schuster, 1996.

Goldman, Peter, Tom Matthews, and the *Newsweek* Special Election Team. *The Quest for the Presidency: The 1988 Campaign.* Austin TX: Touchstone Books, May 1989.

Green, Fitzhugh. *George Bush: An Intimate Portrait*. New York: Hippocrene Books, 1989.

Haldeman, H. R. *The Haldeman Diaries: Inside the Nixon White House*. New York: G. P. Putman's Sons, 1994.

Hoover, Herbert. *The Memoirs of Herbert Hoover*. 3 vols. New York: Macmillan, 1951–52.

Hoyt, Austin (producer). *Reagan: American Experience*. Washington DC: PBS, 1995.

Johnson, Lyndon B. *The Vantage Point*. New York: Holt, Rinehart, and Winston, 1971.

King, Nicolas. *George Bush: A Biography*. New York: Dodd, Mead, 1980.

Kissinger, Henry A. *White House Years*. Boston: Little, Brown, 1979.

Koch, Doro Bush. *My Father, My President: A Personal Account of the Life of George H. W. Bush*. New York: Warner Books, 2006.

Lash, Joseph P. *Eleanor and Franklin*. New York: W. W. Norton, 1971.

Leuchtenburg, William E. *The Life History of the United States*. New York: Time-Life Books, 1976.

Manchester, William. *One Brief Shining Moment: Remembering Kennedy*. Boston: Little, Brown, 1983.

McCullough, David. *Truman*. New York: Simon & Schuster, 1992.

Morgan, Ted. *FDR: A Biography*. New York: Simon & Schuster, 1986.

Morris, Willie. *North toward Home*. Boston: Houghton Mifflin, 1967.

Naftali, Timothy. *George H. W. Bush*. New York: Henry Holt, 2007.

Nixon, Richard. *The Memoirs of Richard Nixon*. New York: Grosett and Dunlap, 1978.

——. *Richard Nixon in the Arena: A Memoir of Victory, Defeat, and Renewal*. New York: Simon & Schuster, 1990.

——. *Six Crises*. New York: Simon & Schuster, 1990.

Novak, Robert D. *The Prince of Darkness: 50 Years of Reporting in Washington*. New York: Crown Forum, 2007.

Parmet, Herbert S. *George Bush: The Life of a Lone Star Yankee*. New York: Scribner, 1997.

Post, Robert C., ed. *Every Four Years*. Washington DC: Smithsonian Exposition Books, 1980.

Reagan, Ronald. *An American Life*. New York: Simon & Schuster, 1990.

——. *The Reagan Diaries*. Edited by Douglas Brinkley. New York: HarperCollins, 2007.

Schlesinger, Arthur M., Jr. *A Thousand Days: John F. Kennedy in the White House*. Cambridge MA: Houghton Mifflin, 1965.

Schlesinger, Robert. *White House Ghosts: Presidents and Their Speechwriters*. New York: Simon & Schuster, 2008.

Schweizer, Peter, and Rochelle Schweizer. *The Bushes: Portrait of a Dynasty*. New York: Doubleday, 2004.

Smith, Richard Norton. *Thomas E. Dewey and His Times*. New York: Simon & Schuster, 1982.

Truman, Harry S. *Memoirs*. Garden City NY: Doubleday, 1955–56.

White, Theodore H. *In Search of History*. New York: Harper & Row, 1978.

———. *The Making of the President 1960*. New York: Atheneum, 1961.

Wicker, Tom. *George Herbert Walker Bush: A Penguin Life*. New York: Viking, 2004.

INDEX

Other works by Curt Smith

Mercy! (Potomac Books, 2012)

A Talk in the Park (Potomac Books, 2011)

Pull Up a Chair (Potomac Books, 2009)

The Voice (Lyons Press, 2007)

Voices of Summer (Carroll & Graf, 2005)

What Baseball Means to Me (Warner Books, 2002)

Storied Stadiums (Carroll & Graf, 2001)

Our House (Contemporary Books, 1999)

Of Mikes and Men (Diamond Communications, 1998)

Windows on the White House (Diamond Communications, 1998)

The Storytellers (Macmillan Company, 1995)

A Fine Sense of the Ridiculous (Diamond Communications, 1994)

Voices of The Game (Simon & Schuster, 1992)

Long Time Gone (Icarus Press, 1982)

America's Dizzy Dean (Bethany Press, 1978)